integrative learning and action

STUDIES IN EDUCATION & SPIRITUALITY

Peter Laurence and Victor Kazanjian
General Editors

Vol. 3

PETER LANG
New York • Washington, D.C./Baltimore • Bern
Frankfurt am Main • Berlin • Brussels • Vienna • Oxford

integrative learning and action

a call to wholeness

edited by

Susan M. Awbrey, Diane Dana, Vachel W. Miller,
Phyllis Robinson, Merle M. Ryan,
and David K. Scott

PETER LANG
New York • Washington, D.C./Baltimore • Bern
Frankfurt am Main • Berlin • Brussels • Vienna • Oxford

Library of Congress Cataloging-in-Publication Data

Integrative learning and action: a call to wholeness / edited by Susan M. Awbrey ... [et al.].
p. cm. — (Studies in education and spirituality; v. 3)
Includes bibliographical references.
1. Learning, Psychology of. 2. Education—Philosophy. I. Awbrey, Susan M. II. Series.
LB1060.I556   370.15'23—dc22   2006004970
ISBN 0-8204-5750-7
ISSN 1527-8247

Bibliographic information published by **Die Deutsche Bibliothek.**
Die Deutsche Bibliothek lists this publication in the "Deutsche
Nationalbibliografie"; detailed bibliographic data is available
on the Internet at http://dnb.ddb.de/.

Cover illustration: M.C. Escher's "Sphere Spirals"
© 2006 The M.C. Escher Company-Holland.
All rights reserved. www.mcescher.com
Cover design by Lisa Barfield

The paper in this book meets the guidelines for permanence and durability
of the Committee on Production Guidelines for Book Longevity
of the Council of Library Resources.

Emotional Intelligence © 2006 Daniel Goleman
Spirituality in Business and Life © 2006 Peter Senge
© 2006 Peter Lang Publishing, Inc., New York
29 Broadway, New York, NY 10006
www.peterlang.com

Printed in the United States of America

Contents

PART FOUR: INTEGRATIVE LIVING AND ACTION

Credits and Permissions

The required credits and permissions are entered in the order they occur in the book and are preceded by the page number.

Poems

Page 9. "You must give birth to your images..." from *Letters to a Young Poet,* by Rainer Maria Rilke, translated by M. D. Herter Norton. Copyright 1934, 1954 by W. W. Norton & Company, Inc., renewed © 1962, 1982 by M.D. Herter Norton. Used by permission of W. W. Norton & Company, Inc.

Page 12. "But yield who will to their separation..." excerpt from "Two Tramps in Mud Time from the *Poetry of Robert Frost* edited by Edward Connery Lathem. Copyright © 1969 by Henry Holt and Company, copyright 1936 by Robert Frost, copyright 1964 by Lesley Frost Ballantine. Reprinted by permission of Henry Holt and Company, LLC.

Page 18. "My Life is not..." from *Selected Poems of Rainer Maria Rilke,* page 31, a translation from the German and commentary by Robert Bly. Copyright © 1981 by Robert Bly. Reprinted by permission of HarperCollins Publishers.

Page 20. "Still, what I want in my life..." from "The Ponds" in *Blue Pastures*, Copyright © 1995 by Mary Oliver, reprinted by permission of Harcourt, Inc.

Page 21. "There is only the fight..." excerpted from "Little Gidding" in *Four Quartets,* Copyright © 1942 by T. S. Eliot and renewed 1970 by Esme Valerie Eliot, reprinted by permission of Harcourt, Inc.

Page 29, 34. "The Stars spoke once to man..." from *Verses and Meditations*, Copyright © 1961, reprinted by permission of Rudolf Steiner Press.

Page 157. "Quick now, here, now..." excerpted from "Little Gidding" in *Four Quartets*, Copyright © 1942 by T. S. Eliot and renewed 1970 by Esme Valerie Eliot, reprinted by permission of Harcourt, Inc.

Page 162. "Me from Myself—to banish..." reprinted by permission of the publishers and the trustees of Amherst College from *The Poems of Emily Dickinson*, edited by Thomas H. Johnson, J642, Cambridge. MA: The

Illustrations

Page 33. "Islamic Cosmology—Man and the Macrocosm" reprinted with permission from the Turkish and Islamic Art Museum, Istanbul, Turkey. Manuscript number 1973. Printed in *Islamic Science: An Illustrated Study* by S. H. Nasr, World of Islam Festival Co. Ltd, Westerham Press, Ltd, Westerham, Kent, UK, 1976.

Page 34. "Phaenomena" from the manuscript *Aratus*. Reprinted by permission of Bibliothèque Nationale de France. Printed in *The Star Hunters: The Quest to Discover the Secrets of the Universe* by D. Mammana., Mallard Press, 1990.

Page 41. "Initiation: The Coming Evolutionary Inflection" by Duane Elgin. Used with permission of Duane Elgin 2006 and retrieved from the website: www.newhorizons.org/future/elgin2020e.html, 1999.

Page 43. "Jacob's Ladder" from *Kabbalah: Traditions of Hidden Knowledge* by Z'ev ben Shimon Halevi, Thames & Hudson, London and New York, Copyright © 1979.

Page 49. "Rosicrucian Path of Initiation" from *The Mirror of Alchemy* by Gareth Roberts. Reprinted by permission of The British Library. BL1032c.3 (1) Plate III. Printed in *Sites of Mystery and Imagination: A Journey Through the Occult Heritage of Europe* by C. Walker. Hamlyn Press, London, 1990.

Note on the Cover Illustration

The cover illustration is based on M. C. Escher's *Sphere Spirals.* It is also the logo for CILA (the Community for Integrative Learning and Action). The spiral is often used as a symbol of evolution and unfolding and is a fitting symbol for integrative learning and action. The spirals evolve from a unified state, and diverge into separate components before reunifying. This pattern mirrors our human evolution. Most primal cultures, for example, had an integrated worldview, where the dimensions of matter, body, mind, soul and spirit were undifferentiated. Later, separations took place into a dualist cosmology of matter and spirit through the world's religions in the axial age, with spirit more valued than matter. No such hierarchies were present in the primal cultures. With the birth of modern science, a reverse dualism emerged with matter given prime place and spirit devalued or even ignored. Nevertheless this separation has led to a much greater depth of understanding of all the components of the fragmentation, so that we now have the possibility of reintegration with a deeper level of insight. The spirals could also represent the separation of different areas of knowledge such as art, science and spirituality (the Kantian Big Three in Wilber's terminology), and the reconvergence that may be possible among them. We could also view the spirals as an evolution from simplicity in the pre-rational and non-rational eras, to complexity in the rational scientific age and in the western enlightenment, and to a new simplicity on the "other side of complexity" in Oliver Wendell Holmes' phrase, or to trans-rationality. The symbol also conveys a global perspective appropriate to an integrative cosmology that must incorporate many different philosophies and worldviews. Finally, it represents the microscopic nature of life through the double helix as the fundamental building block of DNA, and the large-scale structures of the universe in the spiral galaxies.

Introduction: A Call to Wholeness

**Susan M. Awbrey, Diane Dana, Vachel W. Miller,
Phyllis Robinson, Merle M. Ryan, and David K. Scott**

> *Learning to Know*
> *Learning to Do*
> *Learning to Live Together*
> *Learning to Be*
> > From *Learning: the Treasure Within, The United Nations Educational, Scientific and Cultural Organization* (UNESCO, 1999)

The quest for wholeness—in knowing, in being, and in action—is a quest that has been joined on many fronts. This book represents a call to wholeness by poets, organizational theorists, scientists, lawyers, educators, philosophers, administrators, and contemplatives. They all write about the ideas and institutional structures that have separated us from a world alive with meaning. This book challenges us to reawaken to that living world and come to our senses in all their fullness.

The call to wholeness can be heard in the above quotation about the future of education from a multinational study group of the United Nations Educational, Cultural and Scientific Organization (UNESCO). The emphasis in Western education, and thereby in living and work in Western society, has been on the first two components: learning to know and learning to do. These dimensions are important, but they should not come at the expense or neglect of learning to live together or of learning to be. Taken together, all four components create wholeness, a kind of integrative learning, especially necessary in light of the problems created by the success of our rationality.

Many people have written about the isolation and loss of community within educational institutions and about the loss of passion created by alienation from the purposes of our work. Some believe that this is the price paid for a free and autonomous life. Some believe that this is the price paid for material comfort and technological progress. However, the writers gathered in this book reject the inevitability of the fragmentation of knowledge, the desiccation of the spirit, and the corruption of global ecosystems. In diverse ways the essays in this book speak to a desire for a different world—for a different way for learning and being that draws on the full spectrum of human potential of cognitive, aesthetic, emotional, spiritual, and kinesthetic intelligences in order to create a wiser global society. The authors in this book emphasize the importance of reflecting on the deeper meanings of our lives, our ultimate concerns, for the sake of renewed participation in the emergence of wholeness.

In higher education, issues of meaning and purpose in living are intentionally separated from the pursuit of knowledge. While public and focused conversations about the purpose of education come and go in cycles and revolutions, qualities such as love, empathy, wisdom, intimacy with life, mindfulness, appreciation, reverence, and the emergence of human wholeness are often not considered in educational reform and organizational change efforts. What can it mean, then, to transform education or the workplace through a reemergence of meaning, values, and spirituality? Does it mean an appeal to irrationality? Does it propose replacing science with religion? Does it imply there is one set of values that all students should be indoctrinated to believe?

The call to wholeness is life based, not limited to any particular faith or religious tradition. The purpose of this book is not to promulgate a particular sectarian viewpoint, but to create a space for reflection on how we come to understand the world, how that in turn determines the way we act, and how our actions affect the world. It is a space for reflecting on whether the world we are creating is the one in which we want to live and the one we want to pass on to the generations that follow.

A common theme in this book, whether implicit or explicit, is the connection of science, art, and spirituality. This connection is not unexpected because the origins of fragmentation and loss of wholeness originated to a large extent in the Enlightenment with the dissociation of these three knowledge spheres, the three core strands in every culture throughout history. Kant pointed out that science, art, and spirituality had to be differentiated, and this differentiation was key to modernity by allowing each sphere to pursue its own truth without violence and domination from the others. As Ken Wilber has noted, scientists and artists could now work in freedom without accusations of heresy from one another. This freedom was the great gift of modernism and the Enlightenment; it led to the dignity of modernity. Disillusionment with modernity occurred not because of this differentiation, but because of the dissociation that subsequently led to the rise of scientism and the idea that only a rational, analytical approach to knowledge is valid. A deeper insight into the relationship of the Kantian Big Three will be important in overcoming the divisions in society, for it is their separation that has contributed significantly to the alienation of human beings in the universe. Fortunately there are signs of a new integration as the essays in this book suggest.

Another important theme involves the practices that could situate the learner in a different relationship with the self and the environment. Contemplative and mindfulness practices, as well as some reflective and questioning practices, seek to bring the learner into a more direct relationship with the moment, providing either a more spacious mind or a more focused mind, but a mind that is nonetheless more receptive to direct apprehension and relationship with the object of study or with people in the environment. Such practices can position the rational mind in a larger awareness through which other forms of information and knowing may be revealed. Many colleges, universities, health care organizations and corporations are experimenting with contemplative practice and mindfulness as a means of creating more integrative workplaces, enhancing the capacity for integral consciousness, and reducing stress. Many examples appear in the essays that follow.

The call to wholeness has attracted leaders in education and business who have grown weary of the fragmentation and isolation brought on by modernity and postmodernity, as well as the social and environmental consequences that have resulted from the loss of primal connection to a universe alive with meaning. They seek new ways of working, new ways of learning, new ways of knowing and being together. As these individuals gather, momentum builds: conferences, institutes, publications, Web sites, and dialogue circles have emerged. Individuals who thought they were alone in their discomfort, alone in their hunger for wholeness, marvel to find themselves in an ever-expanding community of hope for the future.

The essays in this book speak directly to the possibility of holistic engagement in life. By exploring this theme in education and the professions, the authors in this volume offer an understanding of the term "integrative." They suggest that by cultivating ways of understanding that incorporate but reach beyond intellectual knowledge, we can actually feel in our hearts a concern for the living organisms in this world, and we can enter into a felt-in-the-heart relationship with the "objects" and "abstractions" of our studies. If nurtured, this way of relating can develop a broader perspective and a more acute awareness of how our academic or professional pursuits are affecting the complex web of life. According to surveys on spirituality in higher education conducted by the Higher Education Research Institute (HERI) at the University of California at Los Angeles, there is widespread interest in these dimensions of learning among students and faculty in a variety of colleges and universities.

We have come to see that the many perspectives found in this volume are intrinsically connected. The authors attest to the potential for human transformation and the possibility that education, both formal and non-formal, can play a more conscious role in creating an awake, aware, and enlightened society. We hope that the essays in this book will be valuable in showing that the interest in integrative learning and action and in spirituality as a vehicle to advance our understanding is becoming widespread.

Section I: In the Prologue, a conversation between Margaret Wheatley and David Whyte, chronicles how we have come to the current nexus of beliefs. Wheatley and Whyte discuss the "coming together of two powerful elements that have been split asunder in our psyche." In this wide-ranging conversation the authors poetically examine how we can "keep all of our empirical powers, all of our intellectual beauties, our rigor, and still make room for the unknown, the spacious and the numinous."

Section II: In Integrative Epistemology, the essays examine the nature and roots of the split between normative and descriptive worldviews. Jennifer Gidley notes that the system of knowledge a people hold is tightly bound to their culture. She describes how universities in the West have forsaken epistemology and ontology for the single-minded pursuit of methodology. Gidley examines the ways in which thinking can be transformed from dualistic instrumental rationality to a more integral consciousness. Arthur Zajonc examines the oppositions of faith and reason, belief and knowledge, and religion and science. He theorizes that spirit resides on both sides of these dualistic relationships and that it animates each. He calls for a new map that better integrates and represents the relationships. Eugene Halton looks at how human awareness has narrowed from an organic/participative consciousness to a civilizational consciousness due to the dehumanizing machine we have made of life. Our task, according to Halton, is to rediscover and preserve that "inner ecology" of the human soul in the face of this dehumanizing machine and to create a new civilizational framework that honors our state within the natural world. Bruce Wilshire takes up a similar theme in his essay. He describes how, while factual knowledge has grown, our mode of being aware has contracted and congealed—narrowing, detaching, objectifying.

Section III: Integrative Learning addresses the impact of the modern paradigm on higher education. Diana Chapman Walsh focuses on university students and frames her discussion within the post-9/11 world. She discusses the coherence and sense of meaning that students need in order to thrive in higher education. Walsh suggests that to provide meaning, universities need to identify core values—human values, institutional values, and academic values. Riane Eisler takes a different look at how we create conditions that support the development of meaning, purpose, connection, and caring. She compares cultural models of domination and partnership and their implications for education. Daniel Goleman discusses the relationship between leadership and Emotional Intelligence (EQ). He defines EQ as how well we sense and handle our emotions and those of others. Such abilities are especially significant aspects of leadership and career success.

Section IV: In Integrative Living and Action the authors provide insight into how a more integrative perspective can be achieved. In his essay on mindfulness practices, Jon Kabat-Zinn asks, how often are we fully present in our lives instead of fragmented? Is it possible for us to learn to tune the human instrument, the mind and the body, in such a way that we remain fully awake? Steven Keeva's essay is about the lack of being present in our professional lives. Relating this theme to the legal profession, he describes seven types of separation that cause a sense of alienation. Keeva describes the inner journey of hope that can restore the ability to "feel" one's life. Peter Senge also discusses the disconnection of work from the deep underlying motivations of employees. He describes the role dialogues can play within organizations in unveiling underlying meanings. Senge provides examples of dialogues that focus on how we live in organizations, our desire to use our lives well, and the quest to find meaning in our work. Finally, Mark Kriger examines the issue of meaning and purpose in the work place. He suggests that different levels of being and domains of voice can be revealed through the use of well-timed, appropriate questions within the organizational context.

Several years in the making, this book had its origins in a landmark conference, held in June of 2000 at the University of Massachusetts Amherst, called *Going Public: Spirituality in Higher Education and the Workplace.* This conference expanded space for serious dialogue on the transformative potential of spirituality and contemplative practice in public institutions. In addition to many new essays, edited versions of several keynote speeches from the conference are found in this volume. In parallel developments, a passion for integration brought together a group of faculty and staff members of the Five College community in western Massachusetts, with representatives of Smith College, Mt. Holyoke College, Amherst College, Hampshire College, and the University of Massachusetts Amherst. The group has formed the Community for Integrative Learning and Action (CILA) in order to continue advancing an integrative agenda, particularly in higher education. With contributions from several CILA members, this book also represents the vision of the CILA dialogues over the past three years as well as previous work on integrative universities by faculty and administrators from the University of Massachusetts Amherst, Oakland University, and the Massachusetts Institute of Technology. We are particularly grateful to our colleagues in CILA: Anthony Arcari, Frederique Apffel-Marglin, Karen Barad, Herbert Bernstein, Mirabai Bush, Christopher Carlisle, Katja Hahn-D'Errico, Carolyn Jacobs, Nigar Khan, Mark Kriger, Peter Laurence, Clifford Matthews, Michael Munson, Thomas Murray, Jonathan Podolsky, Gregory Prince, Theodore Slovin, David Thom, Banu Subramanian, Burton Woolf, and Arthur Zajonc.

Together the essays in this book challenge us to chart a new integrative course for the future. They are designed to expand our thinking and to reenlist our hearts in the journey of learning and living. We hope they inspire your own journey.

The editors wish to acknowledge the support of the Harold Grinspoon Foundation in preparing this work.

Sodexo — what do you
say when James G.
asked why you ≠
know

⎫ meeting w/ Neal
    Tom
    Dick

[
motion sent

✓ affirms intention all along for recreation education

always intended to build
]

B [Talk to Dan   **Part One**   Bartlett ¯
    biology never LEED

✓ [Ask Neal ⊕
    Executive C -   *Prologue*

✓ [Jim's #   Tell Janet
                                    + Tony

B (email Neal sent   2 things I felt
                                most imp
✓ (Administration Bldg -

    pornography   Was I only one that
                                  wanted bldg?

Can tell you not how BoT
feels, but how I feel —

    Internationalization
    Ethics
                    Think it's
                    pretty imp   [I ≠ want to be Pres
                    OFFC read about   anymore, but I will
                          meetings -   because it is only
                                        avenue I have to do
                                        something imp for
                                        people.

A Conversation on Spirituality

Margaret J. Wheatley and David Whyte

> *You must give birth to your images*
> *They are the future waiting to be born*
> *Fear not the strangeness that you feel*
> *The future must enter you*
> *Long before it happens.*
> *Rainer Maria Rilke*

MJW: I want to start with a question. This is a conference on going public on the fact that we are spiritual beings. The question I would like to pose is what, or who, called you here? I believe Rilke's answer to what or who called you here is the future (Rilke, 1934).

The question as to where the future comes from is theological. Do we make it up, is it given, or does it come from another place? For now, I would like us to sit with the question of what or who called you here. If it is the future that called you here, if it is the future moving through you, if it is images that come to you about how things should be simpler, things should be easier, things should be more humane, things should make more sense, things should be more beautiful. If any of these images are in you, then it is really interesting to wonder why they are in you and where they come from. In my own theology, I believe that each of us has these images of spirituality in education, of being whole in our work. I believe these images are being spoken through us right now. We are not inventing them. That is a theological statement, which I am just going to leave with you.

DW: One of the beautiful ways that Meg works and poses questions is that she uses plain language. Like a great photographer, she is able to shift the frame ever so slightly, so that you move from an ordinary, or even just a good perspective, to a great perspective. I think particularly that the emphasis on what we are called to and the images that are being called through us at this time are really very germane to the whole subject of this conference around going public with spirituality, particularly in public institutions, because in this country it is enshrined in the Constitution that there will be a great separation between any particular religious inheritance and the political world of the state. And I think that is really quite a healthy and remarkable thing.

It comes directly out of the awful experience in Europe of the seventeenth century when people were killing each other over religion. Literally millions of people died during the Thirty Years War in the late 1600s. Out of that experience, people were absolutely allergic to these questions that made people actually do violence to one another. Out of that experience was born

the reaction of the Enlightenment. The Enlightenment way of separating ourselves from what seemed like an impossible and uncontrollable portion of
our psyches is what, in a sense, we have inherited to this day. While this dynamic is very healthy, I still believe that a movement is possible toward
spirituality in the workplace and in our educational environment because
now we have to create a language that is based on an imaginative participation in the world.

That is exactly what all the international corporations have to do now,
where they have people who are Hindus, Jews, Muslims, Atheists, Episcopa-
lians, all sitting down together in the same room. You cannot use language
that brings out in anyone any kind of allergic reaction. I think one of the
great languages against which we have no defense is the language of the poetic imagination. Amazingly enough, that language lies right within the heart
of our great institutions, our great educational institutions. If you think about
the way that poets such as Rilke, or Dickinson, or Frost, or Coleridge, or
Keats looked at the imagination, you see a tremendous coherence over time,
and you see this understanding of the imagination is not just the ability to
think up new things or the ability to think up new strategies. The imagination
is actually a kind of inborn faculty inside each human being whereby we are
able to place ourselves in incredibly complex environments without having
to divide the world up in order to do it. So the imagination, according to
Rilke, is in that line. Say it once again, Meg.

MJW: The future must enter you long before it happens.

DW: That's lovely. The future must enter you long before it happens. What
Rilke is speaking to there is the artists' need to be beyond the horizon, at
least partially, in their work. If you ever get an artist whose work is completely within the horizon, that artist will usually work only in cliché but
would not be disturbing enough to work in whatever new territory we are
actually being born into. A great poet like Coleridge will say that the ability
to think up new strategies is the secondary imagination and this he would call
the fancy. However, the primary imagination is the ability to actually create
living images in language; images that literally have a life of their own and
that can go their own way in the world. I think this is exactly the territory
that we are moving into.

In some ways, we have become collectively tired of ourselves. I often
think that a time-honored way for any individual human being to change is
just to arrange to get really fed up with who you are and what you are doing.
If you can do that, you are half way to changing, almost tumbled into the
next dispensation.

The primary imagination forms language which will be life-like, and
which will place us in an ecology of belonging that we are attempting to cre-

ate in our institutions. We all realize now, in a way, that whatever our inherited language is in our organizational world, be it public or private, it is too narrow to enable us to live in the new life that we intuit, the kind of oceanic life lapping at our shorelines. Whatever inherited language we have is not large enough for that world. Wittgenstein said a marvelous thing. He said that you cannot actually enter and participate in any world for which you do not have the language. If you do not have the language to describe, to actually participate, to join the conversation, then you are actually living in exile from your time.

I think one of the great hallmarks of our time is that anything that is not life like or based on relationship, on true human relationship, is being swept away, whether it be the Berlin Wall, apartheid in South Africa, the old Soviet system, or the old corporate system that we have in the West. I often think that the moment the Berlin Wall fell, we knew instinctively that the nearest thing we had to an Eastern European dictatorship was a Western corporation. And the game was up for us. That was when we started to investigate our old shadows. We could no longer just project them over that wall onto another entity. Everything now is about conversation, about participation, about life-likeness.

There are a couple of lovely lines from Keats, who had a tremendous sense of participation in the world. He had an astonishing, innocent vulnerability that was incredibly powerful; at twenty-four years old, by the time he died, he had already written himself into the forefront of English letters, just from his courageous willingness to live at the frontier. He said a marvelous thing in one of his letters, "I am certain of nothing but the holiness of the heart's affections and the truth of the imagination." So he really preceded the whole psychological investigation of the twentieth century by a good hundred years because if there is anything that psychological studies have clarified over the century it is the fact that the identity of individual human beings is predicated, ironically enough, on belonging. An individual human being is actually no human being at all. Individuals are somehow in exile from the rest of the world. What brings a human being alive is a sense of participation in the conversation of life with others, with the great things of the world, with the trees or landscapes or skies or cityscapes, and that this conversation is the way by which a human being comes to understand the particularity of their own gifts in the world.

There is a lovely piece by Frost, who used to visit the town of Amherst every year and taught there for quite a while. It is just a brilliant investigation of this whole coming together of what seemed like two opposing thoughts. The poem is called "Two Tramps in Mud Time." "Mud Time," as you probably know, is the time here in the old Northeast when the snows melt and the itinerant workers would get back on the road, going from farm to farm looking for work. Frost is in his farmyard chopping wood. And Frost loves chopping wood, and he loves the weight of the ax, learning the grain of a particular wood and the whole rhythm of the thing. Suddenly in the midst of his activity, out of his peripheral vision he sees two travelers coming toward the corner of the farmyard, and he knows instinctively that they are looking for work. He says a marvelous thing in the poem that, if someone has a need to do the work, no matter how much you love it, you should hand over the ax. That is what his intellectual mind says, but he is not quite able to do it. You can feel him in the poem, swaying backward and forward, and you really do not know in the poem whether he gave the ax over or not. I don't think he did. The whole scene breaks open out of this tension of wanting to give the ax, wanting to keep his work, when he says (Lathem, 1969):

> *But yield who will to their separation,*
> *my object in living*
> *is to unite my avocation and my vocation*
> *as my two eyes make one in sight.*
> *Only where love and need is one,*
> *and work is play for mortal stakes,*
> *is the deed ever really done*
> *for Heaven and the future's sakes.*

The remarkable thing in there is the way you feel this coming together of two powerful elements that have been split asunder in our psyche. Which I think is exactly what is germane to this time together. When he says "yield who will to their separation," it is quite a radical beginning to the final declaration of his poem. He is saying that you can prepare all your life for your work, especially if it is in a public educational institution. Quite often you have some kind of call, as Meg said, that would put you through all the academic work you have to go through and all the interviews and all the financial sacrifices and all the late night studies, burning the midnight oil. When you think of everything you have put yourself through to get to the threshold of your work, it is quite astonishing that when we enter it, most of what we do seems to stand in the way of the very thing that drew us into the work in the first place.

Frost is saying that human beings have this astonishing ability the Greeks called *enantidromia*, the ability to follow anything up unthinkingly until it turns into its exact opposite. One of the astonishing things about the academy, for instance, is that the original meaning of that word comes from the oak grove which was outside the city of Athens and that was the academia. That was the one place you could go and talk about seditious things, radical things, which, if spoken within the polis, within the walls of the city, you could be killed for. The academy was originally the place of radical declaration. It was the place where the frontier was actually being forged, not so

break orthodoxies

much forging our strategic way of being in the world, but forging our identities in a philosophical mode. The astonishing result is that the academy has actually become the polis. It is the place where you cannot say many things.

What Frost is saying, in a way, is that we, as a species, are called homo sapiens, the wise human being; but we should be called *homo forgettens*. We forget so easily what it means to be fully human. Frost has this incredible image, which is so brilliant because it is so simple. He says, "yield who will to their separation." The moment you get to work, after all those sacrifices, could be the very moment you forget why you came into it in the first place. "Yield you will to their separation; my object in living is to unite my vocation and my avocation; as my two eyes make one in sight."

Latin words: *vocation, avocation.* The root of the word *vocatis* is voice and, loosely translated, means to have a voice in the world. Human beings use their voice like animals and birds use their plumage, their feathers, or their fur. Animals have all these astonishing displays in the world; human beings have their voices. When you think about it, we are constantly explaining ourselves to others. Here we are, Meg and I, explaining ourselves all this evening. We never will finish. We shall go right up to the end of our lives. And who knows what lies on the other side? We will get to whatever that land is on the other side of life, and then think that all the explanation will be over; and they'll say, no, there's a meeting starting just down the corridor, and you're just in time for it. You'll say, I thought it was all over, and they say, no, it's just beginning. I often think the reason we have to have so many meetings in the workplace is because at the last meeting I didn't quite explain who I was, and what I was about. And neither did anyone else. So we have to have another meeting. I think one of the first rules you learn about the art of the imaginative conversation is that there is no one conversation that you can have that will eliminate all the other conversations.

This brings me to another point—almost all of the ways that we organize things, whether in the public, academic world or in the private, corporate world, originate almost exclusively from the masculine side of the psyche. There is nothing wrong with the masculine psyche; it has great powers in the world. The only problem is that it is only fifty percent of reality. Conversation has not been one of the great loves historically of the masculine psyche. A young man, at the beginning of a relationship or a marriage, is constantly surprised that, even though we had a conversation last week, we have to have one again this week and it seems to be about exactly the same thing as the conversation before. The forlorn hope of the masculine psyche is that you can have one big conversation at the beginning of the relationship and then you can go six or seven years before anything real comes up. But no, this person keeps drifting before your eyes. Part of the way the masculine psyche forms itself in the world is through difference. Differentiating from mother, differentiating from family, differentiating from society. The intimacy of the conversation actually causes the young man to feel as if he is going to die. He literally, physically, feels that he will not survive. That is why he looks the way he does.

So the whole inherited way that we think work gets done creates this conversation-free bowling alley, with nothing living in the corridor. Then we hurl ourselves down it. I often say in today's world that by the time you get to the end of the alley, things have moved. However, a masculine psyche says, "I don't care; at least I had peace and quiet."

Finally he learns that the conversation is not about the relationship; it is the relationship itself. The conversation between our vocation and our avocation; the conversation between what is hidden inside us and everything we have to deal with in the nitty-gritty outer world; the conversation between other worlds that we only intuit; the conversation between our theological and spiritual inheritance and our strategic and empirical minds. This is where the real harvest is going to be.

No one particular religious inheritance or language is needed. We need to bring ecology of experience together, bring them all into conversation, whatever that conversation is—and this will be the new dispensation. That will be the harvest; that will be our next step. It has to do with an understanding, as Meg says, that wherever we get to in the end, you cannot arbitrate human experience ultimately through scientific explanation. There is another kind of language, enshrined in our great liberal arts that will explicate and create that conversation, the live relationship that will be the proof of the pudding in a way.

MJW: I would like to take a number of the themes you introduced and place them in the academy.

I was really aware, as you were talking, David, that those of us who went into the academy went in from a sense of love. I am going to play with Frost's images here. We saw a need. At the moment when we chose to work in higher education, love and need were one. Then we woke up to realize we were working within an institution that had forgotten many of the things you just spoke about, forgotten how learning takes place, how knowledge is developed, and has chosen, as our whole Western culture has, only one way to know, through the scientific method, through empiricism. So many of us who pursued what was the liberal arts, and with this love and need suddenly found ourselves beholden to explain what we were experiencing in scientific terms, even though they could only be explained through the language of the imagination, through poetry, theater, and music. However, we were suddenly in an institution, like all institutions in Western society that insisted on scientific language.

One of the things I know from many different traditions, but I know deepest in my being, is that the experience we call spiritual cannot be described in the current scientific language of our time. It cannot be described in terms of measures, standards or statistical data because it is always a unique, profound experience that is only known to the individual. The only way to express that experience is through a form of language that is not finite; languages not fixed but open to multiple interpretations. That is where the language of imagination comes in; it comes in the need to capture in one perfect image, or one haunting song, or one piece of drama, when I say, "Yes, I see that experience, I know that feeling." The language in which spirit needs to be expressed, in which spiritual experience needs to be expressed, is not presently available to us in the academy.

Is that something you would agree with? Whenever we try and take that experience and represent it in the traditional terms of statistics or standard measurements, then we completely lose the experience. We may—and this is the real dilemma—we may gain credibility among our colleagues, but we lose the experience. How do you describe the numinous in terms of statistically validated research?

I want us to see that we are in a very difficult place, where love and need are one, and the work is play for mortal stakes, where we are right now in our professional lives, whether as faculty, staff, administrators or students. We are trying to bring forth an experience that we call spirituality and trying to bring it forth in an institution which has named the language by which it will see and accept human experience; and the language is simply not big enough. It is not the right language.

However, in the tradition of the original academy and the oak grove, and even in our present institutions, we still have the language of imagination. Not so much in the sciences as in our liberal arts, music, dance, poetry and literature and theater arts. (It might be in philosophy even. I just have a really hard time reading it.) But these yearnings, these great questions that have circulated for centuries in the academy have now been relegated, like everything else in our dominant scientism of Western culture, as something we can do without. The more focused we are on technical training, the more we see everything represented by scientifically validated terms, and the more we fail to see that we already have a language for expressing what we need to know.

We already have the language of imagination. We already have poetry and music. We already have the great traditions and explorations of the human soul. However that language has been relegated now to a kind of quaint irrelevancy. I speak a fair amount at universities and colleges, and I worry about how little reverence and honor are given to the liberal arts, which I would rather call the human arts. Let us call them the only language we have for expressing the deep yearnings of the human heart and these great explorations of the human experience. It is actually up to us, those of us who are in the academy in one way or another, to realize the images that are speaking through us. The future that is speaking through us will not find honest and valuable expression if we stay limited to the current language predominantly honored in this culture. We cannot express these yearnings through the language of science. We are leaping eagerly; we are so hungry for explanations of the power of love, the power of relationships, looking for a sense of belonging. We are all so hungry for that globally. However, we are still looking to our scientists to explain to us why it is so.

Why do we have this longing for relationships? Quantum physicists could tell you why we have this longing, and it is wonderful to read it in science. But if we allow that to be the sole source of validating authority, that relationships and belonging are necessary for us, then I am fearful. I do not know if it was Einstein who said never use science to explain God, because the science will change, and then where will you be?

I wish we could take our sense of love and need of vocation and avocation, our sense of strangeness, our sense of the future speaking through us and realize that we must simultaneously reclaim a language that has been devalued. It is this language that is so richly abundant in the academy but not honored any longer.

DW: I like the shading of meaning you were bringing in at the end, of qualifying the fact that there is nothing wrong with science itself. It is one of the great faculties by which human beings place themselves in the world. I remember my science classes in my teens, learning about the precision of the world through studying chemistry, physics, and biology. What you are saying is really important; where we fall down is making science the final arbiter of who we are and what we are about in our general conversation in the world. We do not do it in our private conversations. I am not sure scientists actually do it in the inner, private conversations of their hearts before they walk into the laboratory, before they write papers or before they speak in public. However, somehow a kind of gravitational field spreads out in the world where we feel like the last word has to be from science.

As a young boy I was always called by poetry and by mythology and the great stories of the world. When I was twelve or thirteen, I was also called by Jacques Cousteau sailing across our little black-and-white television set. He seemed to be beckoning toward this enormous world. But I discovered in order to get on the good ship *Calypso* and to follow the life of a dolphin, I would have to give up all my subjects that I loved dearly which were English, History, French, and Art. I had to put myself into what, for me, were the salt mines of biology, chemistry, and physics. But that star was so clear over the horizon that I really felt I must follow it. So I put myself into what, for me, was a very hard road to hoe. I went to University in North Wales and studied marine zoology. When I emerged, I was lucky enough to get a job as a naturalist on the Galapagos Islands. I lived there for two years at the center of the zoological world. It was really an astonishing and amazing gift. Everything I wanted to happen, happened. Everything I dreamed of actually happened to me in those islands. I had the life I wanted at the center of it all.

But there I had an amazing experience. When I first got to those islands (and I know it is an old joke) I discovered that none of the animals had read any of the zoology books I had read. I found that my powers of observation, once I actually got to the experience itself, had been narrowed by my education. It was a strange irony because I could not have found myself on those astonishing shores without all the years of species identification, morphology, ecological genetics, the Krebs cycle, and all those ideas you get to know and love at 2 a.m. Once I got there, my educational inheritance was like a grid superimposed over the world. In fact, sometimes the lines of that grid were so thick that I could barely see anything at all underneath. Anything that disappeared behind those shadowed lines seemed not to exist anymore. When I first got to those islands, I found I had to apprentice myself to the silence and the phenomenology of attention, what happens to human beings when they start to pay profound attention in profound silence. Then a whole sense of relationship begins to open up of which you were unaware before, when you were totally immersed in your two-dimensional, empirical investigation of the world.

In most of our great native traditions around the world, whether they are old native European traditions, or old native North American traditions, South American traditions, African traditions, they all speak about living in parallel worlds all at one time. You are never just in one world at all. I had an early apprenticeship of this with my Irish mother, actually, because my father is from Yorkshire, a very practical, down-to-earth world where a spade was a spade, or a bloody shovel, as they sometimes say. My mother's world was totally opposite. My father had one clock in the house, which told the time for everything he did. My mother had six or seven clocks, which all told different times for different activities. There was one clock to go to bed with, set at a certain time, ten minutes fast or fifteen minutes slow. There was a clock to catch the #26 bus out back; there was a clock to catch the #11, there was a clock to go to work. All of these parallel times occurred at the same time in our house. My mother was able to live in the midst of this total incongruity of logic. Hegel would have been totally at home with my mother.

In the Irish tradition, there is always an understanding that whatever name you have given to anything, it is always just the surface name. When you go below the surface, the name will change totally. Even to this day in the west of Ireland, you can be in a pub with a fellow for two or three hours, have the greatest conversation, and you suddenly remember what it is like to have a really good conversation, to investigate the world, to hear things said in a way which actually investigates the subject created between you, but then dismiss it and move on to the next topic, all in one phrase. It is just quite astonishing. At the end of the time, you realize that you have no idea who he was, what he was doing, where he was going, or where he had come from at all. And you barely knew his name. A reluctance persists in old cultures to actually have a name mentioned. It is considered very, very forward and almost an affront to a person's mystery that you would actually try to label them with some kind of name or other.

The English have told stories about the Irish for centuries, in order to show that the Irish psyche is somewhere other than planted on the ground. In fact, though, this is actually a template for a different kind of wisdom, a different kind of way of placing yourself in the world. Upon examination we find that, whatever name you carry on the surface, the deeper you go into your identity the more that will change. There is a lovely scientific analogy in oceanography. If you follow the Gulf Stream across these shores, right across to the British Isles, it flows west to east. However, as you drop down through layers of salinity and temperature, you find that there is actually a spiral in the current, called the Ekman Spiral. By the time you get down to a certain depth an equal current goes in exactly the opposite way. In some ways this is an exact depiction of the average human being. Whatever they say to you on the surface, you know a current goes exactly the opposite way somewhere inside them. Only in someone like Rilke, who had the whole ecology of the experience right, will the whole spiral be there. On the surface, we use scientific language to say I have got to get the balance of my work and life right. The fact that we have already distinguished work from life is a very bad sign. We say we have our "work/life" issues, but Rilke would not talk about balance, because that is the strategic mind attempting to cut things into two. He expresses this in a poem (Rilke, 1981):

My life is not this deeply sloping hour,
in which you see my hurrying.
Much stands behind me; I stand before it like a tree;
I am only one of many mouths,
 and at that, the one that would be still the soonest.

I am the rest between two notes,
which are somehow always in discord,
because Death's note wants to climb over –
But in the dark interval, reconciled,
they stay there trembling.
 And the song goes on, beautiful.

Rilke is saying we are always trying to be the notes. That is how I arrived in the Galapagos, trying to be the notes, literally the scientific notes. However, he is saying, if your focus is absolutely on the notes, what you do is to cram all the notes together and the silence, the spaciousness, is squeezed out. So what you have in the end is not a piece of music, but something that resembles the sixty-cycle hum of an old rusty refrigerator—which you only notice when it switches itself off. Moreover, you have been talking in the kitchen for a good forty-five minutes and did not realize how much will power you had to use to speak to that other person until the refrigerator stopped. Then you realize how tired you are.

That is exactly how we place the empirical mind in the hierarchy of experience. We have placed it too high. There is nothing intrinsically wrong with the scientific mind. It has astonishing beauty, an astonishing way of investigating the world; great understanding of phenomenology and the particularity of the way difference plays out in the world. However, it is meant to be a good servant to the soul's desire in the world. The soul's desire has to do with belonging. It is meant to be a way of belonging in deeper and deeper ways to the astonishing phenomenon we call creation.

So if you look at the whole postmodern way forming our investigations of the future, particularly if you look at the way that technology is undergoing an inversion of its own, it is actually taking us to the place that the old mythologies had arrived at thousands of years ago. Ireland, for instance, is pretty adaptive to the world of software because, when you think about it, the Irish psyche already understands, as many native psyches do in the world, that the surface name changes the deeper you go into the experience. Already you have a precise description of an operating system! It is exactly the way an operating system works in the computer. The surface icons and names that we see on that two-dimensional interface are absolutely and totally different from the ones that are functioning deep inside the whole system, bringing the image to us, to the frontier of the way we can actually pay attention to them.

One of the great challenges we have to apprentice ourselves to now is the unknown. Meg is asking us how to keep all of our empirical powers, all of our intellectual beauty, our rigor, and still make room for the unknown, the spacious and the numinous, in the midst of that language, and fill it out with music again so that it will not hold us and imprison us. Of course, we already have all this wisdom. Meg is saying that we already know exactly what we have to do. We know who we have to be. However, we have not lived those images fully out in the world yet. All of those old disciplined apprenticeships to silence, to the numinous, are there in our great contemplative and artistic traditions, if we can really take them seriously and not reduce them to metrics every time. We must attempt to live out the questions, as Rilke would have said, and bring the kind of eldership of identity back into our academic institutions. We are halfway there.

MJW: David, I have a poem for you. It is from Mary Oliver. I was thinking of it as you were describing your experience in the Galapagos. It is very similar to a description that I heard from one of the Apollo astronauts, Edgar Mitchell, who had the experience of going to the Moon, looking at the Earth, having been trained as a brilliant scientist at MIT. In looking out at the Earth through the shuttle window, he experienced the Earth as a living being and felt that nothing in his training had prepared him for that experience. There was no way he could explain what he was feeling and seeing in the language of his discipline because it was numinous, because it was spiritual. That is why he formed, as some of you may know, the Institute of Noetic Sciences, just to inquire into all of the dimensions that science cannot help to explain.

So Mary Oliver dealt with this at the end of a lovely description of a morning at a pond. She says (Oliver, 1995):

> ...
> *Still, what I want in my life*
> *is to be willing*
> *to be dazzled—*
> *to cast aside the weight of facts*
>
> *And maybe even to float a little*
> *above this difficult world.*
> *I want to believe I am looking*
> *into the white fire of a great mystery.*
> *I want to believe that the imperfections are nothing—*
> *that the light is everything—that it is more than the sum*
> *of each flawed blossom rising and fading. And I do.*

We're still in this domain in which we now have to take that longing, that mystery, that experience, and express it in terms of research. It might not be possible, and there is the edge I want to hold us to. We want to open up the institution to the experiences we have had, that are by their very nature mysterious and numinous. We want to make it possible, for students and for colleagues, to have similar experiences. However, this is impossib'e if we accept the terms of the institution. We are not going to learn how to do it if we stay within the empirical tradition of the academy.

However, if we go to the contemplative tradition, or if we go to any mystical experience, we would find the means. Then we are in this great dilemma, which is also a dilemma in science right now, that there are certain kinds of experiences inexplicable through traditional science, through the traditional epistemology of science. One prominent domain where I have encountered this in science is in consciousness research. Consciousness cannot be understood if we approach it through objectivity because it is such a deeply personal experience. If science stays interested in consciousness as a field of scientific inquiry, you actually have to think about the underlying epistemology of science. How do we know consciousness? Well, we do not know it using the same tools that we use to know other phenomena.

However, what if the images that are speaking through us are also much bigger—about finding very different ways of knowing, very different ways of expressing what we know. This is new territory. How do we get there from where we are right now in the culture of scientism, where we use science to explain everything? What if part of the future that is speaking through us is this much greater work of not accepting the current terms of how we describe experience? What if part of our work is to be brave enough, not just to come out of the closet as spiritual beings, but to be brave enough to realize that we are existing in a culture that cannot yet, has not yet, provided us with processes for seeing things that we know are essential to us?

Now you will not get any credibility for this in traditional academic journals. I think it becomes an enormous choice for us in our professional lives—how far are we willing to push this? How much of the system can we change? What gives me the greatest hope is to realize that the future is speaking through millions of us right now, and speaking to more and more of us. I personally take a lot of courage just from knowing how many of us there are. Sometimes, especially if you are trying to develop a paper to be refereed, it might be difficult to look up, to lift your head away from the computer for a moment, and realize that something much bigger is being asked of you, being asked of all of us. It does take courage right now to step out, but something is moving underneath us. The future is insisting that we hold on to these images. I take real heart in that.

I'm going to quote from another poem, a phrase from T.S. Eliot's "The Four Quartets." It centered me in this work. In the poem Eliot starts to reflect on all of the great ones who have gone before us, and how he just cannot compare himself to them. He just comes up lacking. They were so much better writers, poets, people who championed the causes of freedom. He says (Eliot, 1936):

> *There is only the fight to recover what has been lost*
> *And found and lost again and again: and now, under conditions*
> *That seem unpropitious. But perhaps neither gain nor loss.*
> *For us, then is only the trying. The rest is not our business.*

DW: Could I pick up on that? Because I would say that in some ways we must stop looking for the answers too early in the process. We must learn to wait until the conversation is actually harvesting itself. Change, like everything else, becomes a burden on us. And so, when we are faced with our overly concrete organizations, we can suddenly feel terribly burdened by them. Visions of our refereeing committee come before our eyes, and our Ph.D. guardians, the organs by which our papers go out into the world, and the ways we are vetted by media magazines as to whether we are a good university or not.

I think Eliot is saying that you actually must get involved in the conversation. You bring whatever frontier you have arrived at into the conversation with all the other frontiers that are occurring. You do not do the work of change at all. The conversation does the work. No one has to change, but everyone has to have the conversation. And all of the changes will come out of the conversation. Whatever the frontier, all you have to do is put yourself at that edge and join the conversation wholeheartedly, then everything has actually already changed.

In the Old World, you asked for coordinates; you wanted to know exactly where you were. In today's world, you can have as many coordinates as you want and you can still starve in place, because you do not really know how to live on the land. So how do we ask radical questions of ourselves in our own lives? First of all, it is to bring our vocation and our avocation together to create a kind of wholeheartedness. If your vocation is your own voice in the world, your avocation is that voice that calls you, whether you have any choice or not, and that voice always rests in mystery. You are sensing some system which is larger than you, some ecology of belonging to which you belong, but you have no idea how you fit into it yet. Immediately you begin the conversation between whatever your avocation, your longing, is and whatever calls you and whatever you are called to be; you have already set up a dynamic, a tremendous dynamic, between the future and the past. Already things are beginning to occur which are having tremendous effects.

One of the great questions to ask ourselves, whatever the immobility of the institutions within which we work, is to constantly be asking about your own sense of horizon and to be putting yourself at some frontier where there is a sense of vulnerability and the unknown. In those arrivals, much of the work we want is already occurring because, according to Coleridge and all the great genius minds—Emily Dickinson too if you read her work really closely—in our great literary traditions, they say that the imagination is actually a kind of substrate of belonging responding to the gravity field of the way we are actually made in the world. Naturally it is constantly looking to fit into this astonishing complexity in the only way that you can fit, and no one else can. It is trying to live out the one life that no one else can live in your stead.

The other astonishing aspect about human beings is that they are the one part of creation that can refuse their own flowering. They can refuse to be themselves. We are the only creatures we know with this capacity. Then, as

Rilke says, life will seem too cheap because of living out someone else's life instead of your own. This is what kills us about failure. When you get to your deathbed, the failures that kill you are the ones where you were trying to live out someone else's life. The failures where you were trying to live out your own life are not failures any more at all.

MJW: David, I would like to hear you talk more about something you said earlier when we were speaking privately—that change is always accompanied, or brings forth, a sense of betrayal, personal betrayal, betrayal to the institution, betrayal to everything. I was really stunned when you brought it up, because you named something that I feel personally and I see in a lot of people when speaking about giving birth to these images, and allowing the future. We realize there are all these tugs, and one of them is the rather unusual feeling that we are betraying those we love, or we are betraying the things that have sustained us, the tradition. I wanted you to say more on this subject.

DW: Yes, that comes from the phenomenology of the path. We have to familiarize ourselves with the difficulties of life. We have the strange illusion that if we only put our feet in all the right places, then God will smile on us and look after us. But if you look at reality, if you look at history, and literature and theater and art, everything about life is saying, no matter what you do, you have no immunity against the great losses and traumas. There is no life you can arrange for yourself whereby you will not be held accountable, where you will not feel pain, exile, loss and death. The great religious traditions of the world take great pains to tell us that.

However, among the ways in which society is organized, or we tell each other about reality, is the need to be some simulacrum of yourself in order to deserve the life you want for yourself. One of the difficult portions of existence is that, whenever you change, then always there will be a sense of betrayal, either from others around you, who expect you to be exactly as you were, because you actually constellate a part of their universe, or even a part of yourself. When you take a courageous step forward you find enormous parts of you holding back. Because quite often we have dedicated our identity to elaborate complexity, which we think is absolutely necessary in order to live and to be ourselves. When the complexity starts to atomize on the surface, you actually feel as if you are dying. I think what is so radical about Meg's work, *A Simpler Way*, is the understanding that the simplest thing is often the most difficult thing to do because it is quite often the most courageous thing to do. Whenever you are taking a courageous step, you always feel that you are stepping onto a surface which will not hold your weight, and that you will actually plummet through that meniscus into the depths below and drown. Whatever you know in your own heart, that you know already in your own heart, through an image of what you think is true and best in your work, and the institutions that you came to serve for that work, then you should increase the intensity of your gaze upon it. It is like following a star. In fact, there's a lovely etymological root to the word "desire." It comes from the old Latin word meaning, of the star. So to have a desire in life is, literally, to follow a star. A star above the horizon will take you through tremendously difficult territory on the surface.

There are many organizations we go into, and we are sure that everyone believes that everyone else is just a highly paid extra in our careers, and we also believe that they have been shipped in by the busload, at great expense, every day, just so they can take the next step on the career ladder. Other people are just simulacrums of their own experience. A great sign of spiritual maturity is the admission that other people have lives of their own, engaged in this astonishing conversation with life, and everyone is engaged in their own particular way. The privilege is the conversation itself. So one of the things I think is occurring is our moving from a parent-child relationship in our institutions to an adult-adult relationship with creation, with one another. One of the radical changes our institutions could make, particularly our public education institutions, is admit that the world is alive and that we are in conversation with it. Everyone needs to realize the world is not just there for us to study.

This essay was produced from the transcript of a dialogue between Margaret J. Wheatley (MJW) and David Whyte (DW) at the Conference "Going Public: Spirituality in Higher Education and the Workplace," University of Massachusetts Amherst, June, 2000.

References

Eliot, T.S. (1936). *The Four Quartets*. New York: Harper Brace.

Lathem, E. C. (Ed.) (1969). *The poetry of Robert Frost*. New York: Henry Holt.

Oliver, M. (1995). The Ponds. *In Blue Pastures*. New York: Harcourt Brace.

Rilke, R. M. (1934*). Letters to a young poet* (M. D. Herter Norton, Trans.). London and New York: W.W. Norton.

Rilke, R. M. (1981). *Selected poems of Rainer Maria Rilke* (R. Bly, Trans.). New York: Harper & Row.

Part Two

Integrative Epistemology

Spiritual Epistemologies and Integral Cosmologies: Transforming Thinking and Culture

Jennifer Gidley

The Stars spoke once to man
It is World-destiny
That they are silent now
To be aware of the silence
Can become pain for earthly man

But in the deepening silence
There grows and ripens
What Man speaks to the Stars
To be aware of the speaking
Can become strength for Spirit Man
Rudolf Steiner

The culture of a people is intimately connected with their type of thinking and system of knowledge. In Western culture, universities have been the official guardians and transmitters of those systems of knowledge for the past 1,000 years or so. A crucial question to be addressed here is whether universities have sufficient foresight today to spearhead essential changes in thinking and culture, or whether they are merely "credentialing the status quo" (Wildman, 2000). The twentieth-century university model had its rightful place in the context of nineteenth-century industrial and social progress, and nineteenth-century Western linear rationality. Centuries of instrumental rationality have led to an atrophying of imaginative vision and subsequent technologization of culture throughout Western society, but particularly within universities. They, in turn, have become obsessed with methodological issues and technical detail. The resultant disconnectedness from community and culture of much dry academic thinking today parallels a process of cultural degeneration and fragmentation.

Looking at the conceptual trilogy of methodology, epistemology and ontology as ideally representing a balance, we must recognize that contemporary universities have all but forsaken the latter two constructs. Universities need to move beyond methodology to a dialogue of epistemologies, encompassing the deeper sense of multiculturalism, and beyond that to reflecting on their own ontology, to their very purpose of being. However, it is proposed here that even this is not enough. If universities are not only to survive the complex political, economic, and social chaos that present trends suggest will occur in the coming decades, but also to be active in transformation, then they need to reflect critically on their underpinning worldview (Gidley,

2000). If universities of the future are to rise to the challenge of being agents of transformation, they will also need a more extensive, inclusive cosmology—an underpinning system of knowledge comprehensive enough to take in and give meaning to the complex, global problems we have created. In the growing complexity of current global crises, there is an urgent need to access higher order ways of thinking and knowing if we are to avert environmental and cultural catastrophe.

Even so, in spite of some positive signs of change afoot, the orthodox academic world still seems obsessed with the need to categorize, to label, and to fragment knowledge into its smallest atoms. It is not content with divisions into the disciplines of science, philosophy, humanities, theology, and so on. Even within disciplines, it must divide and fragment exponentially into branches of philosophy, specializations in science, while society follows suit with denominations of religion, and with sects and cults within those. If we are to rise above current global conflicts, and even terrorism, universities as the "guardians of knowledge" must become stewards of practical wisdom by committing themselves to integral approaches to knowledge through fostering inclusive cosmologies and the cultivation of imaginative/integral thinking. This will require an epistemological shift in thinking to encompass the types of spiritual knowledge systems inherent in the "Perennial Philosophy."

This essay explores how thinking may be transformed from the dualistic, fragmenting, and conflict-producing instrumental rationality of the past to a higher-order integral consciousness that has the capacity to transcend and include pluralistic worldviews and to generate diverse, yet inclusive, cultural futures (Wilber, 1995).

From the perspective of the discipline of futures studies, the scientific, intellectual mode looks at the future as a trajectory of existing trends—an empirical model. This concept binds the future to the present and colonizes its potential. The youth-futures research suggests that the young have taken in and are disempowered by the negative potential in the existing trends, fed also by negative images through the media of fearful futures. A society with no vision, no imagination, cannot progress, cannot transcend the limitations of the present. The ability to imagine better worlds is crucial to creating better worlds, as is well known from the research of many futurists (Boulding, 1998; Slaughter, 1994; Inayatullah & Wildman, 1998).

So was intellectual rationality a mistake? An aberration? On the contrary, it was exactly the appropriate and necessary stage of consciousness for humans to discover their freedom and their ego-nature. Intellectual rationality has been a powerful tool for increasing the scientific knowledge of the natural world that has developed since the Enlightenment, and in a sense its development has been one of the major accomplishments of Western civilization. Its limitations, however, become greater the further we move beyond the material manifestations of reality, from the physical sciences into the life sciences, and especially into the social sciences. Its categorical nature leads to dissection and fragmentation of knowledge rather than synthesis and integration. In this regard it is extremely limited in its ability to know the human psyche. Even so, orthodox psychology tries to emulate natural science in its approaches. This is the failure of much contemporary psychology.

If intellectual rationality has led to academic and cultural fragmentation, the question must be asked: "Can the rational intellect itself be the tool for reintegrating the divided disciplines?" It is argued here that it cannot and that new ways of thinking, speaking, and creating meaning need to be found, which lift our consciousness into communion with the spiritual world for inspiration. I would go further to suggest that, in our endeavors to create the new modes of thinking and speaking required to spiritualize our consciousness, the closest forms we have at present are poetry, mythology, movement, and art. For the intellect it is a complicated, convoluted effort to try to integrate "separate" disciplines such as science, philosophy, and theology. What language can be used? "Theologizing science?" "Empirical religion?" "Philosophical methodology?" Conversely, using the artistic imagination, we may create inclusive cosmology mandalas (maps or models) that stimulate the imagination to perceive this interweaving.

A Macrohistorical View of Thinking: Cosmologies of the Past

The term *cosmology* is used very broadly to mean worldview, including our view of the universe and the place of human beings in it. It will be argued that there is an important link between the major cosmological models underpinning macrocivilizational periods and the type of thinking associated with these eras.

The seminal theories of Richard Tarnas (1991) suggest that the present dominant worldview of our culture leaves humans alienated on all levels: cosmologically—in terms of our worldview; ontologically—our understanding of the nature of being; and epistemologically—how we arrive at knowledge. Tarnas's research on the history of Western philosophy further supports the views of Willis Harman (Harman, 1988) and the work earlier of Rudolf Steiner (Steiner, 1923/1990), who claimed that human consciousness would reach a crucial turning point throughout the twentieth and twenty-first centuries. In all these perspectives, it is argued that a crucial shift occurred in the sixteenth century with the declaration by Copernicus that the earth was not the center of the universe. In order to understand the significance of this shift for all aspects of human development and culture, it is necessary to look back briefly to how humans viewed the world before Copernicus. There were two key aspects of earlier pre-Copernican Western cosmologies and these aspects are also found in the cosmologies of traditional non-Western cultures.

- The universe is symbolically represented in holistic, usually circular, mandala forms.
- The imagery within the mandalas consists of hierarchies of living beings representing different aspects of the earth and cosmos.

These two aspects are evident in Figures 1 to 4 below.

Figure 1. Tibetan Cosmology—Mandala of the Maitripada
At the center is the deity Samvara (or Cakrasamvara) the Secret Lord of Mt. Kailash—
Samvara means "Supreme Bliss." "Inner freedom begins where the opposites have ceased to
exclude each other in continuous conflict" (Lauf, 1976, p. 173).

Through the symbols and artistry in these pre-Copernican cosmologies, everything was viewed as a whole and, furthermore, humans were seen to be at the center of this whole worldview/cosmology, as if embedded in a great cosmic womb surrounded by living beings of all dimensions. The Western view of the universe before Copernicus (when science and religion were still united) was based on the Ptolemaic model, which held that the earth was the center of the universe. Ptolemy based his cosmology on the thought of Aristotle (c. 300 BC). This unitary, cosmological archetype, sometimes referred to as "the great nest of being" (Wilber, 2000), is illustrated conceptually in Figure 5, which depicts the centrality of man's place, using the well-known image by Robert Fludd (Godwin, 1979) of man as microcosm in the macrocosm (Gidley, 2001).

Figure 2. Islamic Cosmology—Man and the Macrocosm
Miniature depicting man in the bound cosmos, surrounded by the heavens, each corresponding to one of the prophets; the zodiacal signs; the lunar mansions that symbolize the letters of the secret alphabet; and finally, the angelic realm which is above all space and therefore beyond the visible cosmos and itself the gate to the Divine Presence (Harmony with the Metacosmic Reality) (Nasr, 1976).

Figure 3. Medieval Zodiac (Time: Rhythm and Repose)
From early medieval manuscript, Italy (von-Franz, 1978).

Figure 4. Ptolemaic Cosmology
The medieval view of the zodiac, France, circa AD 1000 (Mammana, 1990).

From the present-day scientific perspective, it is argued that in these earlier "prescientific" times, humans were primitive and childlike and merely
imagined a world of Gods and spirits because they were not intellectually
mature and developed enough "to know reality scientifically." However,
from the perspective of a spiritual epistemology (or Perennial Philosophy), it
could be said that in the times represented by such cosmologies, humans
were in closer communication with the spiritual hierarchies, but that later the
spiritual beings guiding human development stepped back so that humans
could become free. From both these perspectives it is evident that this "stepping back of the Gods" paralleled the development of rational thinking. The
spiritual alienation experienced by contemporary humans was highlighted by
Rudolf Steiner in the following poem written in 1922 for his wife (Steiner,
1961):

The Stars spoke once to man
It is World-destiny
That they are silent now
To be aware of the silence
Can become pain for earthly man

But in the deepening silence
There grows and ripens
What Man speaks to the Stars
To be aware of the speaking
Can become strength for Spirit Man

COSMOLOGY I
Past – Pre-Copernican, Pre-Rational

TYPE OF THINKING:

- Pre-Rational, Pre-Logical
- Pictorial, Sentient

Figure 5. The Human Being Within the Cosmic Womb: The Premodern Condition.

COSMOLOGY II
Present – Copernican, Rational

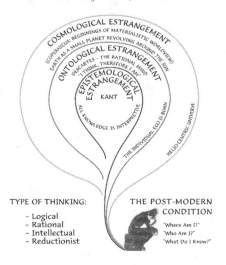

TYPE OF THINKING:

- Logical
- Rational
- Intellectual
- Reductionist

THE POST-MODERN
CONDITION

"Where Am I?"
"Who Am I?"
"What Do I Know?"

Figure 6. The Human Being, Hurled Out of the Cosmic Womb: The Postmodern Condition.

Cosmology of the Present (Western Worldview)

The triple alienation described by Tarnas (1993) as the post-Copernican double bind will now be explored in more detail. When Copernicus declared that the earth (and by default, human beings) was not the center of the universe, the heliocentric cosmology model was born, leading to cosmological estrangement. In the seventeenth century, the ontological estrangement from our own being came with Descartes' *cogito ergo sum.* The realization that "I think, therefore I am," meaning in essence I am an intellect, nothing more, led to a further depersonalization and mechanization of thinking. Finally, in the eighteenth century, building on these new rational/materialist foundations, came the epistemological estrangement from Kant's conclusion that all human knowledge is interpretive, that the world has no reality save what is perceived by the mind that views it (Tarnas, 1993). The diagram (Figure 6) is an attempt to illustrate some of the key features of this stage of human culture and consciousness. In this diagram, the image of man chosen to represent the postmodern, alienated, rational man is the sculpture of Rodin's thinker.

In parallel with these events, cultural power was shifting from the church to science as the new authority. By the seventeenth century the battle was on and by the eighteenth century, science had won. Prior to the developments mentioned above, which in a sense hurled mankind out of the cosmic womb, science and religion existed hand in hand, often woven together in art. Once intellectualism became underpinned by a reductionist, materialist worldview (as opposed to a divine one), spirituality was relegated to superstition and sidelined as faith (as opposed to knowledge which was "scientific"). No longer regarded as a sphere of knowledge, religion lost its status to science that had become by then "scientism." Hence, the dynamic dualism of science and religion gave way to the monism of science as the one true way of knowing. However, science without its divine moorings soon led to philosophical nihilism. In a sense the nineteenth and twentieth century "antiphilosophies" of nihilism and postmodernism are the logical extensions of this triple alienation of the human spirit.

With all these developments, the Western worldview has become increasingly rationalistic, materialistic, and reductionist. The mode of representing a cosmology became denotative rather than connotative, and with this process there was a subsequent decline in the artistic life and imagery of cosmological representations. Therefore, we lost beauty when we severed intellect from its divine source. What was once regarded as the starry heavens, the home of all the spiritual beings who surround humans, became a dark void, filled with dead planets, gaseous balls and black holes. Representations of this field became lists of numerical calculations and linear charts.

Our attempts over the past 300 years to understand the nature of the cosmos, the planets, solar systems, and galaxies, have been dominated by a materialistic worldview and reductionist methodology. However, the attempt to understand the esoteric nature of the cosmic bodies using physical instruments is analogous to trying to understand the human mind by studying a corpse.

Psychosocial Implications
of a Materialist Cosmology

The full sociocultural and psychological implications of the dominant materialist worldview have been gradually seeping into the human soul over the last of three centuries. In many ways the twentieth century could be seen as the low point in this regard. From a psychological perspective the litany of symptoms, exhibited by many young people in the "most developed" nations, exemplifies this disillusionment with great poignancy. Research shows that many young people of the West increasingly manifest high rates of depression (15% to 24%), eating disorders, and other forms of mental illness (Bashir & Bennet, 2000). Comparative studies, primarily in OECD (Organization for Economic Cooperation and Development) countries, indicate that when the numbers for all mental health disorders are combined, including ADHD, conduct disorder, depression, anxiety, and so on, as many as 18% to 22% of children and adolescents suffer from one or more of these disorders (Raphael, 2000). In Australia there have been increases in youth homelessness and school truancy that have created an underclass of "street kids" disenfranchised by society, yet often by the young people's own choice. Increasing numbers of youth are committing suicide and other violent crimes at an alarming rate, and are expressing a general malaise, loss of meaning and hopelessness about the future (Gidley & Wildman, 1996; Eckersley, 1993). Youth suicides among young males (ages 15 to 24) in Australia have doubled in the past twenty years (Mitchell, 2000, p. 194). Sohail Inayatullah (2002) refers to these phenomena as symptoms of "postindustrial fatigue." Personally, I regard them as symptoms of the "malaise of materialism." Under the impact of globalization, it can be expected that the "developing nations" will catch up to the West's sorry statistics in the near future (Gidley, 2002).

We might ask: Has the great Western civilization project been a huge mistake? Richard Tarnas believes that our current predicament is not an error or an imperialist-chauvinist plot, but part of a greater design. This view is supported by other grand theorists such as Rudolf Steiner (1968), and contemporary thinkers such as Duane Elgin (1993) and Ken Wilber (2000) as the remainder of this essay will demonstrate. Although the postmodern predicament may seem depressing, from another perspective it can be seen as an essential step in the development of human consciousness—a step toward the freeing of the human ego. The evolution of human consciousness, by way of the rational intellect which Western civilization has spearheaded for better or worse, will be further discussed below. However, what has happened to spiritual knowledge during the age of the dominance of science and intellectual thinking? Has it vanished or merely gone underground?

The Perennial Philosophy—Hidden Stream of Cultural Transformation

The Perennial Philosophy is that primordial wisdom of mankind whose traces are found everywhere, except in the modern and postmodern Western materialist paradigm. Not only is this wisdom the prerogative of churches and temples, but rather it can be transferred through a lineage of creative individuals. This unbroken lineage has, throughout every generation in history, expressed itself in ways appropriate to the challenges of the time and place. The following list includes some examples given by the Lindisfarne Fellows: the Theosophy of Yeats and Steiner, the Freemasonry of Mozart, the Alchemy of Fludd, the Hermeticism of Bruno, the Sufism of Ibn Arabi, the Kabbalism of Rabbi Moses de Leon, and the Neoplatonism of Plotinus. The hermetic texts on which some of these are based go all the way back to the most ancient Egyptian teachings of Pythagoras and Hermes Trismegistus (Lindisfarne Association). The esoteric Christian stream of mystery-knowledge centers also includes the Cathars, the Rosicrucians, and more recently the Anthroposophists.

From the perspective of these spiritual epistemologies, the cultural evolution of the human race has been a descent of humans from a spiritual homeland (Golden Age, Dreamtime, Eden) deeper and deeper into matter, through several major cultural epochs. Interesting links can also be observed between the various major cultural periods, the architecture and the thinking of the time. As demonstrated in Figure 7, twentieth-century Western architecture is overall the least artistic and integrated, with a predominance of square boxes, that reflect the structure of intellectual thinking.

From a Buddhist perspective, the Perennial Wisdom is referred to as the Shambhala Warrior teachings (Trungpa, 1984):

> The Shambhala teachings are founded on the premise that there is basic human wisdom that can help to solve the world's problems. This wisdom does not belong to any one culture or religion, nor does is come from the West or the East. Rather it is a tradition of human warriorship that has existed in many cultures at many times throughout history.

Figure 7. The Fall from Spirit into Matter.

The way in which this Buddhist wisdom could underpin a wise civilization is well illustrated by the following quote by E. F. Schumacher: "A Buddhist sees the essence of civilization not in a multiplication of wants but in the purification of human character" (Zajonc, 1997).

Esoteric Anthropology

In a contemporary attempt to develop what might be a new human image within the paradigm of Perennial Philosophy, Sheldon Isenberg and Gene Thursby (1984–86) introduce the concept of esoteric anthropology. In their view the Perennial Philosophies provide a significant response to the critiques of modernity while also transcending the postmodern despair of relativism. They offer two alternative approaches within the perennial stream: one which preserves the orthodoxies of traditional religions and one which promises freedom from their psychic bonds (Isenberg & Thursby, 1984–86). These two types of Perennialists are referred to as:

- **Devolutionists** (Traditional Perennialists)—those who believe traditional religions are the only authentic carriers of the Perennial Philosophy.
- **Evolutionists**—the Perennial Philosophers who believe that authentic mysticism is possible apart from the historically established traditions. Isenberg and Thursby refer to Oscar Ichazo (whose scientific mysticism goes beyond Aristotelian logic and Hegelian dialectics to trialectics) and to Ken Wilber as being significant contemporary evolutionists. They also refer to the "evolution of consciousness" work of Rudolf Steiner (Spiritual Science) as interpreted by Owen Barfield.

Robert McDermott (2001) from the California Institute of Integral Studies also discusses the debate within Perennialism between the traditionalists and evolutionists in a series of articles (McDermott, 2001a, 2001b, 2004). He refers to himself as espousing a "spiritually based evolutionism." He explores Rudolf Steiner's evolutionist position in a discussion of the different types of empiricism of Steiner and William James. He refers to Steiner's work as a comprehensive "spiritual epistemology," based on transformational empiricism informed by imaginative thinking, as a "method for generating spiritual, including philosophical and moral insights that can be known to be simultaneously individual and universal" (McDermott, 2001b, p. 6).

Although, in the light of the above, it seems evident that in terms of official culture spirituality had lost its place to science, it has been carried underground by the Perennial Philosophers who have carried a parallel responsibility for the evolution of culture and consciousness. In a sense the Romanticism movement was the visible peak of this underground movement—perhaps a little ahead of its time. Scott (2000) cites Tarnas as referring to a reemergence today of Romanticism with a "new vigor."

The Initiation of the Human Ego or "I Am"

There are many different views on where humans stand today. Many believe that the human race and earth as we know it will come to an end before too long, that we will exhaust resources and/or there will be massive catastrophes. The two extreme views are represented by Duane Elgin's "Crash or

Bounce" scenarios. A contemporary Perennialist, Elgin (1999) speaks of the present crisis of humankind as a "self-inflicted initiation"—a rite of passage that could lead human beings to a new relationship with one another and with the Earth. He speaks of the possibility that we may either crash or bounce, and of four likely stages of denial, innovation, initiation and bounce (see Figure 8).

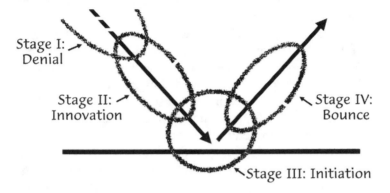

Figure 8. Evolutionary Initiation and Bounce.

Other Perennial Philosophers have a similar view that we are at a low point and will bounce or climb back out of our crisis, also seeing the present time as a time of initiation. Rudolf Steiner's spiritual epistemology includes the concept of conscious evolutionary development and regards the present stage of heightened materialism as a low point. This is the "no growth without crisis" theory in which we had to be thrown "out of the nest" and rejected by the Gods for our own development and freedom. In this view, which is an extension of the bounce theory, the crises of the twentieth and twenty-first centuries described above relate to the development and freeing of the human ego. Crucially though, the individual human ego, if it is not to lead humanity into an abyss of self-centered materialism, needs to be transformed by a higher order, spiritual consciousness or "higher self." Frithjof Schuon, cited in Isenberg (1984–1986), described the human ego as the great double-edged sword. "He alone among terrestrial creatures is free to go against his own nature" (p.14). Soren Kierkegaard was also aware of the dangers of the "free human ego" devoid of spiritual grounding:

> The most tremendous thing that has been granted to man is: the choice, freedom. And if you desire to save it and preserve it there is only one way: in the very same second unconditionally and in complete resignation to give it back to God, and yourself with it... (quoted in Campbell, 1968, pp. 197–198)

The Vertical Dimension

That there is a vertical dimension to our ontology may sound a little flippant at first. However, it is fundamental to the idea that we can "bounce." The bounce idea also implies that we are at a low point because if we believe that we are already at the top of the evolutionary ladder (as in the Darwinian view), then there is nowhere to bounce to. Even so, foundational to our materialistic and postmodern philosophies is the belief that hierarchical levels of existence including consciousness are part of the old "pre-scientific," traditional religious belief systems, and therefore died with God. On the other hand, the vertical dimension of humanity stretching from the physical to the spiritual has always been foundational to the Perennial Philosophy as discussed earlier. This vertical dimension has long been referred to as the Great Chain of Being. E. F. Schumacher, in discussion with Fritjof Capra, described what he called "a fundamental hierarchical order consisting of four characteristic elements—mineral, plant, animal and human" (Capra, 1988, p. 228). He related these also to four qualities— matter, life, consciousness, and self-awareness. Schumacher maintained that the differences between the levels represented fundamental jumps in the vertical dimension or "ontological discontinuities." Such ideas are also part of the comprehensive spiritual epistemology of Rudolf Steiner, which will be further explored in the next section. Harman expressed a similar view when he explored four levels of science (physical sciences, life sciences, human sciences and spiritual sciences), in which only the first is really well developed in the West (Harman, 1988). In this context it is not surprising that the horizontal rather than the vertical dimension is favored by Western science because in this first level (the physical level) it reigns supreme and consequently, it is easier to deny the existence of the other levels. Ironically, the vertical dimension and the ontological levels within it have always been acknowledged and respected by the Perennial Philosophers and mystics and have been symbolically represented by the metaphor of the ladder or steps (see Figures 9 and 10). St John of the Cross (1959) refers to the secret ladder as secret wisdom in his sixteenth-century classic of spiritual initiation—*Dark Night of the Soul.*

Types of Thinking—Three Major Layers

If the vertical dimension is applied to types of thinking we may consider three major layers—the prerational, rational, and post/transrational. These can be contextualized into a broader framework of human development where the human potentiality has nine major parts: three body related, three mind/soul related and three spiritual. This vertical layering of the different aspects of the human being (Figure 11) is found in a slightly varied form in many of the Perennial Philosophies (Eastern and Western), as already discussed. Similar taxonomies may be found in Vedanta Hinduism, Mahayana Buddhism, and the Kabbalah (Bjonnes, 2001), while Ken Wilber (2000) cites dozens of such frameworks in his book, *Integral Psychology*. In spite of the numerous different taxonomies for examining the developmental layering of the human being, the model presented here is chosen because it contains many linkages to other fields and includes the theory that different levels of consciousness are developed in humanity during different major cultural periods. Hence it supports the main thesis of this essay that the culture of a people is intimately connected with its constituents' type of thinking.

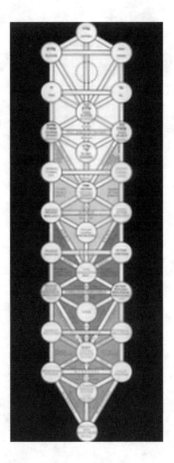

Figure 9. The Tree of Life (Jacob's Ladder)
According to the Kabbalah, the Tree of Life (or Jacob's Ladder), represents where the four worlds (of the Jewish Cosmology) interpenetrate the whole of existence.

The four worlds are:
The World of Emanation (White for Radiance)
The World of Creation (Blue for Heaven)
The World of Formation (Violet —Union of Heaven and Earth)
The World of Action (Red for Blood and Earth) (Halevi, 1979).

Figure 10. Jacob's Ladder—An artistic representation, painted by William Blake, circa 1800, England (Purce, 1974).

A Framework for Depicting the Developmental Layers
of the Human Being

Body	Mind/Soul	Spirit
Physical Body	Sentient Soul	Spirit Self
(Mineral)	Prerational/Prelogical	(Transformed Astral)
	Picture thinking	Psychic
	EGYPTIAN	
Life/Vital Body	Intellectual Mind/Soul	Life Spirit
(Vegetative)	Rational thinking	(Transformed Vital)
	Logical thinking	Subtle
	GRECO-ROMAN	
Emotional/	Consciousness Mind/Soul	Spirit Man
Astral Body	Vision-Logic	(Transformed Physical)
(Animal)	Transrational	Causal
	Imaginal/integral thinking	
	PRESENT ERA	

Table 1. A Linear Model of Layers of Human Development.

From the point of view of cultural development, the aspects that most concern us in our recorded history are primarily related to the three mind/soul functions or thinking types:

- From a Western perspective, prior to the Greco-Roman times, humans thought primarily in a pictorial manner—the hieroglyphic writing of the ancient Egyptians is indicative of thinking more steeped in images than the more abstract Greek and Roman alphabets. The Egyptian period (prelogical, prerational) covered approximately 3,500 BC—1,500 BC.
- The newborn logical powers of, for example, Aristotle, in a sense heralded a new stage of human consciousness from picture (or prelogical) thinking to logical, rational, intellectual thinking. The intellectual, rational thinking developed during the Greco-Roman period of approximately 1,500 BC–AD 1,500.
- Finally we encounter the consciousness thinking (post-rational or trans-rational thinking) characteristic of our own era (AD 1,500—present and future). Some of the great souls of the Renaissance period expressed the first glimmerings of this stage of consciousness (the multifaceted, integral human), but the next few hun-

dred years would see intellectual thinking become more instrumental, materialistic, and reductionist, and finally completely fragmented and alienated from its source.

With any new development in human evolution, there are always the initiates who come before, while the majority of humanity may take hundreds, even thousands of years to catch up. As a new stage breaks through, the time of most resistance from the old is encountered.

The trans-rational, imaginal/integral thinking that we need to develop in the present era, if we are to rise to a new, conscious accessing of spiritual wisdom, was called by Steiner "consciousness soul." In this view, imagination can be seen as a first step in transforming the thinking from matter-bound intellect to spiritual consciousness. The three stages of imagination, inspiration, and intuition are virtually universal concepts found in many spiritual paths (Steiner, 1967, p. 58). The development of imagination is thus a vitally important, yet neglected, part of education at all levels. This concept can apply to personal development, as well as laying foundations for a spiritual transformation of culture, beginning with developing our thinking beyond the categorical intellect to encompass imaginative consciousness. This same process of conscious, imaginal, and spiritually embodied thinking has been identified by several other contemporary thinkers. Essentially it involves a reinvention of human values to reincorporate the sacred. This approach is aligned to Thomas Berry's (1988) "post-critical naveté," Morris Berman's (1981) "participatory consciousness," and David Tacey's (1995) call for a "postmodern spirituality." Wilber (2000) and Scott (2000) call it "integral thinking." Futurist Tony Judge (1998) calls it higher coherence.

As an example of how information may be imaginatively transformed, the diagram in Figure 11 is an attempt to present the information of Table 1 in an integral rather than a linear way and illustrates how such an image could be synthesized with the "great nest of being" metaphor.

Although many contemporary thinkers are becoming increasingly aware of the need to stretch consciousness to new levels, the processes for achieving this evolution are often not so clearly accessible. It is suggested here, however, that the processes for attaining such development of thinking to higher levels of consciousness have been known in the secret knowledge centers. Perhaps now, in this time of global planetary crisis, is the time for them to be unveiled for all. By awakening our thinking with the ideas found in the perennial philosophies or spiritual epistemologies, by contemplative practices, by artistic work to stimulate the imagination, and sometimes by "grace," we can all develop our consciousness and ultimately our cultures to move beyond fragmented, materialistic thinking to multilayered, pluralistic, and inclusive integral cosmological models. Crucially, it involves a shift from solely "brain centered" thinking to "heart and brain centered" thinking.

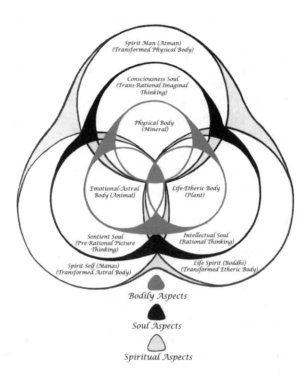

Figure 11. Layers of Human Development—An Integral Psychology Model.

Steiner also stressed the importance of the rational intellect. He insisted that we use the same rigorous thinking of the natural sciences to come to know our own inner natures and that of the outer, unmanifest, spiritual world. Through this, as well as contemplative practices and artistic practices, spiritual consciousness will come. These thoughts are echoed in Peter Russell's comment: "I believe that when we delve as fully into the nature of mind as we have into the nature of space, we will find consciousness to be the long-awaited bridge between science and spirit" (Russell, 2000). Some might argue that we are returning to the past and to prelogical thinking, but Wilber (1990) refers to this potential confusion as the "pre/trans fallacy" whereby no distinction is made between the prerational and trans- or post-rational type of thinking. There is, however, a crucial distinction: pre-rational, pictorial thinking was largely by unconscious revelation. Trans-rational, integral thinking includes all the earlier stages and transcends them in full consciousness (Wilber, 1995).

Integral Cosmologies for Reintegrated Futures

In this final section I suggest a conscious approach to the "bounce" model, although it is a work in progress. I propose here that it is entirely possible, using a spiritual epistemology to reverse the process of threefold alienation described by Tarnas (1991), to resituate the consciously evolving human being back into an inclusive cosmology where indeed the earth has meaning again and, from a spiritual perspective, becomes again the center of the cosmos.

In the same way that we can not regress to prerational thinking, we can not revert to pre-Copernican cosmological models. In searching for new images for a "*post* Post-Copernican" cosmology, we must not go back to the old circle, and we cannot ignore the developments of science. There will be no one future cosmology, as there will be no one future—mine may be full of images created from my experience. It is often said that "the Spiritual beings clothe themselves in different images depending on who is looking at them." We need not deny our Cartesian rational thinking, nor revert to old, absolutist, and pre-Kantian "truths." However, by using our own individual interpretive framework, we may endeavor to create new cosmological models for the future. As Tarnas (1991) stated: "The human mind is ultimately the organ of the world's own process of self-revelation" (p. 434). In this spirit perhaps we could move beyond Descartes, "I think, therefore I am" to a new dictum, "I am, therefore I create."

In an attempt to uncover any existing integral cosmologies from the Perennial Philosophies which might provide a starting point for our own creations, I have chosen to present two models developed by the Rosicrucians, both because of their universality of symbols and their artistic beauty. The Rosicrucian cosmologies illustrated in Figures 12 and 13 are examples of reintegrated systems where mankind is "outside" the cosmic womb yet part of it. Universal symbols are contained, including:

- the macrocosm/microcosm idea
- 'as above so below'
- living spiritual beings as part of the planetary and zodiacal systems
- the four elements/directions
- the vertical dimension by way of steps

Figure 12. Rosicrucian Cosmology
From the Museum Hermeticum (the most influential of the alchemical-Rosicrucian texts—published in 1677). The picture is believed to be the illustration for the oldest known alchemical text, the Emerald Tablet, supposedly written by Hermes Trismegistus. According to the Rosicrucians, the nature of the cosmos (or macrocosm) is visualized as a reflection of the lower world (microcosm). "As above so below."

Figure 13. Rosicrucian Path of Initiation
Important themes include the seven steps, the mystical cave, the signs of the zodiac, the four elements, representing human beings "outside the circle" (cosmos), yet with steps to take in consciousness to reunite with the cosmos (Walker, 1990).

It is possible that these illustrations may be ridiculed by some scientists as being full of superstitious meaningless symbols. However, similar to the mathematical formulae of physics, the symbols in these images are intensely charged with meaning for those who are initiated into their secrets.

Beyond Dualism to Inclusiveness

As mentioned in the introduction, one of the most limiting features of rational, intellectual thinking is its categorical nature that leads to fragmentation and a narrowing of options. Indeed, when it comes to presenting cosmological models, the basic dualism underpinning the Western worldview tries to force a choice between the old, "prescientific" Ptolemaic, geocentric model, and the "scientific," Copernican, heliocentric model. At the heart of the dilemma is the intellectual way of thinking, the categorical mode of Western intellectual thinking. When binary logic dominates we have tremendous difficulty dealing with paradox—"If one thing is correct the other must be incorrect." Compare this with the modes of speech used by Eastern mystics as devices to point beyond those pairs of opposites by which all logical thought is limited. For example, in the Zen Koan we hear of "the gateless gate," the "full void." The closest we have to it in Western linguistic concepts is the oxymoron, deriving from the Greek "pointedly foolish" which somehow does not command the status it deserves. It is merely a literary device rather than a path to spiritual awakening. I would like to suggest that the idea of the Koan gives us a clue to a reintegrated view using these two apparently conflicting cosmological models as a point of departure. I suggest that these two views are not in conflict and are, in fact, complementary views—the Copernican model explaining the physical universe and the Ptolemaic model being more applicable when we take into account the evolution of culture and consciousness incorporating the spiritual hierarchies as viewed by the Perennial Philosophies. These two cosmologies are in juxtaposition; neither is wrong but just incomplete. The potential power of bringing such an imagination to our scientific observation is captured by Tarnas (1991):

> It is only when the human mind brings forth from within itself the full powers of a disciplined imagination and saturates its empirical observation with archetypal insight that the deeper reality of the world emerges. (p. 434)

It is interesting to note that, although Western science began to come to terms with such complementarity in the twentieth century in the area of quantum physics, it still feels most comfortable when this paradoxical behavior of reality is restricted to minute particles (microcosm). There is still great controversy over whether the paradoxes found in quantum mechanics can be applied to the universe as a whole (macrocosm). Earlier, Rudolf Steiner (1970) proposed the notion that, before too long, people would again come to an understanding that the Ptolemaic model of the universe still has meaning when we can move beyond a materialistic worldview. Interestingly, a similar view is taken by quantum physicist Werner Heisenberg in his essay on scientific and religious truths. In a discussion of the different types of language used to express religious and scientific ideas, Heisenberg, cited in Wilber, speaks of the

> ...precision-oriented language of natural science...(which)...tries to give its concepts objective meaning. But religious language... (closer to that of poetry)...must avoid this cleavage of the world into its objective and its subjective sides; for who would dare claim the objective side to be more real than the subjective? (Wilber, 2001, p. 43)

Heisenberg also states:

> In the astronomical universe, the earth is only a minute grain of dust in one of countless galactic systems, but for us it is the center of the universe—it really is the center. (Wilber, 2001, p. 43)

Ironically, some of the latest developments in astronomy are beginning to have some resonance with these seemingly heretical ideas. At a conference held in 1973 in Poland, to celebrate the 500th birthday of Copernicus, a concept was presented that had the potential to turn astronomical thinking full circle. First put forward at this conference by the astrophysicist and cosmologist Brandon Carter, the Anthropic Principle in astronomy has been gaining ground and even developed several versions. While it is beyond the scope of this essay to expand on the "weak Anthropic principle," the "strong Anthropic principle" and the "final Anthropic principle," the basic thesis is an attempt to explain the "observed fact that the fundamental constants of physics and chemistry are *just right* or *fine-tuned* to allow the universe and life as we know it to exist" (Barrow & Tipler, 1986).

In summary, it is argued here that, while the Copernican system is undoubtedly true for the physical universe, the Ptolemaic system, which placed the earth (and thereby humans) at the center has more meaning from the perspective of the evolution of culture and consciousness. In this light the inclusive, future cosmology model developed here as a starting point in a new dialogue of cosmologies, incorporates this complementarity principle at the macrocosmic level as illustrated in Figure 14.

In this proposed model for a future-oriented integral cosmology, each of us as human beings is at the center of our own interpretive, creative cosmology: "I am, therefore I create."

While this approach may evoke the fears and risks of megalomania and terrorism, these are with us already and will not be overcome by the simplistic dualisms of "us and them." Notwithstanding also the tremendous structural obstacles many people around the planet are faced with today, we each have the choice and responsibility to begin our conscious evolution. If as a species we are to survive the materialistic age, we are obliged to lift our thinking beyond matter-bound intellect via one of the spiritual epistemologies. Through the imaginative process of higher order trans-rational thinking, we will be able to see beyond dualistic logic, to live with and embrace paradox and to begin our transformational tasks. The networking of change through a critical mass of innovative individuals and organizations can act as a human trampoline to facilitate the civilizational bounce that will be needed as materialistic culture collapses.

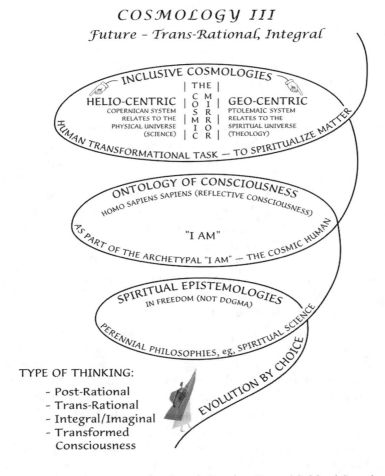

Figure 14. The Human Being Steps in Freedom Toward Spiritual Consciousness.

I would like to acknowledge with much gratitude the assistance of Alli Lawlor in transforming my graphics into their current form. I also wish to thank David K. Scott, for encouraging me to further develop these ideas, originally presented orally at the 2nd International Philosophy, Science and Theology Festival in July 2001, in Grafton, Australia.

References

Barrow, J. D., & Tipler, F. J. (1986). *The anthropic cosmological principle*. New York: Oxford University Press.

Bashir, M. & Bennet, D. (Eds.). (2000). Deeper dimensions: Culture, youth and mental health. *Culture and mental health: Current issues in transcultural mental health.* Parramatta, Australia: Transcultural Mental Health Centre.

Berman, M. (1981). *The reenchantment of the world.* Cornell, NY: Cornell University Press.

Berry, T. (1988). *The dream of the earth.* San Francisco: Sierra Club Books.

Bjonnes, R. R. (2001). Koshas: The state of the mind. *New Renaissance 10*, 7–9.

Boulding, E. (1998). *Building a global civic culture: Education for an interdependent world.* Syracuse, NY: Syracuse University Press.

Campbell, J. (1968). *The masks of God: Creative mythology.* New York: Penguin.

Capra, F. (1988). *Uncommon wisdom.* New York: Simon and Schuster.

Eckersley, R. (1993). The West's deepening cultural crisis. *The Futurist, 8–20.*

Elgin, D. (1993). *Awakening earth.* New York: William Morrow and Company.

——(1999). *Initiation: The coming evolutionary inflection.* Retrieved June 20, 2001 from www.newhorizons.org/future/elgin2020e.html

Gidley, J. (2000). Unveiling the human face of university futures. In S. Inayatullah & J. Gidley (Eds.) *The university in transformation: Global perspectives on the futures of the university.* Westport, CT: Bergin and Garvey.

—— (2001, July). *The dancer at the edge of knowledge: Imagination as a transdisciplinary force.* Presented at the 2nd International Philosophy, Science, and Theology Festival, Grafton, Australia.

——(2002). Global youth culture. In J. Gidley & S. Inayatullah (Eds.) *Youth futures: Comparative research and transformative visions.* Westport, CT: Praeger.

Gidley, J. & Wildman, P. (1996). What are we missing? A review of the educational and vocational interests of marginalized rural youth. *Education in Rural Australia. 6, 2,* 9–19.

Godwin, J. (1979). *Robert Fludd.* New York: Thames and Hudson.

Halevi, Z. (1979). *Kaballah: The tradition of secret knowledge.* New York: Thames and Hudson.

Harman, W. (1988). *Global mind change: The promise of the last years of the twentieth century.* New York: Warner Books.

Inayatullah, S. (2002). Youth dissent: Multiple perspectives on youth futures. In J. Gidley & S. Inayatullah (Eds.) *Youth futures: Comparative research and transformative visions.* Westport, CT: Praeger.

Inayatullah, S. & Wildman, P. (1998). *Future studies: Methods, emerging issues and civilizational visions.* A multimedia CD ROM. Brisbane: Prosperity Press.

Isenberg, S. R. & Thursby, G. R. (1984–86). Esoteric anthropology: "Devolutionary" and "evolutionary orientations." In Perennial Philosophy. *Religious Traditions*, 7, 9, 177–226.

Judge, A. (1998). From information highways to songlines of the noosphere. *Futures 30*, 1998, 2/3, 181-187.

Lauf, D. I. (1976). *Tibetan sacred art: The heritage of tantra.* Berkeley: Shambhala Publications.

LindisfarneAssociation. http://www.pacweb.com/lindisfarne/goals.html

Mammana, D. (1990). *The star hunters: The quest to discover the secrets of the universe.* New York: Mallard Press.

McDermott, R. (2001a). *Philosophy as spiritual discipline.* Retrieved May 2001 from California Institute of Integral Studies. Web site:http://www.ciis.edu/pcc/FAULTY/philosophyasspiritualdiscipline.htm

———(2001b). *William James and Rudolf Steiner*. Retrieved June, 2001 from California Institute of Integral Studies. Web site: http://www.ciis.edu/pcc/FACULTY/william james-andsteiner.htm

———(2004). *From mysticism to a modern spiritual philosophy*. Retrieved November 2004 from California Institute of Integral Studies.Web site: http://www.ciis.edu/pcc/FACULTY/mcdmysticism.htm

Mitchell, P. (2000). *Valuing young lives: Evaluation of the national youth suicide prevention strategy*. Melbourne: Australian Institute of Family Studies.

Nasr, S.H. (1976). *Islamic science: An illustrated study*, UK: World of Islam Festival Publications Co, Ltd.

Purce, J. (1974). *The mystic spiral*. New York: Thames and Hudson.

Raphael, B. (2000). *Promoting the mental health and well-being of children and young people*. Canberra: Commonwealth Department of Health and Aged Care.

Russell, P. (2000). *From science to God*. Sausalito, CA: Author.

Scott, D. K. (2000). Spirituality in an integrative age, in V. H. Kazanjian, Jr. & P. Laurence (Eds.) *Education as transformation: Religious pluralism, spirituality and a new vision for higher education in America*. New York: Peter Lang Publishing.

Slaughter, R. (1994). *From fatalism to foresight—educating for the early 21st century: A framework for considering young people's needs and responsibilities over the next 20 years*. Melbourne: Australian Council for Educational Administration.

St John of the Cross. (1959). *Dark night of the soul*. New York: Image Books.

Steiner, R. (1923). *The evolution of consciousness as revealed through initiation knowledge: Lectures*. London: Garden City Press.

Steiner, R. (1961). *Verses and meditations*. London: Rudolf Steiner Press.

———(1967). *The stages of higher knowledge*. New York: Anthroposophic Press.

———(1968). *Microcosm and macrocosm*. London: Rudolf Steiner Press.

———(1970). *The spiritual hierarchies and their reflection in the physical world*. New York: Anthroposophic Press.

———(1971). *Theosophy*. New York: Anthroposophic Press.

———(1990). *Toward imagination: Culture and the individual*. New York: Anthroposophic Press.

Tacey, D. (1995). *Edge of the sacred: Transformation in Australia*. Melbourne: Harper Collins.

Tarnas, R. (1991). *The passion of the western mind*. New York: Random House.

———(1993). The western mind at the threshold: Astrology and the post modern crisis. *The Quest*, 25–31.

Trungpa, C. (1984). *Shambhala: The sacred path of the warrior*. New York: Bantam.

von-Franz, M. (1978). *Time: Rhythm and response*. New York: Thames and Hudson.

Walker, C. (1990). *Sites of mystery and imagination: A journey through the occult heritage of Europe*. London: Hamlyn.

Wilber, K. (1990). *Eye to eye: The quest for the new paradigm*. Boston: Shambhala.

———(1995) *Sex, ecology, spirituality: The spirit of evolution*, Boston: Shambhala.

———(2000). *Integral psychology: Consciousness, spirit, psychology, therapy*. Boston: Shambhala.

Wilber, K. (Ed.). (2001). *Quantum questions: Mystical writings of the world's greatest physicists*. Boston: Shambhala.

Wildman, P. (2000). At the edge of knowledge: Toward polyphonic multiversities. In S. Inayatullah & J. Gidley (Eds.) *The university in transformation: Global perspectives on the futures of the university*. Westport, CT: Bergin and Garvey.

Zajonc, A. (1997). Buddhist technology: Bringing a new consciousness to our technological future. In *Seventeenth annual E. F. Schumacher lecture*. Williamstown, MA: Williams College.

Science and Spirituality—
Finding the Right Map

Arthur Zajonc

Every object, well-contemplated, creates
a new organ of perception in us.
                                        Goethe

Why has it proven so difficult to clarify the status of spirituality and its relation to science? In part, it is due to a confused cartography, a false map. That
map looks something like this:

Faith......vs.	Reason
Belief.....vs.	Knowledge
Religion...vs.	Science

In one column there is faith, belief, and religion. In the other, opposite
faith many people would place reason. Following that logic, in contrast to
belief we would have knowledge, and opposite religion, science. This common scheme is not entirely mistaken. It provides a useful set of distinctions,
certainly for our public and social life, perhaps even for aspects of our intellectual life. The faith/reason interplay and debate have endured for centuries,
possibly since the time of the early Church, and certainly since the Reforma-
tion.

However, I do not wish to explore the classic tension between religion
and science, faith, and reason. Instead, I will focus on the following three
questions: first, the status of spirituality—the spiritual life, the spiritual dimensions of our lives and our world. Where are these to be located on this
map? Second, what is the relation of spirituality to science? This question
invites a review of our perspective on science itself. Third, following on the
latter point, might our understanding of knowledge or "knowing" be enhanced or enlarged? Should we really rest content with our conventional notions of the nature and limits of "knowing?"

Regarding the first question, the nature and status of spirituality, the
common assumption will be that we must choose a side for it on our little
two-column map. It is a classic "either/or" situation. It appears we must
place spirituality either on the side of faith or of reason, belief or knowledge,
religion or science. Naturally, the common choice will be the faith/be-
lief/religion side.

Even this first step, crediting the presumption that we must choose one
side of this proposed divide, seems to us a fundamental error, one that al-

ready yields a false map. I believe that some significant aspect of "spirit" actually resides on and animates both sides of this mapped polarity. Now, inasmuch as spirituality certainly lives within the first column of our map, the column that includes religion, it can figure prominently in the ethical sense of an individual or a community. However, it does so by drawing upon a kind of knowing, rather than on a religious tenet (which might well express spiritual knowing in particular, tradition-specific terms). I therefore take spirituality to be the more fundamental case, and thus more suitable for our discussion of possible links and contrasts with science.

We should acknowledge in passing that the distinction between religion and spirituality may itself seem debatable because the two coincide in many people's practice. I hope the reader will grant us leeway to concentrate on a line of thought we feel requires the distinction, at least up to a point. More-over, we are expanding on our claim that spirituality does have a place on both sides of the map. Thus, spirituality may be distinguishable from relig-ion, but it certainly should not be defined in such a way as to relegate it to a separate, circumscribed niche. For us, spirituality is a term that bears on the most encompassing view of life and human engagements. Our objective is therefore to provide an account of how this may be so. Following advice given by Owen Barfield, I seek to distinguish, but not to divide (Barfield, 1971).

Now, what basis could there be for including spirit and spiritual life in the other column of our map, the column we have characterized as emphasiz-ing inquiry, reason, experience leading to knowledge, science? Sciences such as physics are taken to be ultimate expressions of disciplined inquiry and rational analysis. What possible connection could they have to spirituality?

This same kind of question arises regarding many other dimensions of our lives—aesthetic, ethical, and moral. Where should we locate these on our little map? Following the map's apparent logic, they might seem to involve only feelings, subjective impressions, and opinions. That common assump-tion notwithstanding, might they actually be more akin to knowledge? How? In this essay, I want to step away from specific developments within science and religion, aesthetics and ethics, and argue instead for an acknowledgment of their common root. I maintain this root consists in a common cognitive source—specifically, an active and refined use of appreciation and insight.

It is precisely such capacities that constitute the heart of science and the quest for knowledge. If we omit them from our definition of either spiritual-ity or the knowledge project, we will have arbitrarily defined out much of what we care about most. By including the role of insight, we recover a sense of the basic nature of all the items in our little map, and can find a more sat-isfactory way to redraw it.

Seeing a Sunset

Imagine that we are standing on a hillside in some natural setting, viewing a sunset. The sun will soon dip beneath the horizon, and some clouds hang low in the sky. The sky overhead remains an intense blue. However, as the sun sets, both the landscape and cloud-filled horizon are wonderfully transformed by a series of shifts in color. The last streaming sunlight dances across the landscape, and the clouds show first, perhaps, the most tender touch of pale yellow, and then gradually change over the course of some minutes to an increasingly intense orange and then red. Not only the clouds, but the entire landscape before us is thus transformed. The sunset scene makes a powerful impression, aesthetically, perhaps even spiritually, fascinating us and drawing us into a deep rapport with the world, with various facets of our existence as they are felt in this special moment.

While we are immersed in this experience, a certain kind of thought might intrude: "This display is remarkable, spectacular, and the moment—the engagement—meaningful in some elusive way." So it is natural for us to wonder, "Hmm … what is present here? What is happening here?" That question, which is concerned with large matters of existential significance as well as intellectual curiosity, might then be further sharpened to concentrate on natural processes: "How does this happen?" Then further, "What is the scientific mechanism?"

The easy, unconscious restatement of our wonder as a request for a predictive or causal account of a phenomenon is a fairly modern quirk. We should be aware of the steps taken here, and of both the enormous advantages and the somewhat regrettable tradeoffs. The advantages are obvious to us at this point in history, but the tradeoffs have become harder to appreciate or even define, and so they now seem negligible, "metaphysical."

Can we remember when we first asked things like, "Daddy, why is the sky blue?" or "Why is that cloud so red?" Then too, our questions may have been pointed, concerned with some observed particular that struck us as remarkable. Through our questions, we sought answers that would help us deal with what we were meeting directly in the world. We wanted to clarify this meeting so we could turn back to it with greater acceptance and appreciation.

This orientation toward questions and answers—and omniscient mothers and fathers—seems so natural for children as they relentlessly quiz their parents. It is doubtless naïve in some respects, but it nevertheless retains a connection to an issue that is important for us all. Let us see how it might have been respected and served if our hypothetical parent were a scientist, or scientifically informed. How would "Daddy's" patient explanations have sounded, and how would they have addressed our original concern, if offered at various periods in these last few, increasingly scientific, centuries?

In the eighteenth century, Daddy might have said something like: "Well Mary, light is really made up of tiny corpuscles or particles; and the big ones give rise to red sensations, while the small ones yield blue sensations. As these particles stream through the clouds, you see, the blue ones are absorbed and the red ones get through." So an eighteenth-century Mary would be expected to consider her untutored perception of the red sunset in terms of that explanation and think, "Oh, that's the reason the sunset clouds look red— only the red particles are reaching me."

This kind of explanation, due to Newton, served well for quite a while. However, scientists gradually began to realize for various reasons that the corpuscular model is not a satisfactory way of thinking about light. So another picture then came into vogue, to the effect that "light is a wave." Specifically, that light is a wave within something that used to be called the "luminiferous ether." This view was especially popular in the late eighteenth and early nineteenth centuries, and persisted right through the nineteenth century.

The luminiferous ether was conceived to be a subtle material body that pervaded all of space. It could support light waves, in a manner similar to the physics involved in sound propagation through air. The waves traversed the luminiferous ether, which spanned the distances intervening between objects and observers with waves, reached our eyes ... and so we could see. Again, there was an attendant explanation of the color differences: the long wave lengths and the short wave lengths give rise to the different colors, some being absorbed and some not, *et voilà*—a magnificent sunset!

Again, a happy resolution of at least some aspects of Mary's concern— but only until scientific research failed to support this "luminiferous ether" notion. In the wake of the justly famous Michelson-Morley experiments, we scientists reluctantly rid physics of the "ether" altogether. However, we still liked the "wave" idea, and it was in fact a very powerful way of thinking. Only, what then was waving? If there was not any water or air or ether— there was just nothing there. Try to think that thought— something is waving, but there is nothing there to wave, no medium. So, it is like trying to catch a wave and surf your way in to the beach, only there is no water to carry you. We are dealing here with an entirely different conception of the wave nature of light.

We might say that we have shifted from an ontology of matter (be it corpuscles or ether) to an ontology of force. This mysterious thing called light, which used to be considered as particulate, and then as luminiferous ether waves, is now recast as electromagnetic waves, waves within something called the "electromagnetic field." Even if this field is still seen as analogous to the discarded "etheric medium" of the past, the crucial difference is that in this case it has become more abstract and requires a primarily mathematical treatment. Michael Faraday suggested a nonmathematical version of this sort of shift forty years before experimental data necessitated such a change in thinking. James Clerk Maxwell developed the abstract theory for it in the 1860s.

The "electromagnetic field" is an extremely powerful conception in physics. In fact, it was so remarkable that even the originators of this concept such as Maxwell and Lorentz could not quite bring themselves to accept its implications fully, and so clung to some kind of ether hypothesis (Zajonc, 1993; Cao, 1997). It was really only after these great physicists died and we were well into the twentieth century that the "ether" was finally abandoned, and electromagnetic waves were accepted as traveling through space without the support of a material medium.

Of course, by the turn of the century, the specific issue of sunset colors could already be explained by Mie scattering and Rayleigh scattering. Here the basic idea involves the incidence of electromagnetic waves on polarizable particles in the atmosphere, which sets up little electric dipoles that oscillate and give off their own electromagnetic waves. These secondary fields interfere with the original incident waves, with the result that the differential cross section depends on the fourth power of the frequency of the electromagnetic wave's vibration. This is all very complex but works beautifully— at least until we start thinking about light from the perspective of quantum mechanics!

Remember where you are on the hillside, entranced by the sunset, holding a poignant question about it that is prompted by your elation and curiosity. Perhaps you are disappointed or annoyed by the answers your solicitous parents are offering and feel that they miss your point. Perhaps you are feeling distracted and hope Daddy will not tell you any more about this physics stuff. Perhaps, though, Daddy's skillful summary of physics exposes you to more marvels than even your original experience and question encompassed, and starts you on the way to your own scientific calling. Perhaps both of these reactions arise, leaving you feeling subtly torn.

So, as we gaze enraptured by the sunset, the scientific answers may seem irrelevant to us or they may help us to appreciate its glory and the wonders of the world's phenomena even more. They may even accomplish the latter splendidly and still miss something important. Much depends on how the scientific view itself is understood, the extent to which it is taken— or presented—as an exercise of insight and an aid to appreciative participation in the phenomena.

We must remember that even the electromagnetic conception we have described is still only physics circa 1905, a hundred years ago. Quantum mechanics and quantum field theory have since arisen and added to our understanding of light and its interaction with clouds, so the electromagnetic waves, which we thought of as unsupported waves of the energy of the electromagnetic field, have since been reconceptualized in terms of a quantized field in which photons are created and destroyed in the scattering process.

So for us living in the twenty-first century, answers have become quite abstract. "And yes, Mary, that's the reason why the sunset sky turns red! That's what's really happening here."

Science Is Wonderful ... But What Is It?

Physics is a very beautiful field. It is the love of my intellectual life, especially this area last mentioned above, quantum optics. Overall, what has been briefly sketched here is part of the real story of how physicists have understood light since the eighteenth century. It is clearly an elaborate and marvelous theoretical framework, one which has changed repeatedly to give us the best account of light we can manage at any given time. Furthermore, it is very illustrative of the scientific enterprise in general. Note that while science yields an account, this process of explanation may never be fully completed—so far, it has kept changing, undergoing refinement.

The first and simplest lesson we should probably draw from this story is that it's best to be modest in our pretensions to understanding the world. It's not only that we ordinary mortals don't understand, for example, the nature of the light that streams through that beautiful sunlit landscape. Even Albert Einstein was keenly aware of his theory's limits. In 1917, when as a young scientist he had finished his papers on both special and general relativity, he set a task for himself: "For the rest of my life I will reflect on what light is" (Wolf, 1979).

Decades later, not long before he died, he wrote:

> All the fifty years of conscious brooding have brought me no closer to the answer to the question of what are light quanta. Of course today every rascal thinks he knows the answer, but he is deluding himself. (Wolf, 1979)

Whether or not physics undergoes radical change indefinitely, we can be quite certain that our last account, which reflects the most modern physical theory about the light quanta—even that will continue to be refined, and probably will be overthrown in radical ways. While this theoretical evolution is of tremendous importance, and leads to profound understanding, what is the nature of this understanding? What does it really involve, all along the way? What fuels it, what does it yield for us, and what might it obscure if we're not careful?

Returning to the sunsets—both they and our human visual capacity, perhaps even our actual appreciation of their colors and beauty, have been the same for millennia. Even granting that differences of culture, language (including color terms and color categories) and worldview are also involved and doubtless influence certain features of our appreciation, we believe much has remained the same, especially at the fundamental level: recognizing the basic colors, feeling a sense of wonder and curiosity and connection. On the other hand, in the past three hundred years physicists have certainly produced a fascinating series of quite different accounts of sunsets' splendors.

The process of doing science is largely about generating models for things like light—for what light is, how it interacts with the atmosphere, and so forth. Without model-making, there could be no science. However, if we take this particular aspect of scientific praxis too literally, and if we focus on the model-making enterprise itself too exclusively, we then make the mistake mentioned earlier—we define the search for knowledge too narrowly.

What is essential, and thus proper, in our model-making, our theorizing? This question might help us find the right way to handle theories, one that frees us in certain respects. Obviously we can't renounce the use of formal theories; we will remain scientists in that sense. Perhaps we can and should handle such theories more lightly, without exaggerated commitments. If we see that this is so, we may then move easily from one theory to the next, always being prepared for further advancements or refinements.

Even more importantly, we may come to a new view of our knowledge projects, a way of understanding what science is really about, that could accommodate the aesthetic, ethical and spiritual dimensions of our lives. If, however, we define science as the only knowledge project, and as being primarily concerned with models, all knowledge is captured within or restricted to those models. The knowledge project is then—I think unfortunately—reduced to the modeling project. We thereby also leave out some other, very important aspects of both the phenomena and the scientist *qua* knower.

Early Modern Articulations of "Really Knowing"

In 1851, Henry David Thoreau stood on a hillside, viewing just the sort of sunset we've been discussing. It was Christmas evening. He writes in his journal:

> I, standing twenty miles on, see a crimson cloud on the horizon. You tell me it is a mass of vapors which absorbs all other rays and reflects the red. But that is nothing to the purpose. What sort of science is that which enriches the understanding, but robs the imagination? If we knew all things thus mechanically merely, should we know anything really? (Thoreau, 1906, pp. 155–156)

Here Thoreau alerts us to a major tension, a contrast he describes as holding between "understanding and imagination." At stake here is the difference between a form of understanding that he calls "mechanically merely," and what it would be to comprehend something incisively and satisfactorily. Thoreau seeks more than just to know via a narrow preoccupation with the models and postulated mechanisms of physics. He wants also to know through what, in the parlance of his time, he calls the faculty of imagination.

The "imagination" that Thoreau so prized—and which he claims might reveal the sunset to him more fully than a mechanical account by itself— certainly also has a central and active place in the life and practice of a scientist. By clarifying this faculty's nature, scientific role and relation to the world, we may establish that science does more than proffer merely mechanical accounts. Thoreau's friend and mentor R. W. Emerson raises the challenge succinctly, "And never did any science originate, but by a poetic perception" (Emerson, 1903–04, pp. 364–365).

Despite the great difficulties involved in defending such an assertion, we think what is at stake is so important that we must reopen the inquiry—how might Emerson have been right? Note that what lies behind his point applies to commonplace insights and sensibilities, ethico-spiritual and aesthetic responses, philosophy, and to the practice of science. Much has changed since the romantic philosophical vision of Emerson and Thoreau. In addition, our contemporary view of nature and science cannot possibly be traded away for a return to those nineteenth-century yearnings. Still, though, Thoreau and Emerson also offer us glimmerings of a critical and timeless issue.

We find related clues in other authors, cultures, and periods. Thoreau and Emerson struggled to articulate and defend a point that for them and many others over the centuries has remained inchoate, an awkward fledgling. Now its explication must be made more mature, and integrated more fully into our modern understanding. Much new work is needed, but it should not be undertaken without acknowledging the early but extremely provocative attempt by Johann Wolfgang von Goethe.

Goethe was a genius of an unusual kind, who sought a harmony of view concerning the scientific, poetic, and personal domains. He made a remarkably concerted attempt to engage the question—how we can understand science and the knowledge project in general, in ways that would also be open to the spiritual dimensions of our lives? Thoreau and Emerson both read Goethe in the original and admired him enormously as the most modern and exemplary genius of their day. To Emerson Goethe was the ideal poet-savant who saw the harmonizing of science and poetry as not only desirable, but essential. Goethe's whole nature was a living refutation of the false map.

Goethe soared to fame with the publication of his short novel *The Sorrows of Young Werther*, which has been called the first bestseller in Europe. One admirer was the young Duke Karl August who invited Goethe to Weimar where he would not only live and write for the remainder of his life, but he would became a minister in the Duke's government. In this role Goethe's responsibilities spanned the gamut from director of the Jena stage to head of the regional mining operations. The breadth of Goethe's portfolio reflects the wide range of Goethe's interests. Although his fame rested on his literary productions—his lyric poetry and plays especially—his mind was absorbed in the mysteries of nature. This led to energetic studies in botany, biology, geology, meteorology and optics, and which lasted for most of his adult life. Indeed he felt that his contributions as a scientist would eventually be seen by posterity as more significant than his work as a poet. While Goethe made specific scientific discoveries, especially in botany and anatomy, of greatest interest to us is his philosophy of science. It was developed gradually out of his long practice of observation and experimentation, and benefited enormously by his relationship with his more philosophically minded friend Friedrich Schiller.

First of all, Goethe was critical of the model-building enterprise as an end in itself. In his *Theory of Colors* he wrote:

> The investigator of nature should take heed not to reduce observation to mere notion, to substitute words for this notion and to use and deal with these words as if they were things. (Goethe, 1970, p. 283)

In a short essay on science Goethe stated:

> A false hypothesis is better than none at all. The fact that it is false does not matter so much. However, if it takes root, if it is generally assumed, if it becomes a kind of credo admitting no doubt or scrutiny this is the real evil, one which has endured through the centuries. (Goethe, 1952, p. 239 and Goethe, 1981, HA 13, p. 51)

In the terms of our example, we are standing there on the hill in the early evening, immersed in our experience of the sunset, but we unconsciously drift from its vibrant presence to words, notions, concepts. Then we deal with those concepts and words as if they were the thing itself. So in fact, we have stopped looking. Unless we are aware of these concepts' limits and their source in our capacity for insight, and are careful to note ways they may aid our direct participation and enlarge our discernment—we are effectively not there anymore.

The same dislocation and truncation of appreciation can occur in many other domains, even the interpersonal sphere. When looking at one another, we sometimes see only in terms of social conventions, memories and descriptions, words and concepts, and perhaps ideas drawn from psychology, politics or medicine or a hundred other disciplines. We meet, understand, and interact with each other in a way that is very complex but remains "mechanically merely" as opposed to really.

Over the course of his life, Goethe went to great pains to explain why, both as scientists and as human beings, we must avoid this mistake. From his standpoint, the problem is not that we use a description, convention, model, or hypothesis, but rather that it acquires a dominating force:

> Hypotheses are like the scaffolding erected in front of a building, to be dismantled when the building is completed. To the worker the scaffolding is indispensable, but he must not confuse it with the building itself. (Magnus, 1949, p. 229 and Goethe, 1981, HA 12, p. 432)

Models and hypotheses are like scaffolding—do not confuse the scaffolding with the building itself. Once we have succeeded in raising the mature insight, we must take down the scaffolding so we may see the building directly. Without doubt we need stepping stones, intermediate stages, conceptual aids, in order to gain a fuller and more direct view, a direct engagement with the building. However we should not confuse the latter with any of the former.

Here Goethe uses a wonderful German word, *das Wesen*. He says:

> Yet how difficult it is not to put the sign in place of the thing. How difficult to keep the being (das Wesen) always livingly before one, and not slay it with the word. (Goethe, 1981, HA 13, p. 452)

We must gain and retain access to what he calls *das Wesen*, the being, the building itself, whose character is reflected in the theory or scaffolding, but should not be equated with the latter at all, and is thus not limited to the narrow, antiseptic version of what we moderns typically consider a "phenomenon." So we honor theory and the theoretical enterprise of normal science, but at the same time we do not want to adopt a fundamentalist attitude toward that science. We do not want to interpret knowing and knowledge of a thing as being equivalent to our possessing a scientific model of it.

We seek an approach to science that is honest about its nature and sufficiently respectful of the world being studied that it can accommodate more of the phenomenon's actual character. Granted, this agenda is both complex and problematical, possessing many controversial points. However, these difficulties should not intimidate us into settling for less without even considering the possibilities. With this commitment, spirituality may also be accommodated—not as involving only faith, but as part of the knowledge project, as relevant to true knowing.

Goethe' s own work contains some useful hints about how this might be achieved. In addition to being a great romantic poet, Goethe also made many significant contributions to the study of color, plant morphology, and human anatomy. His approach to these apparently quite disparate fields exhibits a vision that was clearly indebted to his study of novelistic technique. Drawing upon that experience, he says that attempting to formally define the inner nature of a thing is not the only or best option:

> What we perceive are effects, and a complete record of these effects ought to encompass this inner nature. We labor in vain to describe a person's character, but when we draw together his actions, his deeds, a picture of his character will emerge. (Goethe, 1995, p. 158)

Goethe, the novelist and playwright, knows one does not capture and convey a person's character by trying to define it, but rather by showing it, enabling the reader to directly apprehend that person's actions and responses to life. Confronting first the effects or actions, we readers can eventually come to see more, the person. Turning his attention toward Nature, Goethe retains this same conviction. Persons must do their jobs as observers, as empiricists, and one could say, as experiencers, knowing that they cannot just open their eyelids and let the whole world flood in and be known. One must engage the world actively and systematically, seeking out its effects, and then the phenomenon will begin to reveal itself more completely and coherently. Its nature will shine through its effects. Attaining a more full and incisive cognizance of these effects is the goal of applying the scientific method.

In dozens of treatises and also in his correspondence with Friedrich Schiller and others, Goethe explored this view's application to science. While modern science and philosophy obviously supercede much of that eighteenth-century account, I think Goethe saw and emphasized an important point that nowadays tends to be lost:

> There is a delicate empiricism which makes itself utterly identical with the object, thereby becoming true theory. But this enhancement of our mental powers belongs to a highly evolved age. (Goethe, 1995, p. 307)

This is an extremely condensed statement of many of Goethe's ideas about science. "A delicate empiricism"—there is a way of engaging the world of phenomena, the world of experience, which is both fully active and delicate. We thereby make ourselves "utterly identical with the object" of study, we move into the phenomenon, we do not stand off at arm's length. We maintain the best kind of objectivity when we engage and become identical with the phenomenon. Thus we "become true theory." What could Goethe possibly mean by being identical with the object, by becoming true theory? Are we not separate from the objects of our knowing? Isn't a theory just a formal statement, a generalization, an abstraction?

Goethe says that true theory, true knowledge, arises for us in that moment and through that delicate empiricism, because by staying with the phenomenon, insight into its fundamental nature may arise. This more participatory form of insight is what he calls "the *aperçu*." Then, though, he cautions, "But this enhancement of our mental powers belongs to a highly evolved age." A person cannot just passively acquire the aperçu. First we must work to enhance our powers of discernment. As a physicist struggling with a scientific challenge, or as a person seeking maturity or moral integrity, we must evolve, developing new capacities of insight so we may integrate more fully with the phenomena of life as they actually present themselves.

This very brief account of an alternate view of the knowledge project posits that knowing is more capable of refinement and discernment with respect to the phenomena than is usually supposed and thus need not be set altogether apart from more spiritual forms of beholding. Applied to science, this view does not overemphasize theoretical models, but rather respects the cognitive source that gives rise to them and also, in the end, completes them.

Developing Our Capacities to See

The tension between the theory and presuppositions of modern science on the one side, and the alternate possibility of a science—or a new approach to ordinary science—based more on insight, is itself creative. It can challenge us to clarify both perspectives, examining each with the other in mind. In the process, we may also begin to see our way to a bridge between ordinary science and other domains of knowing, and even significant fundamental overlap between them. The common element is an active insight that is appreciative, intimately connected with its object through a process of rigorous engagement and exploration.

Ambiguous figure—an old lady or a young maid.

Some psychological research has also centered on the phenomenon of figure-ground reversal, and other ways in which we can switch between two views of an ambiguous figure. The reader is probably familiar with the picture above, in which one can make out either the face of an old woman seen close up, looking to the left, or the profile of a young girl at a distance turning away from the viewer (her chin becomes the old woman's nose, her necklace becomes the mouth).

Our present interest in such ambiguous materials should not suggest that we think the world itself is usually so ambiguous, but only that they illustrate the role of active decisions and selective attention in perceiving. While not ambiguous, the world is rich in content and features on many levels that may be of interest for various reasons. In addition, the discernment of specific phenomena in that rich presentation depends on both our attention and our sensitivity. The latter are themselves iteratively informed and refined by interaction with the world. With received knowledge and with the theories ("scaffolding"), we may fashion to represent such complexities. Our own degree of maturity and personal development in appreciating the possibilities are also involved in "insight."

This was Goethe's point—what is the real, or essential, phenomenon? We must practice something like his method to bring out the real phenomenon so that we may appreciate it better. Having done this in the classroom, or by thinking deeply, reading or watching some instructive film or television program at home, we must then practice seeing instances of that same phenomenon in the world at large. Only thus may we truly cultivate a fundamental "insight" and may we expect to find a corresponding enrichment in our own selves, in our way of being, as a result of entering the world more appreciatively.

True beholding, true theorizing, requires the active cultivation of an appropriate sensibility. Goethe says, "Every object, well contemplated, creates a new organ of perception in us" (1995, p. 39). Working our way into a deep engagement with the world, using care and contemplation, eventually creates an organ for perception, and changes us in the process. This is as true of the artist as it is of the scientist. In fact it applies equally well to the spiritual contemplative, or to anyone seeking to be a better person in the spiritual sense. In any of these spheres, such disciplined engagement and contemplation yields a deepening of capacity and maturation, enabling us to see more of what is there.

One delightful story to this effect is about Paul Cezanne, the great post-impressionist painter. Over the period of a generation Cezanne made many studies of Mont Sainte-Victoire near Aix. The story has it that his son found this repetition incomprehensible, and asked, "Father, why are you painting the same thing?" Cezanne's not very forthcoming reply was, "I could stand here for six months and paint this scene again and again and again." In a letter to his friend, Emil Bernard, he essentially said, "Nature is the true teacher, and we must make ourselves concentric to her" (Cézanne, 1976, pp. 327, 303 and 306).

This "becoming concentric" is quite a wonderful notion. The point is partly that we start out eccentric, "off-center." Then through that constant patient inquiry by which something is well contemplated—as Goethe put it—not only do we paint pictures or contrive models, but we actually find the world. We create new organs of perception; we make ourselves concentric to that which we are beholding. When we finally succeed, an element of true theory is made plain. Perhaps we also find something of ourselves in this engagement with the world.

In discussing this idea an anecdote about Rilke comes to mind. Rilke passed through an exhibition of paintings and, standing before a painting by Cezanne, felt at a loss for quite some time. Finally, though, his capacities became adequately sharpened by the encounter, and then Rilke is rumored to have exclaimed: "Ah, now I have the eye and I can see it!"

To some extent I am advocating a new approach to knowledge, different from that of standard science. We can all develop a Goethean methodology appropriate to our various domains of inquiry. Science itself after such an evolution would differ in some important respects from the science of today. However, because the essence of Goethe's approach is the refinement of engaged insight, and since insight stands at the center of normal science, what I propose does not abandon science, but rather deepens and extends it.

What I find most important about Goethe's ideas is his realization that, without turning away from our engagement with the world, we can ascend from initial, unfocused and naïve impressions to a direct appreciation of an archetypal phenomenon (Urphänomen). This is not metaphysics, but rather the opposite—enhanced, appreciative presence. Especially concerning what we take to be "real" or of the greatest relevance, we should not then look for something further behind that Urphänomen. However, Goethe was well aware of Eckermann's comment:

> ...the sight of a primal phenomenon is generally not enough for people; they think they must go still further; and are thus like children who after peeping into a mirror, turn it round directly to see what is on the other side. (Eckermann, 1964, p. 147)

I suggest that this caution applies to science as well, but not that science itself is intrinsically misguided. Science does not need to make the mistake of "looking behind the mirror," attributing existence to its models and theoretical terms. Furthermore, once the basic phenomenon is discovered, there is still more we can legitimately do as scientists—Goethe's cautions do not rule out the further development and proper use of models.

Goethe's approach thus stands in a complex but complementary relation to the scientific theories I summarized earlier in this paper, where the stated objective is often thought to involve just the framing of a successful candidate for an underlying mechanical or efficient cause (such as Rayleigh and Mie scattering). Many of the same terms Goethe mentioned still figure in such a standard scientific account but with a different emphasis: I start with light and optics (rather than with the human eye and its interactions with light, as in Goethe's case), and again there is a turbid medium affecting the light's passage, and so on. However, I then also move on to the search for a model that predicts which wavelengths of light will be seen under particular conditions. So in the case of the sunset, long wavelengths of light are predicted because the short wavelengths are understood to be scattered away.

Goethe would respond that while this might or might not be true (and it really might be true!), it is missing an important point—what we are always dealing with, first and foremost, is an actual encounter, an arrangement of phenomenally engaged entities. More specifically, we are confronting perceived relationships between these entities, not just analyzing them in isolation (a situation which can never really exist) or hypothesizing things and workings that may lie behind them. The fact that we can gain fundamental insights about phenomena without leaving them or our engagement with the world behind is a major discovery. Our reading of Goethe suggests that it is an important aspect of any real understanding, particularly that which is involved in science.

Insight's greater scope can be useful and important. This is precisely the point I sought to make by raising the example of the small girl, gripped by both wonder and curiosity as she witnessed the sunset's display of colors. Her father's explanations, drawn from physics, may address part of her interest. Goethe's own color theory and methodology can also help along similar lines, as we have indicated with our summary of his account.

However, I believe Goethe's point goes farther than that, in ways that address other features of the girl's interest. It is not just a supplement to the standard scientific way of explaining certain colors or characteristics of the sunset that might have caught her attention. It is not even limited to looking at the same phenomena, in some sense, or to "phenomena" at all. For it is intended to aid our direct participation in a larger context, discovered by more emphasis on what is "actual" and apprehensible by mature sensibilities. This context has been called the "Being" dimension by some modern Western thinkers. The phenomena and the situation in which they manifest would thus be seen as an expression of Being, not just of physical principles and causal connections.

At least an incipient understanding of Being was probably involved in Goethe's concern for balance between science and human values, and in his emphasis on always keeping "the being" (das Wesen) "livingly before" us. The ordinary ontology explored by science, or even defined by it, may itself come to be seen as an excerpt from a more fundamental ontology of Being. The latter also seems to be the source of some aesthetic, value-oriented and spiritual sensibilities. Goethe commented that he who has art and science has religion also.

Here we find ourselves at the crossroads, facing two intersecting and inseparable worlds—one supporting propositional meanings, the other sheer meaningfulness. Because this latter dimension is found within manifest phenomena, our awareness of it can easily be heightened by the latter, especially in situations of particular beauty or which carry a strong existential charge of various sorts. Moreover, the experience of Being does not seem to be a mere affect, but—like science—bears on issues of ontology.

Examples

Let's consider some examples. Suppose you are interested in the phenomenon of motion. You might find a small dense object like a ball and throw it upwards, catch it, throw it from hand to hand, and toss it to someone else, catch it, and so on. You would probably notice that these motions involve trajectories and velocities and also depend on the object's weight. However, throwing and catching and tracking paths of motion are all pretty intuitive, and so you might stop there. This would be an example of a preliminary, naïve engagement with the phenomenon.

If you happened to become more curious about the laws of motion you might persist, examining the phenomenon more systematically to determine its essential features and conditions. How hard do you throw the object? Does it make any difference if the air is removed from the room? How do size, shape, and weight affect the motion? Various factors of this sort can be tested; data can be collected and analyzed. You might even begin to formulate some descriptions or mathematical equations that summarize the data's correlations.

However, the latter enterprise of quantitative treatment and theory formation is best kept in relation to something else—fundamental insight. Insight suggests the theories but also brings us into an increasing intimacy with the phenomenon itself, eventually penetrating to the recognition of its essential character. We discern the fundamental phenomenon that is expressed within the particular effects.

For the case of laws of motion, particularly planetary motion, one of the early modern scientists who unconsciously followed this exploratory path with great success was Isaac Newton, whom Goethe criticized for overemphasizing the abstract side of science, and who did in fact originate the modern quantitative, formal and abstract approach to science that Goethe opposed. However, while Newton developed this now-standard approach, he also necessarily drew upon the same source that concerned Goethe. Consider, for example, Newton's discovery of what we call the universal law of gravitation.

The young Newton had left Cambridge and returned home to Lincolnshire to avoid a plague that was raging at the time. This several-year break from school constituted what he called the "miraculous years," during which he claimed to have had all the best thoughts of his life (an assertion that might have disturbing implications for college teachers).

Imagine Newton out in his yard, picking apples or whatever he was doing during this time off from school, when something remarkable occurs. (At least, this is the legend, and Newton was one to supply the legends and help them along.) An apple dropped from a tree, and Newton says that when he saw this fall, he simultaneously saw that it was the same thing as the moon passing slowly overhead. Note that he had not derived any equation. He just saw a basic similarity. The moon's motion around the earth, which he had been pondering, he saw in that moment to be the same as the apple falling. Now, if you are like most students of physics—you will probably find it very hard to see such a thing. The point is far from obvious. However, he saw it. Can you imagine the exhilaration of suddenly entertaining this thought, through the power of insight—that the motions of the world and of other worlds all work this way?

Remember, he had not made a computation yet. To prove his point, in general, he had to invent the calculus (which was also accomplished during this same vacation from school) and also do much more theoretical work to formulate the issue in precise, scientifically cogent terms. So to convince himself and his colleagues, he needed formal definitions and tools that had not even been invented then, but still, he definitely saw something essential. In Goethe's terms, Newton had become so directly and insightfully connected to his experience, he participated in some fundamental feature of the apple's fall. Moreover at that moment, because he had been so concerned with celestial motion, like that of the moon around the earth, he also saw these two things as the same in some important sense.

This is the kind of moment for which physicists live. In essence, it bears on what we all live for, whether we are scientists or not. A person does not become a physicist in order to solve differential equations, or to play with quantum field theory; the latter are just useful tools, aids to an enriched understanding and appreciation of the world. A similar point applies to musicians, or builders, or politicians, or teachers, or parents. What we really seek is enhanced, appreciative participation in the significance of life and the world.

Another example from my own personal history made an enormous difference to my own understanding of these matters and to my own priorities in life. In 1975, when I was a graduate student, I and two other students were working on a problem in atomic physics, time-of-flight analysis of electron impact excitation of helium to metastable states to be exact. This problem seemed intractable—the time-of-flight spectra could not be analyzed. I had read the literature on the subject and found no help. One night I told my wife, Heide, that I was going out for a walk, and then I went out the door and started strolling down the dark street. Soon an image started to form in my mind, a growing sense of a pattern. Suddenly, I saw all the different geometrical features of the problem clearly—things hung together in a way I had never seen before. Of course, part of my excitement was that no one on the planet had ever seen them before either. Thousands of students repeat some of Newton's experiments every year, straining to see what he had, but in this case I was the lucky first.

The next day, I tried to explain my insight to my advisors and struggled to convince them that it really did make sense. Eventually I noticed something happening to them too—they began to put aside their old ways of thinking and to see it with me. Now, we did not have a new language or set of conventions to discuss my idea properly in the formal sense. We stumbled around with the old language, and scribbled and drew on the blackboard, but we did not have a derivation, only a "co-seeing," a growing convergence in joint participation. Then, at a certain point, we were all there together. This was tremendously exciting. Our work acquired a heightened form of meaning. In my opinion, that is the heart of science. Of course, subsequently, as always happens in situations like this, we performed more experiments, wrote papers on our discovery, and so forth—all important parts of scientific practice. However, the core element was that cognitive act, that special moment of *aperçu*.

Several times in my professional work in laser-atomic physics or the experimental foundations of quantum optics, I have been privileged to enjoy fundamental and appreciative engagements with facets of our world. In each case, it was clear to me that in addition to filling out a description and advancing some physical theory in particular ways, I was also making contact of a sort that was akin to what happens in other domains, including the aesthetic, ethical, and spiritual. These experiences have shed a light over my whole life. Insight into the phenomena, and appreciation of the connection to a full life—these were the concerns that Goethe held uppermost in his work on science. Not just the models, but the *aperçu*, the discovery, the epiphanic dimension of knowing. Knowing as fundamental participation, not as a deduction or solution of an intellectual puzzle, but as a special kind of seeing.

It is worth mentioning here that the roots of our English language make a related point. In ancient Greek, the word "theory" means "to behold," to see. Goethe urged that we not lose this connection, but explicitly make it the heart of our approach. He gave his own treatment of the blueness of the sky and the crimson sunset along precisely these lines. Writing about such an approach to science, he says:

> The ultimate goal would be: to grasp that everything in the realm of fact is already theory. (Goethe, 1995, p. 307)

and

> The blue of the heavens shows us the basic law of chromatics. Let us not seek for something behind the phenomena—they themselves are the theory. (Goethe, 1995, p. 307)

Thus, his point is that we should not seek to get past the phenomenon to some abstraction, or to a scientific metaphysics based on theoretically reified abstract entities. Rather, we should intensify our engagement with the phenomenon, until the delicate empiricism is accomplished and we become directly appreciative of the phenomenon's essential features. This epiphanic form of "theory" might well prompt the development of abstract descriptions or models, and will probably use them in turn to help us further appreciate the phenomenon with increasing directness. However, it should not be confused with the models. It is something important in its own right, something more. That "more" is vital both for doing science and for living well or living spiritually.

Concluding Remarks

I began by concentrating on what has become familiar to us about science—the development of theoretical models. While honoring that development, I also pointed out that the models' origin, in fact the origin and heart of all science, is actually located somewhere else—what Emerson called a poetic perception. A rigorous consideration of this notion should probably take account of Goethe's work on the nature of science, and his claims that true perceptiveness requires us to fully elicit and engage our world in all its aspects (its "effects"). We allow the world to work on us so that we may change and mature—we are cultivated by that engagement, and then we see the world anew.

That new seeing works back on us again—it is a cycle of becoming "concentric to Nature." The more we mature, the more we see. The more we see, the more we grow, and know—in a complete sense. This is not just an active process, but a creative— even evolutionary—one. Emerson says, "We only see what we animate, and we animate what we see (Pouncey, 1991, p. 31).

Rather than emulating the camera *obscura,* the dark chamber, we must let the creative light of our minds engage and animate or exercise the world, illuminating it so that its nature becomes clear to us. Because this approach yields both good science and more developed human beings, I have become convinced that doing science properly is itself relevant to human maturation—and that it is related at its root to the other disciplines which emphasize a similar maturation. Each of them shares this connection to refined insight.

The practice of science might then include a process something like this: we "exercise" certain aspects of the natural, physical world through well-designed experiments. We collect and correlate data under a wide range of conditions, and gradually gain insight enabling us both to discern what we might call the real phenomenon at issue and to participate appreciatively in its workings. This understanding may in turn be formulated in hypotheses and theories which can be tested and refined, and which further enhance our insight and sharpen our formulations. In this manner, we enter the world more fully and describe certain features of it more rigorously and perspicuously.

Our explorations of other domains of experience will not possess all the characteristics of scientific practice, such as an emphasis on formally stated theories. However, they all involve an interplay between our participation in the world, insight regarding the adoption of an apt perspective, formulations in terms of concepts and ideas, and further (hopefully enriched) participation.

Along the way, we must take care not to abandon the insights for the formulations, not to reify the language and concepts, not to confuse the full engagement with the language. Often we can get so caught up in the formalism that we forget its motivating source. This is doubly regrettable because we then also lose our ability to see back through the formalism to the insightful engagement with the phenomena. Barfield might declare this lapse a kind of idolatry—the image has replaced the sacred dimension that it pictures. The models become idols, whereas they should be vehicles or aids to engagement with their true object.

A certain vigilance is required. We must note and avoid idolatrous tendencies, heeding above all the *aperçu,* the direct, epiphanic engagement. In this way, genuine knowledge is engendered. Preserving it in its true form and sharing it require both education and edification. The phrase "education as transformation" comes to mind. What else could it mean to truly educate? In addition I think this applies not only to others—children or young adults, but to ourselves as adults, on an ongoing basis.

With an educated vision, it really is possible to work our way still further into the world, to stand on the hillside with Thoreau or Goethe, and become "true theory." We should have a confidence that if we do this carefully and responsibly, the domain of participatory experience will become increasingly nuanced, larger, and more accessible. At first it may be confusing, like emerging from the cave that Plato described in the Republic. So we may not see much for a while, nor perhaps will we be able to make much sense of the world we do see. Gradually, though, new appreciative capacities do arise, and our insight will become sharper and its object more articulated. Then fully dimensioned knowledge becomes available within that new domain as well.

By always cycling between the formalisms and direct appreciation, engaging features of our existence at higher and higher levels, we not only respect experience and cede it a prominent place, but we reaffirm the value of the human being in the enterprise. With proper grounding, remaining concentric to Nature, our human capacities for insight become open-ended, free from any sharp boundaries. Our limits are simply the horizons of where we stand now in our efforts to appreciate our life and the world.

This is the common source for all human inquiry—for the artist, striving to see something new and challenging us to see as well; for the spiritual teacher, who can be helpful because he or she speaks from direct experience of the fundamental significance of our existence; for the conscientious scientist, valuing and encouraging an understanding of the theories as grounded in the world, rather than leaving us buried in a passive acceptance of the models. In each case, with preparation, we can share the understanding and feel its authenticity. We can learn to work our way toward this source and live from it. Depending upon our individual natures and aspirations, it will express itself in our various careers and actions, through our scientific research, artistic work, and spiritual practice.

Such a happy situation would be characteristic of what Goethe called a highly evolved age, one that nurtures the maturation of awareness so it can embrace and function more within all the dimensions of our lives. In recent years, more and more people from various sides of the real "knowledge project" have awakened to the challenge of implementing this unifying vision. Perhaps—as we so dearly hope—the spirit of that highly evolved age is already with us now, and may continue to grow and flourish as never before.

In a sense science and spirituality are related because they are both based on ontologically relevant insights. They are both knowledge projects, both grounded in insights, but this is not the end of the similarity. They often draw on the same type of insight, deriving from aspects of the same ontology, one that is not broken into a "spiritual" part versus a "scientific" part. No such compartmentalization exists at the root. The map depicting what is commonly supposed to be a sharp contrast between knowledge projects and more values-oriented concerns must be discarded. New maps of their relation must take account of substantial areas and kinds of overlap.

This essay was based on a presentation Arthur Zajonc made at Salisbury College (March 8, 2000). Together with Steven Tainer, the paper was then supplemented and rewritten into the current version, which features our views on the subject of "insight." I therefore wish to acknowledge the enormous help I had in writing this paper, and I thank Steven Tainer for that help.

References

Barfield, O. (1971). *What Coleridge thought.* Middletown, CT: Wesleyan University Press.

Cao, Y. T. (1997). *Conceptual developments of 20th century field theories.* Cambridge, UK: Cambridge University Press.

Cézanne, P. (1976). *Paul Cézanne letters*, J. Rewald (Ed.). New York: Hacker Art Books.

Eckermann, J. P. (1964). *Conversations with Goethe*, translated by C. O'Brien. New York: Ungar Press.

Emerson, R. W. (1903-04a). *The complete works of Ralph Waldo Emerson, vol VIII.* Edward Waldo Emerson (Ed.). Boston: The Century Edition.

Goethe, J. W. von. (1952). *Goethe's botanical writings*, translated by B. Mueller, Honolulu: University of Hawaii Press.

——(1970). *Theory of colors,* translated by C. Eastlake Cambridge, MA: MIT Press.

——(1981). *Goethes Werke, Hamburger Ausgabe, (hereafter, HA)* Munich: C.H. Beck Verlag. Translations of many of the Goethe passages can be found in D. Miller. (Ed.), *Scientific studies,* Also see *Goethe's way of science*, D. Seamon and A. Zajonc (Eds.), Albany, NY: SUNY Press, 1998.

——(1995). In *Scientific studies Goethe: The collected works,* vol. 12, Princeton, NJ: Princeton University Press 1995.

Magnus, R. (1949). *Goethe as a scientist,* New York: Henry Schuman.

Pouncey, P. (1991). *Teaching what we do.* Amherst, MA: Amherst College Press.

Thoreau, H. D. (1906). *The journals of Henry D. Thoreau.* Francis H. Allen and Bradford, (Eds.). Torrey, Boston: Houghton-Mifflin Co., vol. III.

Wolf, E. (1979). Einstein's researches on the nature of light. *Optics News*, vol. 5, no.1, Winter 1979, pp. 24–39.

Zajonc, A. (1993). *Catching the light.* New York: Oxford University Press.

The Cosmic Fantasia of Life

Eugene Halton

> *"I came into the clearing and asked, jokingly, why he was dancing alone. He stopped, turned slowly around and looked at me as though...surprised by my stupidity...But I'm not dancing alone," he said, "I am dancing with the forest, dancing with the moon."*
>
> Colin Turnbull

Let me tell you the *Good News!* It was in the newspaper: "There is no God..." It may not seem like good news for believers, but it is even far worse for atheists. Let me spin a fantasia.

Imagine a wandering Apache scout and shaman, a master of tracking and camouflage born during the Apache Holocaust in the 1870s, raised in a small band isolated in high desert, invisibly present at the 1922 Encampment of the Apaches on the Jicarilla Reservation at Dulce, northwest of Taos. He sees a paleface there, observing the ritual. I don't mean a mere white man, I mean a really pale-faced, sickly white man, a face touched by death, tubercular.

Amazingly, this warrior and holy man, this "Grandfather" (or teacher), sees in those fatal eyes a deep understanding, an epiphany, a man enraptured, not only of the groove of the ritual, but of creation itself and of the apocalyptic nature of modern civilization. He sees in those eyes a vision oddly similar to his own. He sees the eyes of one truly alive, though fatally involved with a tubercular trajectory. He sees D. H. Lawrence there, a man who would be dead less than ten years later, and who would leave one of the great Holy Books of the Apocalyptic twentieth century, a book he simply titled *Apocalypse*, unpublished at the time of his death.

Back to the news, the facts, as you could have read them in *The New York Times* on October 26, 1924. There is no God, or, at least as D. H. Lawrence put it in his essay, "Indians and Entertainment," after attending that Apache and some other Pueblo rituals:

> There is, in our sense of the word, no God. But all is godly. There is no Great Mind directing the universe. Yet the mystery of creation, the wonder and fascination of creation shimmers in every leaf and stone, in every thorn and bud, in the fangs of the rattlesnake, and in the soft eyes of the fawn. Things utterly opposite are still pure wonder of creation, the yell of the mountain lion, and the breeze in the aspen leaves....There is no God looking on. The only god there is, is involved all the time in the dramatic wonder and inconsistency of creation. God is immersed, as it were, in creation, not to be separated or distinguished. There can be no Ideal God... (Lawrence, 1982, p. 117)

Lawrence understood that the Apache ritual demonstrated what Lévy-Bruhl (1923) termed *participation*, a consciousness of felt connectedness to the drama of all-surrounding life. Lévy-Bruhl claimed that the hunter-gatherer consciousness, or what he unfortunately termed "prelogical mind," does not objectify nature through logical classification, but, "It *lives* it rather, by feeling itself participate in it, and feeling these participations everywhere; and it interprets this complexity of participations by social forms" (Levy-Bruhl, 1926, pp. 129–130).

Lawrence goes on to contrast the participation perspective with that of the spectator consciousness, using Greek drama as his example of the spectator perspective:

> The spectacle is offered to us. And we sit aloft, enthroned in the Mind, dominated by one exclusive idea, and we judge the show....There is absolutely none of this in the Indian dance. There is no God. There is no Onlooker. There is no mind. There is no dominant idea. And finally, there is no judgment: absolutely no judgment....The Indian is completely embedded in the wonder of his own drama. It is a drama that has no beginning and end, it is all-inclusive. It can't be judged, because there is nothing outside it, to judge it....The mind is there merely as a servant, to keep a man pure and true to the mystery, which is always present. (Lawrence, 1982, pp. 119–120)

Now Lawrence's definition of God is not different from what most civilized people mean by God. However, most hunter-gatherers, as Lawrence sensed, do not believe in that conception of God. The Grandfather who observes Lawrence in my fantasia believes in divinity as what Native Americans call *The-Spirit-That-Moves-Through-All-Things*, a seeming synonym for "God," yet ultimately a very different idea. To ignore the difference is to miss the gulf between participation consciousness and civilizational consciousness, contrasting ways of seeing the world, and not only metaphorically. For hunter-gatherers tend literally to see from the entire peripheral field relying on "wide-angle vision," whereas literate and especially modern civilizations rely overwhelmingly on focused vision in everyday life. When one sees from the entire field of vision, motion is easier to detect, and moreover, one feels that one is in the picture, not an outside spectator. These literal visual differences also reflect the difference between a participation consciousness and a spectator consciousness.

Let me put it another way: God is the moment of human alienation from the divine presence of the living universe. That is, the concept of God is the peeling away from direct, felt participation in the creation of the universe, from participation in the Creator. However, the Creator is no spectator, as "God" implies. The Creator did not say, "Let there be Light!" as though a separate entity. The Creator did not create the universe during a peculiar week and then relax. The Creator is incessant creation, creating, creaturing. In this sense the Creator is indeed The-Spirit-That-Moves-Through-All-Things, of whose Presence the entire continuum of Originals through whom we evolved into human beings were intensely aware.

Why must the Creator come before the Creation? If we call a person "creative" on the basis of one painting she has created, was she a creator before she created the painting? Or is the Creator creation-creating? If the concept of "God" is the moment of human alienation from direct participation in the creation, from the presence of divinity in all things, then that which is designated as God is a human creation, emanating from the human penchant for making concepts of all things. Many moderns either see God as separable from and prior to the creation, or as a human fiction, as Marx, for example, claimed. I am claiming something else, namely, that *the divine is not a human-made social construction, but that the "concept of God" is.* Some forms of Buddhism, such as Tantric Buddhism, believe that "God" or the gods are mental fictions. This idea provides a good critical view of how we humans "conceptualize," not simply because our brains are naturally equipped to do so, but rather that our big-brained, rational, conceptualizing abilities are immature, dangerously immature, in the sense that philosopher Charles S. Peirce also drew attention to (Peirce in Halton, 1995a).

Is it possible that the principles of life function are more like a fantasia than like a machine, as the sciences would have it? When one abstracts from the living presence of divinity in all things, one runs the risk of creating a mental fiction God. Call it a Spectator God, or a Camera God who makes "the big picture": a "one-size-fits-all" God. This noun-God seems to me a complete violation of "The-Spirit-That-Moves-Through-All-Things." Now one may say they are the same thing, the unifying concept. However, I believe that the Native American term is more sophisticated, that it calls out the living activity of creation and the unique natures that get lost in the abstraction "God." Such, it seems to me, is what the whole Judeo-Christian monotheistic and idealizing Western tradition has done—Islam as well. This developing and idealizing consciousness has created, to transpose William Blake's words from his poem "Jerusalem,"

> *...An Abstract objecting power that Negatives everything.*
> *This is the Spectre of Man, the Holy Reasoning Power,*
> *And in its Holiness is closed the Abomination of Desolation.*

However, the living self is far more than conceptual reason, even though rational, calculating thought has come to dominate modern life. Humans evolved in reverence and awe at the divinity in all things, and this religious sense does not need a concept of God, nor, in my opinion, did it have one until quite late.

Flight from the Earth

Henceforth I spread confident wings to space
I fear no barrier of crystal or of glass
I cleave to the heavens and soar to the infinite.
(Giordano Bruno in Crosby, 1997)

Hunter-gatherers tend to live in a relation of "human-to-greater-than-human," as David Abram has put it in his marvelous book, *The Spell of the Sensuous* (Abram, 1997). Abram makes an eloquent and convincing argument for the qualities of place as a real aspect of animism, and of how hunter-gatherers attune themselves to the qualities of their environment. He also argues that the development of written language, especially the alphabet and its transmission from Semitic to Greek, is key to the abstraction from the sensuous environment.

Abram (1997) notes that, though Socrates does not write, he claims in Plato's *Phaedrus* to learn only from the city, not from "trees or the country," a good example of city-centrism. Even so, Socrates, though characterized elsewhere in the text as "without place," as *atopoi*, is more ambiguous than this. Socrates is a true pivot between an older, almost vestigial shamanic philosophy, and a new, critical consciousness.[1]

Abram undervalues the role of the city itself and its institutions, other than writing, in that process of abstraction from the animate environment. Civilizational consciousness refocused those energies, beamed them onto a divine or semidivine king connected to a community of gods in the heavens, who were themselves a mirroring of the human community. The invention of divine kingship in the city is also an aspect of the first Megamachine, as

---

[1] Now it is true that Socrates told Phaedrus when they ventured out to the countryside, as written in Plato's *Phaedrus*, that he did not learn from the trees, but from the men of the city. However, at the end of the same dialogue, he offers a prayer to the god Pan, and to the other gods of the place, thanking them and praying for inner beauty. Socrates is a pivot between an older reverential wisdom and a new form of critical mind. He viewed writing as a threat to living memory, but we know this because his devoted student Plato wrote it down. He was much more than a great thinker. One sees the whole being of the man involved in his practice of life and quest for wisdom. Consider his invocation from the ending of *Phaedrus*:

> Beloved Pan, and all ye other gods who haunt this place, give me beauty in the inward soul; and may the outward and inward man be at one. May I reckon the wise to be the wealthy, and may I have such a quantity of gold as a temperate man and he only can bear and carry. (Plato, 1929, p. 329)

Lewis Mumford termed it, a machine which could literally move mountains in its assembling of the pyramids. The Egyptian pyramids were among the earliest manifestation of the Megamachine that is civilization, a machine in those times comprised of mostly human parts. Writing and the scribal traditions were absolutely crucial in the assembling and functioning of these first Megamachines, and continue to be so right down to the present, but so were settled agriculture and the larger populations it produced, centralized bureaucracy and class structure, and standing armies. Mumford claimed that modern culture represents a rebuilding of the ancient Megamachine (Mumford, 1970).

With civilization humankind reversed the relation of the human to greater-than-human world: Now it became a relation of human to lesser-than-human nature, and lesser-than-human should be controlled more than revered. The religious impulse is siphoned from the living nature of things to personified deities. Nature becomes that which is to be dominated by human power. The "struggle for existence" and gods enjoining people to worship them are not universal realities, but historical manifestations of civilizational consciousness and its discontents.

Civilizational structures developed out of settled agriculture at a specific period of history and displaced other kinds of structures, typically neolithic village structures. Most of what we eat today was developed by neolithic domestication of plants and animals, but most of what we believe was first developed by civilizational structures. There were gains and losses, and it is quite reasonable to look at civilizational structures as rationally superior and also humanly inferior to what was displaced. Why would humans embark on a course that made living conditions worse for the vast majority and better for a small elite, for example?

The ancient Sumerian creation myth, *The Atrahasis,* begins with the idea of relieving the gods of work. The new hard-work ideology of civilization is first projected onto the gods, who revolt against their overburden by creating humans. The work ethic is "divinized" by viewing it as relieving the gods, so the labor becomes acceptable by disguising it as service to gods. Struggle becomes humankind's new way of life, a story later echoed in the account of Adam and Eve's expulsion from the garden in Genesis.

Much later again, when the Greco-Judeo-Christian ideals of *polis* and love were systematically inverted in the modern, mechanical worldview, struggle would be further idealized as the basis for Hobbes's "state of nature," and later still, echoed in Darwin's theory of evolution and Freud's theory of the unconscious. The early civilizational consciousness bodied forth new minds to further it, and imbued them with the belief that the city is the earthly center of the universe—as Mircea Eliade put it, an *axis mundi*—and that their labors on behalf of the city are called forth by the gods. *Anthropo-*

centric mind began to see the world as a mirror of human society instead of humans as children of the community of life on earth. With agriculture and civilization, animate mind began its contraction, and the human ego broke its moorings to the tempered, extrarational forms of reasonableness which reached back inwardly through our evolutionary hunter-gatherer past to our primate and mammalian bodies, and reached outward to all-surrounding life. The greater-than-human world of animism began to transform into the great-human-world, whose powers of organized city-states would dominate nature. However, civilization itself was later to undergo a further transformation from a machine-like, specialized, anthropocentric mind to a view that the universe itself is fundamentally a non-living machine, from which life springs accidentally by machine rules and to which the laws of life itself are reducible.

I view this history of consciousness not as progress, but as a contraction of mind (see Figure 1). This contraction brought with it more precise ways of thinking, which are traditionally associated with progress. However, the increasing dominance of rational-mechanical mind—of what I am terming *mechanicocentric mind*—came at a great cost. For it regarded its narrowed domain as a true picture of the world, when in fact it was a partial view that excluded the living, communicative, and purposive human mind as an irreducible reality of nature, and the possibility that nature itself is mindlike. This latter possibility is the reality on which the animate mind is based and is the source of its spiritual beliefs. It is also an idea that the modern mechanicocentric mind claimed to have destroyed. Unfortunately, tragically even, it is an idea irremovably embedded in our very bodies, and its real destruction would be our destruction. Much of the modern clocklike universe was founded in revolt against Aristotle. Galileo refuted Aristotle's physics, but was part of an emerging mechanical, scientific worldview. Hobbes, for example, inverted Aristotle's understanding that humans are by nature community creatures ("political animal," *zoon politikon*) by seeing nature as a greedy war of each against all. Disabled by philosophical nominalism (the view that only individual particulars are real and that general classes, laws, or signs are merely names or conventions for these individual particulars) and by the wars around him, Hobbes falsely projected certain attributes of civilized society, such as mass war and shorter, nastier, more brutish lives, onto "natural" or hunter-gatherer humans. Darwin inherited Thomas Hobbes's antisocial theory of nature, a theory that cannot account for sociality in nature, but which reduces it to an aspect of competitive struggle.

Competitive struggle is a reality of nature, yet one that does not exhaust the dynamics of evolution. Darwin's is an incomplete theory reflecting the partiality of modern mechanicocentric mind. "Evolutionary Love," as philosopher and physicist and founder of philosophical pragmatism, Charles S.

Peirce, called it, is also a reality of nature. Competition is real, as Darwin argued, but mutual aid is also irreducibly real, as Piotr Kropotkin argued against Darwin. Darwin's is a "philosophy of greed," as Peirce called it, which would make evolutionary hate real and love but a human fiction. However, what if love, viewed as general relation, as the working of communicative signs or semeiosis, as sociality, were a real element of evolution itself?

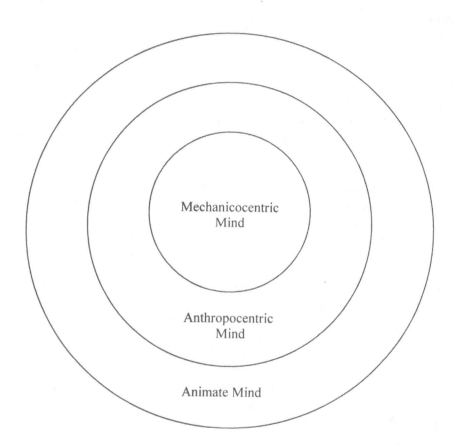

Figure 1. The Contraction of Consciousness.

With modern culture, we deluded ourselves into thinking that the "lesser-than-human" could be determined exactly and controlled at will, like a machine, and that the human could be reduced to it. The greater-than-human world of animism is today complete anathema, and the great-human-world of civilizational consciousness itself gave way to the greater-than-human-machine-world in the modern, scientific-mechanical worldview. Consider that the division of labor, the specially marked ruler, organized military imperialism and mass-killing war, caste/class differences, domestication of other species, agricultural practices, architecture, in short, the major ingredients of what we featherless bipeds like to call civilization, are the original invention of ant colonies. So much for the "progress" of humankind.

This is what confronts us in the *Alien* movies: the giant ant colony we have been making ourselves into by jettisoning our uniquely human bodily capacities for empathy and spontaneity. This mechanical mind-in-formation has continued the abstracting process of the civilizational mind, only adding a new system requirement to its secret teleology, namely the elimination of nonmechanical parts. This involves not only the progressive elimination of the variescence of nature, but the elimination of the variescence of human nature as well. The ultimate goal of this process, a world divested of the nonmechanical, is like the mechanical aspect of the human brain attempting to eliminate its own nonmechanical elements: a kind of infantilization and murderous suicide. What strange ideas. Why and how did they begin? Was it a simple trade-off of short-term farming gains for long-term living?

Now that civilizational structures have dangerously overexpanded to threaten the biosphere, it is high time that we reconsider the whole business of "civilization," and what its limits need to be. It is time to reactivate those ways of human life, whether traditional or modern, which might be of value to a rapidly dehumanizing world that is increasingly civilized, perhaps all too civilized. The hunter-gatherers were aware that there is something more than the mechanisms of civilization available, something more than the divine king representative, or the later, more democratized, divine axial-age representatives, or the scribal word-play to access the Secret Code of esoteric lore. They were aware that each of us has as birthright, that inner gyroscope, that inner voice which connects us to the Creator, through which we get our bearings to find The Way. Each of us has, as birthright, the means to Walk-in-Beauty without intermediary, to walk the path of ongoing creation in touch with the Creator on this earth, attuned to the greater surrounding life in which we participate. Indeed, the only way to find The Way is to find our way and walk it.

Then there is also The Way of Taoism, as the *Tao Te Ching* puts it: "In metaphorical terms, the relationship of all under heaven to the Way is like that of valley streams to the river and sea." This seems to me similar to the Native American idea of the good life: "to Walk-in-Beauty." Beauty, or Tao, is not only change, but is also the ultimate determinant of existence: the intrinsically admirable sea toward which the rivers and streams tend. Yet the path can only be born out of oneself. There is no "one-size-fits-all" Way. For that is the way of idealism, with its ideal model educating ideal selves, determined to live ideal lives and be rewarded with the ideal of an afterlife in paradise. One cannot live from ideals and be true to life; sooner or later the ideal must give way to life or to its repressed opposite. Modern civilization is rooted in the idealization of life that is the Judeo-Greco-Christian tradition, a tradition whose ideals of love and spirit would seem overturned through the anti-ideals of materialism and views of nature as antisocial (Halton, 1995b).

How was it that "knowledge" ever replaced "awareness" as a basis of philosophy? Socrates, with his negating muse of critical consciousness—his muse who spoke the negative to him, *No!* but not *Yes!*—was both continuer of the traditional philosophy as living act, and beginner of the abstracting turn to rational, critical consciousness. It is why, to me, Euripides' play, *The Bacchae*, is possessed of more wisdom than the perspective of Socrates, because Euripides had a deeper appreciation of the tragic nature of rationality *per se*.

A variation on the hunter-gatherer reliance on inner voice and outer attunement to surrounding life is what I see as the best chance of overcoming the globalized megamachine: by the private and public exercise of those organic bodily capacities, such as empathy, spontaneity, and imagination, that were crucial to our transformation into humans in the first place, and those humane institutions we have invented since then, such as human rights. It means creating a new sense of relation to the earth and its limits, something that humankind has avoided from the beginnings of civilization until now.

Myth and Infantilized Rationalization

You may explain the myths away: but it only means you go on suffering blindly, stupidly, "in the unconscious," instead of healthily and with the imaginative comprehension playing upon the suffering. (Lawrence, 1936)

Imagine a small circle of rational mind. It is circumscribed by the larger circle of reasonableness, by animate mind, whose contents include emotional, empathic, instinctive, imaginative, guessing, and other forms of inference; of sensing, evolved throughout the making of humans and in living contact with our mammalian ancestry. The larger circle is more mature, the smaller one still in a state of, let's say, nascent development. It is dependent on that larger circle for optimizing itself (see Figure 2). Now imagine the circles reversed (see Figure 3). This is the modern world, where rationality maximizes itself. As part of maximizing itself, it claims that the universe is a vast machine, and it progressively incorporates that myth into every facet of life. It provides apparent support for that myth, through the workings of its scientific avatars and their world-transforming successes. It evicts teleology from nature, at least on the surface of things, while it secretly enacts the dark rituals of its true, religious, teleological foundation. Not only to negate the organic world, but ultimately to dehumanize the world, to evaporate what is in reality the larger ring of reasonableness, of passionate, animate mind. As it approaches realizing that goal in our time, it becomes increasingly apparent how rational maximization is not optimization, but rather a form of auto-infanticide. For when the mechanical instruments of human purposes, bloated by a progressively infantilizing rationality, the ghost in the machine, are projected into a mythic role as the foundation of all human purposiveness, they become agents of antilife.

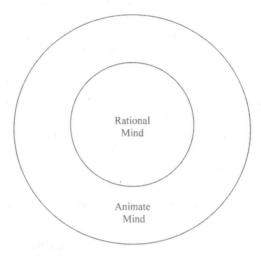

Figure 2. Circumscribed Reason.

Mythic consciousness is more than an illusory way of explaining the world through stories. It is that living effort to connect to and participate in the all-surrounding life of ongoing creation. Myth is the ineradicable dance of life. The chief problem today is how to reintegrate the abstracted and infantilized modern world back into the greater-than-human rhythms that inform myth. A naïve reintegration may not be possible, but that is because rational reason is not yet mature enough to realize why the mythic consciousness of animate mind remains its paradoxical goal to which it must reattune itself. As D. H. Lawrence put it:

> For the whole life-effort of man was to get his life into contact with the elemental life of the cosmos, mountain-life, cloud-life, thunder-life, air-life, earth-life, sun-life. To come into immediate felt contact, and so derive energy, power, and a dark sort of joy. This effort into sheer naked contact, without an intermediary or mediator, is the root meaning of religion. (Lawrence, 1936, p. 146-147)

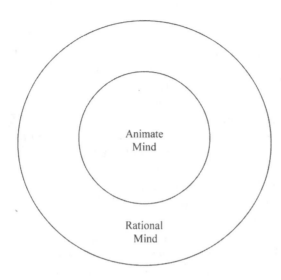

Figure 3. Rationality Maximizing.

The rational, infantilized mind of our time cringes from the task of reintegrating itself with the deeper mind of myth and animate mind. It remains utterly incomprehensive of the depth and maturity of the passions, locked in its dualism of either depersonalized abstraction or hyper-sentimentalism. In my opinion, though, the ultimate goal of this whole development of rationality, from the rise of civilizational structures through our modern world civilization, will be its eventual transformation into instinct within the broader range of human instinctive capacities, a paradoxically "critical" instinct.

Biophilia and the More Dead and Dreary States

> The community of life has worked well on this planet for three billion years—has worked beautifully, in fact. The Takers draw back in horror from this community, thinking it to be a place of lawless chaos and savage, relentless competition, where every creature goes in terror of its life. But those of your species who actually live in this community [The Leavers] don't find it to be so, and they will fight to the death rather than be separated from it. (Daniel Quinn, 1992)

The universe does not struggle to know itself through some Darwinian *homo competitor*, but is more like a cosmic fantasia, dreaming itself into being which we perceive as the Spirit-That-Moves-Through-All-Things. In my view, "dreaming itself into being," or creation, is primary consciousness, in relation to which knowing is derivative, and "dreaming itself into being" is that which all knowing has as its goal, the "final participation," to use Owen Barfield's term, in the creation of the universe.

There is no going back to original participation naïvely without passing through the "crucible of doubt" that is modern consciousness. That trip through the inferno may lead to a "final participation" consciousness. However, how could such a reconciliation of opposites occur, given the still strongly held belief that participation consciousness is "primitive" mysticism, that mythic consciousness was a fog made clear by the Enlightenment, that modern scientific-technical civilization represents an inevitable and unstoppable progress? Perhaps progress is not what it is cracked up to be, when viewed as the contraction of mind involving an overemphasis on the mechanical and rational aspects of reasonableness.

In a sense, we are genetically retarded primates whose prolonged newbornlike physiology is vastly exaggerated over other primates. We glory in our "new-brain" frontal-cortex capacities, our ability to make concepts. In fact, when we began to build vast social organizations which heightened the calculating side of things, when we began civilization, no matter where we began it around the globe, we began to turn the direct perception of The-Spirit-That-Moves-Through-All-Things into a concept, the concept of God. God began the trajectory toward becoming an ideal. The concept of God is the moment of human alienation from the divine presence of the living universe, from the cosmic fantasia of life. An ideal God, an ideal religion, an ideal life, dedicated to the ideal of God, results ultimately in an abomination to life, because one cannot live by ideals. One can only live with ideals, not by them. Idealize Love, and you will sooner or later beget Hate.

The living earth, from which agricultural, civilizational, modern rational mind has severed itself, remains Eden, and remains embedded in our huntergatherer shaped bodies, despite the 10,000-year veneer of civilization. The living earth is that source of intelligence from which infantilized human reason needs to refashion itself if humanity and organic life are to prosper. Intelligence is far more than a happy spiraling progress of human mind and reason. It involves orders of intelligence deeper and more mature than human reason—of instinctive, emotional, dreaming, and spontaneous forms of reasonableness tempered into the human body and sprung from the biosphere in which we evolved.

C. S. Peirce saw that our penchant for conceptualizing is evidence of our immature minds, and that the elevation of this tendency as the foundation of modern civilization is indicative of the thoroughgoing nominalism of the modern mind. Here I am leaving Peirce, though I feel it remains consistent with Peirce, in addressing the potentially suicidal infantilization of modern civilization. This destructive tendency of modern life and of possible ways out was seen even more clearly by Melville and Dostoevsky than by Peirce, in *Moby Dick* and *The Brothers Karamazov*.

Peirce's semeiotic realism, conceived not only as a theory of logic but as a general outlook, is a form of animism that re-introduces the ancient idea, refracted through Peirce's conceptions of science and semeiosis, of the relation of human to greater-than-human. As Peirce put it:

> There is a reason, an interpretation, a logic, in the course of scientific advance; and this indisputably proves to him who has perceptions of rational, or significant relations, that man's mind must have been attuned to the truth of things in order to discover what he has discovered. It is the very bedrock of logical truth. (Peirce, 1998, p. 444)

When one claims that every sign is a living being, as Peirce did, one is again in a living universe, freed from the ghost in the machine death wish that was modern culture, no longer set over against nature but able to reclaim one's place as the universe come alive enacting creation.

When Peirce claimed that each and every sign is a living being, he gave testimony to this animism, but an animism forged from the crucible of doubt that is modern science and logic. His view is one I call critical or semeiotic animism, involving modalities of signification far deeper than conceptual. Even so, it is a form of animism framed in a rigorous logic, one that is far deeper than modern, nominalistic science and logic can allow, a reconciliation far deeper and of more import than a mere "improvement" of modern ways of thinking (Rochberg-Halton, 1986).

Animism, far from being a fogbound, illusory, nature-mysticism believed in by "primitives," is a consciousness of awareness. It represents that attunement to the organic sign-complexus of life, without and within, through which we evolved into our present primate bodies (Halton, 2004). Further, it reveals how our very brains are made, as a living relation of the evolutionarily "newer" human forebrain with the older "greater-than-human" paleo-mammalian and reptilian brain-archives incorporated within us. We are built to live in that relationship of human to greater-than-human brain, yet our modern rationalizing consciousness, the "neonatal" icing on the cake, has made a machine of the tiger and the bird and the snake and the baboon within us, infantilizing us in the name of rational-mechanical scientific progress, to our imminent peril. I see about twenty or so years more of building this globally, electronically, virally, economically, and spiritually interconnected house of cards before it collapses—all gone.

However, a mere throwback to hunter-gatherer ways would not work because eventually it would face the same problems we face today, namely unlimited expanding power. A mere modern or even postmodern outlook will not work either, because it is at base suicidally murderous, or murderously suicidal, depending on your outlook. All this was seen clearly by Melville and Dostoevsky, and by others too, including D. H. Lawrence and Owen Barfield.

In his essay "The Harp and the Camera," Barfield used the analogy of the aeolian harp—which included its wind as part of itself—and hence is a self-playing instrument, to depict participation consciousness. He contrasted it with the camera as symbolizing modern "camera civilization." In Barfield's words:

> We live in a camera civilization. Our entertainment is camera entertainment. Our holidays are camera holidays. We make them so by paying more attention to the camera we brought with us than to the waterfall we are pointing it at. Our science is almost entirely a camera science...and it is already becoming self-evident to camera man that only camera words have any meaning. (Barfield, 1977, p. 76)

The resolution of these seeming opposites—self-playing participation versus being a spectator of the picture—is what Barfield termed *final participation*. We need to develop this final participation consciousness here and now, to develop the abilities to be in the very picture we are depicting. Here and now is where we need to be developing the emphatically grounded abilities to be of our surrounds, while being able to critically depict and correct them or ourselves. We need to refigure the majesty and divinity of the living universe, of the mysterious and miraculous voices of reasonableness that surround us without and within, and to which we must ever attune ourselves. In giving up the organic for the mechanical, we thought we were finding freedom, but it turns out that freedom is found in living in and with the struggles and joys of life, not in escaping from them. Re-attuning ourselves to the organic limits and possibilities of self-originated bodily experience and its generalization to institutional structures is one way to undermine the anti-organic system requirements of the postdemocratic matrix, and of finding that autonomy which democratic society promises.

The Ecology of the Soul

> When the human mind exists in the light of reason and no more than reason, we may say with absolute certainty that Man and all that made him will be in that instant gone. (Eiseley, 1957, p. 482)

At the beginning of the millennium, the idea exists that human culture, human subjectivity, or religion itself can find its freedom in attuning itself to nature by living in an active relationship to the inwardness of nature, thereby becoming the growing incarnation of nature's subjectivity. This idea is typically despised by both natural determinists and cultural determinists, for whom cultural purposes are either survival mechanisms or arbitrary or habitual conventions.

I recently read a commentary on why philosophy seems so underfunded and undervalued. A computer scientist argued that people pay attention to science because it affects technology, and technology is a constant concern of everyone. Concern with the meaning of things is less prominent, found more in those occasional "contemplative moments" of life.

This person, who described himself as a mechanist, precisely depicted what I would call the religion of contemporary life, the one most people practice, regardless of what they preach. It is the religion of external technique, of technomania, practiced along with a near ascetic denial of contemplation. It is the myth that mechanism is real, that the subjective world is unreal, that only what is like a machine in us is real. The seventeenth-century view of mechanism may have been updated with quantum mechanics in physics, but it simply updates the kind of machine it views the universe to be, while still discounting the possibility that general, purposive signs may be irreducibly real.

There is an old name for this religion, which I now apply with a literal meaning as well: *deus ex machina,* the god out of the machine. It is an orthodoxy, like previous religious orthodoxies. Although science claimed to reduce purposive or "mind" understandings of the universe to a mere "god out of the machine" and therefore obsolete status, in fact the underpinning of these theories is a crypto-religion of the literal ghost in the machine.

The *deus ex machina* religion holds that a frozen cinder here, a ball of gas there, a mechanical thing we have not yet discovered somewhere else, are the stuff of which the real universe is made, while the living forms of intelligence which behold that universe and which evolved in that same universe, are unreal *per se*. A living form of intelligence is simply a computer that fornicates and reads the papers, and we have already perfected non-living computers which read the papers, win at chess, and replicate. So it is just a question of finding the undiscovered computer programs of the human automaton and showing how it fits into the dead, gas-ball universe.

D. H. Lawrence identified this scientific narcissism inherent in the modern mechanical universe, when he said in the 1920s:

> How gibbering man becomes, when he is really clever, and thinks he is giving the ultimate and final description of the universe! Can't he see that he is merely describing himself, and that the self he is describing is merely one of the more dead and dreary states that man can exist in? (Lawrence, 1936, pp. 300–301)

Consider Lawrence's implication. The whole modern world is based on an exaggerated projection of those more automatic (hence "deader") inner capacities onto nature, coupled with a denial of vital spontaneity in nature. In other words, the *deus ex machina* religion deifies the Megamachine of death as the ultimate reality of the universe, and in so doing, becomes the great voice of ultimate human self-alienation. For the closer the ghost in the machine moves to its perfection, the more severe will be the reaction of nature. Nature, both outward and inward, can only withstand so many assaults to life from humankind before it must cleanse the slate, so to speak. For as our whole modern world civilization "progresses" toward the achievements of the ants 60 million years ago, the dirty little story that the wondrous universe is but a gasball-filled machine will prove the final ant-trap of humanity.

Animism is no mere fogbound, primitive cult, but a way of *making sense*: life as a living relation and attunement of the human with the "greater-than-human," not simply in some mystical sense, but in the literal bodied-sense of living in deep awareness of the many voices of nature who speak to the hunter-gatherer; the birds who tell of a disturbance in the forest a few kilometers away; the tracks reveal an intimate portrait of the creature, gravitized through some of the 5,000 or so possible pressure indicators of the moving foot, that is more accurate than an X-ray; the plants which heal; the ongoing symphony of these voices that reveal the unfolding of seasons and one's place in the fantastic play of life. We are wired to marvel in nature.

Far from being moving mechanisms with rational guidance systems, *humans are living organs of meaning*, whose bodies are designed to love life, biocultural life, no matter how much we are prepared to kill for it, and whose brains carry the enregistered experience of the evolution of life and consciousness. Many rationalists today would deny the incarnate soul, the living, breathing, sensing spontaneity within us altogether, preferring at most to discuss mind. However, the human soul includes far more than the individual self; it also involves a vast complexus of transpersonal, transhistorical, transhuman memories and experiences, which twentieth-century depth psychology and brain research have served to confirm (Halton, 1992).

The human brain itself is organically fantastic, heavily conditioned by ecstatic mammalian experiences of rapid-eye-movement dreaming, play, and mother-infant bonding. It lives as an archive of evolutionary history, with still-living reptilian, mammalian, and human domains, all in living communication. The "reptilian brain," or brain stem and its automatic processes, is one aspect of a triune brain, a Holy Trinity that is the human brain, our amazing inner archive of the history of life on earth. The paleo-mammalian or "smell brain" is more the basis of the passions. Though the three evolutionary reptilian, paleo-mammalian and frontal neo-cortex layers of the human brain have differing chemistries, they are all in communication. Moreover, the talking, tonguing, "brain," the neo-cortex, our vaunted "human" element, is the baby in this mix. Deny the reptilian and paleo-mammalian portions their due in cultural practices, and eventually you get a rationalized infant, crawling its way around the ant farm of contemporary civilization. The "anima," or soul, the spontaneous intelligence, might be better characterized as an internal community of animals, our inner-brain ecosystem.

"Good and evil" are indeed in the brain, as a cognitive studies researcher might have it. However, that is because the brain itself is an evolutionary incarnation of the laws of nature, and good and evil are more than human conventions, they are realities. Beauty, Goodness, and Truth, what medieval philosophy called the summum bonum and what Peirce's philosophy of semiotic realism demonstrates, are realities of nature, though modern philosophy, disabled by nominalism, has reduced them to mere human conventions, to mere "names," to the nominal.

We became human through dreaming and playing and bonding ourselves to mother forest and mother savannah in all her variescence, and finding our own way within it. We became human, in other words, through our capacity to be more of a child of the earth, more of a "retarded ape," more dependent on the inpouring signs from all-surrounding life, signs which gave us animate mind, for all that surrounded us was indeed life. This is a kind of anti-anthropocentrism of the usual sort, for it realizes that anthropos depends on surrounding life and spirit. When we "progressed" to human-centered environments, progressively to agriculturally based lifestyles and ultimately agriculturally rooted cities, we achieved anthropocentric consciousness in full, though still immersed in cosmos. When we "progressed" yet further, to machine-centered environments, we achieved a specialized form of anthropocentric consciousness progressively equivalent to death, the unbearable enlightenment of being that is mechanico-centric mind, to the mythic ghost in the machine. Man isolated from the living cosmos becomes living death, and eventually, simply death. We have already virtually perfected living death.

Organic awareness was the original end that directed us into humanity. Organic awareness will remain the end of our further development, should we survive, as the age of homo sapiens now completes itself. We can shake off neither the noble savage nor the ancient reptile within, for they live in the very structure of our human brains. Instead, we are faced today, it seems to me, with a daunting task: to figure out how we can not only rediscover and preserve that "inner ecology" of the human soul in the face of the dehumanizing and ever more powerful Machine of Modern Life, but, further, how to body forth those vitalities in the creation of a new civilizational framework, one reattuned both to its limited place in nature and to nature's as yet undreamed possibilities within us.

I am sure of one thing, though, from deep in the center of my chest. Each and every human on this planet possesses the ultimate key to offset that dehumanizing machine we have made of life, and that key is our own bodies and how we live through them. Why should we stay in the prison when the door is wide open?

As the medieval poet Rumi (1997) put it:

> *...We have fallen into the place*
> *where everything is music.*
> *Stop the words now.*
> *Open the window in the center of your chest,*
> *and let the spirits fly in and out.*

Take a deep breath and let it out. Life flows as heaven on earth at each and every moment, if we open our hearts and our awareness and our love and allow ourselves to feel it as it truly is, to feel infinite creation.

References

Abram, D. (1997). *The spell of the sensuous.* New York: Vintage Books.

Barfield, O. (1977). The harp and the camera. In *The rediscovery of meaning and other essays.* Middletown, CT: Wesleyan University Press.

Crosby, A.W. (1997). *The measure of reality: Quantification and western society, 1250–1600.* New York: Cambridge University Press.

Eiseley, L. (1957). *The immense journey.* New York: Random House.

Halton, E. (1992). The reality of dreaming. *Theory, Culture and Society 9* (3), 119–132.

——(1995a). Of life and social thought. In *Bereft of reason.* Chapter 2. Chicago: University of Chicago Press.

——(1995b). The transilluminated vision of Charles Peirce. In E. Halton *Bereft of reason,* Chapter 5. Chicago: University of Chicago Press.

——(2004). The living gesture and the signifying moment. *Symbolic Interaction.* Jan. 2004: 27(1): 89–113.

Lawrence, D. H. (1936). New Mexico. In E. D. McDonald, (Ed.) *Phoenix: The posthumous papers of D. H. Lawrence.* New York: Viking. (Original work published in 1928).

——(1982). Indians and entertainment. In *Mornings in Mexico.* Salt Lake City, UT: Gibbs M. Smith. (Original work published in 1924)

Levy-Bruhl, L. (1923). *Primitive mentality.* (L. A. Clare, Trans.) New York: Macmillan.

Mumford, L. (1967). *The myth of the machine: Vol. I, technics and human development.* New York: Harcourt Brace Jovanovich.

——(1970). *The myth of the machine: Vol. II, the pentagon of power.* New York: Harcourt Brace Jovanovich.

Peirce, C. (1998). A neglected argument for the reality of God. In Peirce Edition Project *The essential Peirce. Vol. 2.* Bloomington, IN: Indiana University Press: 444.

Plato. *The Works of Plato.* B. Jowett (Trans.), I. Edman (Ed.). New York: The Modern Library 1928: 329

Quinn, D. (1992). *Ishmael.* New York: Bantam Books.

Rochberg-Halton, E. (1986). *Meaning and modernity.* Chicago: University of Chicago Press.

Rumi, J. (1997). Where everything is music. In C. Barks (Trans.) *The essential Rumi.* San Francisco: HarperSanFrancisco.

Turnbull, C. (1962). *The forest people: A study of the pygmies of the Congo.* New York: Simon and Schuster.

Ways of Knowing

Bruce Wilshire

> *I believe that it is the destiny of the occident continually to keep bringing into connection with each other these two fundamental attitudes, on the one hand the rational-critical, which seeks to understand, and on the other the mystic-irrational which looks for the redeeming experience of oneness. Both attitudes will always reside in the human soul, and each will always carry the other already within itself as the germ of its contrary. Thus there arises a sort of dialectical process, of which we do not know whither it is leading us. I believe that as occidentals we have to commit ourselves to this process, and recognize the opposites as complementary.*
>
> *Wolfgang Pauli*

Sixteenth- and seventeenth-century Europe was the site of a momentous turn of human history. It was so momentous that we cannot yet encompass its consequences for human life and hence cannot yet grasp its meaning and reality. I am referring to the eruption on the world's stage of modern science and its most intimate companion, modern technology.

Looking back 10,000 years earlier, we locate another momentous emergence, one necessary for the later scientific revolution. This was the appearance of agriculture as a new way for humans to live on the planet. Agriculture itself emerges starkly from a background so primal and fundamental that we cannot date its origins, for it was a way of life evolving out of the pre-human. I refer to the hunting-gathering-scavenging life in a wide-open world, before lands were marked off agriculturally, cultivated, protected, fenced in, before animals were domesticated and herded. All these developments probably occurred before humans decisively marked themselves off from the four-legged, flying, crawling, and swimming creatures—in other words, before human beings segregated themselves.

We forget these archaic hunting-gathering ancestors at our peril, for it was in those raggedly defined hundreds of thousands or millions of years that what was to become the human species adapted, and basic needs, skills, and gratifications formed themselves. Some genes themselves evolved. No matter how adaptable our species is, we forget or defy this residual layer of our human being.

For these dimly known creatures to have survived and perchance to have flourished, they would have had to be aware of what was happening on every side, and in them, every moment. We can imagine that as they moved about sensing, sniffing, probing, following up leads, their dilated awareness quivered and shimmered with alertness. There must have been ritualized ways of being dilatedly alert—of living, surviving, achieving in Nature, moment by moment, season by season, generation after generation.

The topic is indefinitely large and multiform. If we are not to close off in advance possible ways of knowing, we must cast a very large net at the start of the investigation. I suggest this: at the great turning points of human history—agriculture and then, much later, modern science and technology—the scope of human awareness contracted and, in a sense, congealed.

Left at that, my suggestion will appear glaringly counterintuitive, laughably so. For, until I have clarified the radical ambiguity of the phrase "scope of human awareness," to say that it has contracted and congealed will be taken in only one sense. That of course is the sense, dominant since the beginning of agriculture, which intensified, cemented and further constricted since modern science and technology emerged 400 years ago. I mean "scope" construed as the number and extent of entities or events that we are aware of in a world objectified for systematic, long-term, scientific-technological knowledge and, in some sense, control. I mean galaxies upon galaxies, atomic particles after atomic particles, viruses and genes, and so forth.

Understanding Our Scope of Awareness

In my brief account of our Paleolithic ancestors, I have already sketched a very different sense of "scope of awareness." Here it means our subjectivity (though this is a dangerous term)—the scope of each of our lives as beings quiveringly aware moment by moment of what is happening here and now all around us and in us. Instead of pinching down and focusing our awareness on what is to be objectified and measured for scientific and technological control, if ever and whenever we choose to exert ourselves in broader ways of knowing, our awareness is dilated to try to encompass all that is happening around us and in us, here and now, as far out as we can reach in the immediacy of sensory contact, and continuously. Trackers of animals and birds speak aptly of "splatter vision," as they pursue their prey on tiptoe.

In this second sense of "scope of awareness," the keynotes are involvement, dilatedness, sensuousness, immediacy, flexibility, nimbleness, spontaneity, continuity, and an engaged alertness to the encompassing surround at every instant. We might say that in this second sense our alertness is both dilated and relaxed, except that relaxation does not mean loss of quivering, encompassing, continuous alertness! The payoff comes from the fact that this second sense of awareness generates a world as experienced (or world-experienced) in which things of all sorts are more like fellow subjects than they are like objects.

It is this second sense of "scope of awareness" that we moderns have tended to lose. The loss leaves us with only the first sense dominant. Our mode of being aware, even of our being, tends more and more to be the narrowing, detaching, objectifying, and discontinuous sense essential to the objectifications of the mechanistic physics and technology of the sixteenth and seventeenth centuries and their aftermath. So despite the greatly expanded scope of what this science makes us aware—galaxies, atomic particles, genes—our mode of being aware and being tend to contract and congeal. We no longer feel kinship with things as fellow subjects, no longer feel that we belong immediately together with them in the vitality and abundance of the Whole and its shifting ambience, its vibratory being, fellowship, radiance, its presence to us moment by moment. Given scientific stress on the fear that our ancient ancestors must often have felt, we lose a sense of what they probably had and what we have lost.

When our being aware expands, our belonging in an ever-present company of fellow beings, expands and intensifies. This is a cohesive, experiential matrix which supports and nourishes us through time. In contrast, when our awareness in terms of numbers, sizes, and distances of objects expands, the cohesiveness of our lives may disintegrate. An astronomer, say, may relinquish her use of a telescope on Thursday night, not to regain it until Sunday night. However, her tabulations of behaviors of stars begin on Sunday night just where it left off on Thursday night. Her life as an astronomer, though, probably supports her only marginally in her encounter with her mother-in-law, say, on Sunday at noon.

Disintegration of existence and of the immediately lived world is exemplified by a young North American woman's experience of an Internet café in Ecuador. "Internet cafes are frightening places. People without homes, travelers, alone, each trying to connect to something, somewhere." Yes, tapping a few keys and bouncing a message by e-mail off a satellite to be registered nearly instantaneously in another computer thousands of miles away—breathtaking connections between objects. Without doubt, there must be subjects who can understand and send, and subjects who can receive and understand the message, maybe even prize and cherish it.

However, what is the cost? The continuous being with fellow subjects all around us or in front of us, actual subjects in our actual presence is destroyed. The enwombing cohesiveness of the sights, sounds, smells of the place one is in, along with the enticements, opportunities, responsibilities, the cohesiveness of the place—the elemental—deserts us. I mean the cycling continuities of Nature actually going on in every place: the humming of crickets in the warm night air; the methodical hooting of owls at midnight; the rutting and whistling of elk; the splashing of fish as one assembles the fishing rod; the age-old freshness of the dawn; the inexorable appearance of the sun.

I will argue that we need both modes of awareness—both modes of knowing and experiencing a world—if we are to achieve wholeness, integrity, and genuine vitality or spirituality today. We need to cultivate both scopes of awareness, if those of us who work in the contemporary university are to find it tolerable. The contemporary university, this omnicategorizing, segregating, detaching, and objectifying institution, the hardened residuum of sixteenth- and seventeenth-century dualism of mechanistic science: subjects opposed to objects, minds opposed to bodies, cultures opposed to Nature, the "haves" opposed to the "have-nots," and so on.

It is extremely difficult today to grasp the distinction I am making between scopes of awareness. For it is just the objectifying, scientific-technological sense of knowing that has been valorized and conditioned into our nervous systems for millennia, and particularly in the last four hundred years. The conditioning accelerates every day. Have not we all been taught, as if it were gospel, that only when humans settled down and adopted sedentary agricultural ways of demarcating, objectifying, controlling, cultivating, and protecting land did civilizations (the "really human") arise? Fences keep all those others out! Only then did the division of labor arise, allowing gifted humans time in which to specialize, and to cultivate the arts and sciences. We have been taught that with these ways of knowing came expansion of awareness and of horizons; that is, the expansion of objects and events that we are aware of, the amassing of hard facts about the planet never before known.

Scientific Knowledge: Reading the Book of Nature

This limited understanding of awareness, of knowledge and existence is easily understood. With science and technology 400 years ago came explosions in dimensions of the known world. Earth was no longer at the center of the universe, but one small planet far from the center, and rapidly giving up its secrets, as one nook and cranny after another were penetrated by the probes of science and technology. How could anyone looking at the luminous celestial congregations, gathered in photos taken by the Hubble telescope, possibly believe that the scope of human awareness had increasingly contracted and congealed after the agricultural, and then after the scientific-technological revolutions of the renaissance? Surely, we must have left indigenous peoples far behind!

However, I stress that the phrase "the scope of human awareness" is radically ambiguous. For example, how can we be aware of trees; in what ways can we know them? Clearly, we are amassing more botanical and genetic facts about them all the time. We do this through multifarious instrumentation and control; we precisely verify hypotheses about them. In asking what we are aware of, we are asking what we can do with them observationally and experimentally. However, we can also ask, what can we be with them moment by moment, as we stand or walk in a dilated, responsive, and maybe entranced manner in their actual presence? Might we radiantly and gracefully be with the trees? R. W. Emerson (1938/1982a, pp. 42–43) reminds us of this elemental way of being and knowing when he writes that the boughs of the tree in the soft wind nod to him (see his path-breaking essay, "Nature," p. 39 and throughout, and in particular the phrase, "I dilate and conspire with the morning wind," in section III, "Beauty.")

To be sure, scientific truths about objects as objects are intrinsically— not just extrinsically—valuable, and their discovery can be exciting. However, there are other ways of knowing, other intrinsic values and excitements, that scientific methods of knowing and their attendant technologies do, ironically, tend to eclipse.

Let us back up and try to relive, in short compass, the emergence of science and technology in the sixteenth and seventeenth centuries. Without doubt, twentieth- and twenty-first-century science and technology exhibit fundamental differences from the earlier forms, which I will touch on at the close of this chapter. However, it is the earlier emergence of science and technology that has sedimented itself in our lives so deeply. It is the earlier emergence that set the divisions and segmentations of the contemporary university, as the disciplines were formalized and professionalized in the last decades of the nineteenth century.

Galileo put it succinctly: the book of Nature is written in mathematical characters. The stupendous edifice of modern science and technology arose because it limited itself to observable events that were precisely quantifiable. Only some qualities can be correlated with quantities. Traditionally, the most venerated and valued things, events, experiences have been called holy or sacred. Does it make any sense to talk of quantities of holiness or sacredness? Doubtful indeed. Similarly, does it make sense to talk about the experience of dignity in doing one's work well. Just exactly how much dignity does one feel? It is a dubious question.

Let us further explore that modern science had to limit itself in order to ground itself. Immanuel Kant says this in several different ways. In famous lines from the Preface of *Critique of Pure Reason* he writes straightforwardly:

> When Galileo let balls of a particular weight, which he had determined in advance, roll down an inclined plane, or Torricelli made the air carry a weight which he had previously determined to be equal to that of a definite volume of water...a new light flashed on all students of nature. They comprehended that reason has insight into that only which she herself produces on her own plan...[and that] she must not let herself be led by nature, as it were in leading strings. (Kant, 1965, p. 20)

Science, then, in expanding the range of entities as precisely measurable objects or events that we are aware of, is a most sharply focused doing, and belongs with technology in its very essence. We can even say that science is the theory of technology in the broadest sense: that is, science is what we must suppose about objects if we would understand how our techniques for inquiring into them and measuring them, through our technical apparatus, could possibly grasp them.

Subjective Knowing: A Dilated Way of Being

This very action-focused, measuring-focused, constriction of being aware is essential to expanding what science-technology can make us aware of. Moreover, as I said, the discoveries bring their own mode of excitement, perhaps even modes of radiance and effulgence. Nevertheless, a generalized habit of attending to the world in a constricted way is gradually engendered through the culture. What can be experimented with and known through mathematical science-technology is only a subset of what we need to know to live well. What do we need to know if we would relish each morning, each possibility of a new beginning, and what do we need to know to keep open and alit our own shimmering potentialities? For as long as I live, my question addressed to myself is not finally answerable, and this is the case for any self to itself: Who am I? Any self is not finally objectifiable or measurable to itself, or to anyone else.

Science-technology induces a habit of attending and being aware that is objectifying, linear, and utilitarian (no matter how subtly utilitarian). So we know this fact. Now what other facts can we go on to know? Science-technology is most at home with objects pushing each other around, at home with productive causes. However, what came to be called formal causes must also be considered. That is, what something is must include its meaning and value. There is no way of grasping meaning and value without being dilated in our awareness at each moment of the fellow subjects that surround and buoy us, or oppress us, and not just fellow human subjects either. Things with roughly the same meaning and value can be produced by very different means, very different productive causes. In particular, what I will make of myself, or what we will make of ourselves, is not just another knowable fact. In addition, it cannot be achieved through grasping a closed set of productive causes. Potentiality is a quivering and magnetizing openness, an arresting call to our freedom.

This openness in our being aware is all-dilating and all-pervading. It opens us to the past as well as to the future. We can experience time not only linearly and instrumentally, but also in a recuperative manner. The past is in our bones, muscles, and nervous systems, and can be experienced as a com-

muning presence. As did our archaic hunting-gathering-scavenging ancestors, we still can be aware of all living things as fellow congregants, fellow
subjects. Science-technology cannot tell us how best to live with them so that
our presence to each other is a radiant being with each other, or a blessing to
each other. Only a greatly dilated way of being aware of what is happening
here and now and all around us and through us can restore us to the community of beings in which we were, and can still be, rooted. To miss this dilated
way of being aware is to be condemned to loneliness beyond reckoning, beyond calculation and measurement. It is to be rattling around in the lonely
crowd, rushing around, trying to fill up the emptiness.

A member of the Omaha tribe relates:

> When I was a youth the country was very beautiful....In both the woodland and the
> prairie I could see the trails of many kinds of animals and could hear the cheerful
> songs of many kinds of birds. When I walked abroad, I could see many forms of
> life, beautiful living creatures which Wakunda [The Great Mystery] had placed
> here; and these were, after their manner, walking, flying leaping, running, playing
> all about....But now...sometimes I wake in the night, and I feel as though I should
> suffocate from the pressure of this awful...loneliness. (Nabokov, 1992, p. 184)

I doubt that it is only indigenous peoples in their destroyed cultures, who feel
this awful loneliness.

So, in sum, the scope of awareness means not only the number and quantities of objects and events that we are aware of, but a dilation of our mode of
being aware that allows fellow subjects into ourselves. A dilated mode of
being aware which is our living together in shared patterns of being with
each other, shared patterns of being in each other's presence. Contrary to
Kant (at least in the *First Critique*), at times we can and should be led by
Nature.

Local Knowledge: The Way of the Shaman

The greatest dilation in being aware is exhibited in shamanism. Here
practitioners do not use instruments so much as they allow themselves to be
used as instruments. Shamanic healers allow the regenerative powers of the
universe to flow through themselves. This happens in the densest intersection
of the most intimate relations: channeling the presences of paradigmatically
regenerative beings into and through the bodies of the sick. For example,
snakes, bears, and birds are believed to reconstitute themselves out of their
own ashes or from springs that forever run clear after being roiled and
marled.

Shamans know more than they know that they know, and they trust this
knowledge that cannot be put into thematic or technological terms. Black
Elk, Native American shaman and cousin of Crazy Horse, recounted to John

Neihardt his first challenge as a healer (Neihardt, 1979). He had a great vision and a near-death experience at age nine, and now, at eighteen, was called on to minister to a very sick boy. He prepares himself by exposing himself to whatever Nature brings. Alone on a cold and stormy night, he laments for all beleaguered beings, including himself, even for those not yet born. In a vision he sees a four-rayed star herb growing on the side of a ravine. In the light of day he and a companion find such an herb and dig it out carefully. He says he knew he would have need of it in his ministrations, but he did not know how or why he knew.

Included in his preparations there are astonishingly dilated moments and modes of being aware, quivering and radiant moments of his being and of his being aware. He hears a voice calling him, but he cannot locate or demarcate the source in space or time that produced it. It came, he says to Neihardt, "from all over the sky." Again, in another one of his dilations and visions he sees a ceremonial teepee, sewn and painted with "thongs of lightening." The teepee is pinned there on the ground. However, simultaneously, in his vision, he sees its radiant double in the sky. At the close of this paper, I will relate these experiences to nonlocality, superposition, and plenipotent phenomena in contemporary physics. I will also recount Roger Penrose's speculations concerning how a new physics of the nervous system might explain how micro or quantum phenomena could manifest themselves on the macro level of experience.

The scene is set for Black Elk's first cure with elaborate detail, layout, and order (but it is not the objectified and measured precision and not the layout of sixteenth- and seventeenth-century mechanistic physics). Every detail is immensely significant for the Lakota Indians, at their time and their place. The sick boy lies at the northeasterly point of the inner circumference of the tepee. They do not know this point merely as the capital letters *NE* on a map or compass. For, by being conditioned in their bodies over centuries, they experience the north as the place from which come the cold winds that teach endurance. They experience the east as the place where the sun rises every morning, the place they ritualistically engage as the source of new beginnings. If the boy can be bathed in both influences, he may endure and have a new beginning.

Black Elk enters the teepee from the south, the place of heat and life. A drum is played in beats of four, the four orienting and buoying cardinal directions. He proceeds around the perimeter to the west, where he offers his smoking pipe to the authority, the Grandfather. The west where the sun goes down each day and dies before it can be reborn. The west, the talisman of the death that each of us must live some day, and which Black Elk had himself closely visited nine years earlier. For how can the healer heal, call back the sick from the edge of death, unless, in his dilated and radiant awareness, he hosts the presence of death intimately in his own body?

Black Elk moves to the north where he then offers the pipe in address to the Grandfather. Then he drinks from a wooden cup of water with flakes of red willow bark in it. The boy looks up and smiles at him, since each of the celebrants must do their part. Black Elk is on his maiden therapeutic voyage, not fully confident in what he is doing, but with this smile he has a strange feeling; a power is coming up through his feet and legs, the power of Mother Earth supporting and nourishing them. He asks a young woman, a virgin, to take the cup of water to the boy and give him drink. Why a virgin, rather than a pregnant woman? It is because through her the potential of new life is particularly vivid, particularly visceral.

Black Elk proceeds to where the boy lies and stamps on the ground four times. He then proceeds to kneel, to place his mouth on the boy's abdomen in order to suck the north wind that teaches endurance through the boy's body. He rises, asks one of the virgins to assist the boy to rise, then proceeds through the east to the south entrance of the tepee and exits, not waiting to see the effect of all this. The boy's father later told Black Elk that this son lived until 30.

This is exceedingly local knowledge, to use Clifford Geertz's (1983) phrase. This is knowledge of the much-at-once here and now. There are far too many variables and far too many strange sorts of them, for any brand of modern science and technology to control them, and to make precise predictions. It is the art of healing advancing ahead of the science of healing.

However, when such cures work, we should ask why? We should try to help the fledgling science of psychoneuroimmunology onto its feet. Why suppose that the "core reality" of the north wind is only particular passages of air molecules from the north? Why suppose that any such passage of molecules, measurable by a meteorologist's instruments, need be present in the teepee during the ministrations? Why not dilate our awareness on every parameter and suppose that the reality of the north wind for these people at this time includes its typical effects on their neuroimmunological systems: Allowed into themselves, that wind prompts and teaches endurance. Why suppose that a scientific-reductive account of reality is the only reliable one? Maybe in some situations it is the most unreliable. We can hardly state the question adequately, so caught up in abstractions and in reified words are we. But why not the "core reality" of the north wind for these peoples at those times? Why not the reality of universals, on which Emerson and Peirce spoke so penetratingly and eloquently long ago now? (For Peirce, universals are general tendencies in long runs of events.)

Artistic Awareness: Being Alive to Everything at Once

Artistic creation, in its many forms, is an indispensable mode of being aware and of knowing. As Hegel knew, forms of art arise coevally with forms of culture and forms of religion and healing. The impetus to create artistically holds an immense moment of dilation of awareness and of receptivity. The great artist is as much possessed angelically as is Black Elk. Of course, the artist typically leaves a deposit of worked up materials, a working up that requires dexterous skills that are to be understood on a narrower basis than the shaman's skills. Let us call the "fine" arts preshamanic.

Artists leave themselves open. They are alive to everything at once. Alive, as William James put it, to the humming fittingness of things along with each other or to their cacophony. As much flows through their bodies from every side at once, they let it flow out through their paint strokes, their chippings of marble, their fingers on keys, their dances in steps and leaps, or their notes on paper. They render the world for us in its immediacy through their bodies. Oftentimes we cannot catch up to what artists reveal. However, when we do, we know ourselves more deeply than we did before. We settle into ourselves and recognize a reality that is, as Emerson (1838/1982b) puts it, not unknown but strangely familiar. For a moment at least, we are reconnected to our most ancient ancestors, and to their quivering alertness to beings on every side, and to what moved within them. We are restored to our integrity and wholeness, whether or not we can objectify it by some means, or whether we can say how we know what we know. Nevertheless, there is a sense that we know more than we know. We sense or intuit that we belong in the universe, and that we are cared for beyond our ability to adequately acknowledge the gift.

There are many ways of speaking the truth, and we need them all. Not that we can know what they all are. Emerson (1838/1982b, p. 110) put it well: "Speak the truth and the very roots of the grass underground there do seem to stir and move to bear your witness." We are supported and buoyed by reality, contained, and nourished, and we are removed from confusion or madness. It is reassuring to know this, and it is a knowing.

Converging Ways of Knowing

We who live our lives in universities may be tempted by despair. To various degrees, we live boxed in by conceptual segmentations laid down first by agriculture, then by the mechanistic science and technology that come down to us from the sixteenth through the nineteenth centuries. We live and think within an immense culture lag. The disciplinary university reflects mind/body fractures and corresponding fact/value and science/humanities-and-arts fractures inherited from past ages of science and philosophy.

However, if we look around and detect what is actually happening around us, there is much less reason for despair. First, twentieth- and twenty-first-century physics has moved far from the model of the detached scientist simply describing mathematically the moving parts of the cosmic machine. Newton said the universe is a machine with God in its wheels. What does that mean? (Wilshire, 1968). For current physics, it is much less certain that the universe is a machine and that the physicist, the observer, is detached from the observed. What is going on is a much more organismic and inter-participatory system. Instrumentation on the microlevel disturbs and limits what can be known. More than this, creative hypothesis formation in science is not all that different from creativity in poetry, drama, or music. As Niels Bohr put it, science proceeds by image, parable, and metaphor. Perhaps, most of what the scientist predicts must be in principle empirically confirmable in precise quantitative terms at some time or place (assuming that it is not in principle indeterminate). However, experimental physicists and astrophysicists must often be as imaginative and inventive in their testing projects and procedures, as the "pure theorists" are in their own thinking.

Earlier I drew a fundamental distinction between the scope of the objects about which science can be aware (including the dilation of that mode), and, on the other hand, the scope or dilation of our mode of being aware. Today, for many in our culture, it is either one or the other; they cannot have both. This is a terrible impoverishment and disorientation.

As stated above, we live in an immense culture lag. We must not lose touch with what the most creative persons in the world are actually doing today. Let us look at a paradigmatic case of creativity; that of the plant biologist and geneticist, Barbara McClintock. In her work, the exclusive disjunction in modes of being aware begins to break down and release beckons. As detailed in an intellectual biography by Evelyn Fox Keller (Keller, 1983), McClintock looked lovingly through her microscope at her kernels of maize, as if they were fellow subjects. This dilated mode of being aware seems to have been necessary for her to observe, to be aware of what she did discover, e.g., "jumping genes." These observations were later confirmed after much delay, by her "rigorous" colleagues, and she was awarded the Nobel Prize.

Let us now look briefly at one of the most amazing convergences of modes of being aware. Recall Black Elk's perceptions and visions in which he could not locate things as objects in their own time or place. This lack of recognition could easily be dismissed as hysteria, the result of superstition, exhaustion, or extreme emotionality. However, there are parallels in the microreality of quantum physics: nonlocality, superposition, and perhaps plenipotentiality. David Bohm writes of Bell's theorem that entities once closely

associated correlate with each other when far apart, "noncausally" and immediately. Einstein was uneasy even with the thought that this might be true.
However, the evidence does not imply that some influence is transmitted
faster than the speed of light; rather a wholeness may be at work, such that
what affects one part affects other parts instantaneously (Bohm, 1980, p.
175).

Is it possible that these microreality anomalies average out and disappear
on the macrolevel of human behavior? Enter the noted astrophysicist Roger
Penrose to give us pause (Penrose, 1994). All our experiencing is mediated
by some portion or portions of the brain. He thinks that individual neurons
and their synaptic connections are units of reality far too crude to account for
what humans do sometimes actually experience. Black Elk in his visionary
and entranced moments did actually experience things as non-located and
superpositioned.

Penrose supposes that we need a new quantum physics of the brain. He
speculates that the myriad microtubules of the neurons may form a quantum
field that would correlate with mystical or visionary experiences of nonlocality and superposition or fusion. He says we do not yet have such a form of
physics; but he is looking.

How might such fields within the brain correlate with fields in the environment? I don't know, but I want to ask. As John Dewey put it, the basic
unit is not brain alone, or environment alone, but brain-in-body-in-
environment. Thus, environment must include our cultural modifications of
Nature in Nature, modifications and structures that can only be known
through local knowledge of cultures.

Let me close with words I also used at the beginning of this essay from
the twentieth-century physicist, Wolfgang Pauli:

> I believe that it is the destiny of the occident continually to keep bringing into con-
> nection with each other these two fundamental attitudes, on the one hand the ra-
> tional-critical, which seeks to understand, and on the other the mystic-irrational
> which looks for the redeeming experience of oneness. Both attitudes will always re-
> side in the human soul, and each will always carry the other already within itself as
> the germ of its contrary. Thus there arises a sort of dialectical process, of which we
> do not know whither it is leading us. I believe that as occidentals we have to commit
> ourselves to this process, and recognize the opposites as complementary. (Pauli,
> 1994, pp. 139–140)

This idea is remarkable, but Pauli's phrase "mystic-irrational" is unfortunate.
For mystical experiences of union in the community of fellow beings is but
another mode of knowing, another and complementary mode of rationality.
In these cases of convergence, the two senses of "scope of awareness" connect with each other. We are no longer left in a kind of schizoid state. New
hope is generated for a spirituality that is neither obscurantist nor escapist.

References

Bohm, D. (1980). *Wholeness and the implicate order*. London: Routledge.

Emerson, R. W. (1982a). Nature, section III, Beauty in L. Ziff (ed*), Selected essays*. New York: Penguin.

——(1982b). An address delivered before the senior class in Divinity College, 1838. In L. Ziff (Ed.), *Selected essays*. New York: Penguin.

Geertz, C. (1983). *Local knowledge: Further essays in interpretive anthropology*. New York: Basic Books.

Kant, I. (1965). (N. K. Smith, Trans.). *Critique of pure reason, 2nd ed*. New York: St. Martin's Press. (Original work published in 1929.)

Keller, E. F..(1983). *A feeling for the organism*. New York and San Francisco: W. H. Freeman.

Nabokov, P. (1992). *Native American testimony*. New York: Penguin.

Neihardt, J. (1979*). Black Elk speaks*. Lincoln: University of Nebraska Press. (Original work published in 1932.)

Pauli, W. (1994). *Writings on physics and philosophy*. New York: Springer.

Penrose, R. (1994). *Shadows of the mind: A search for the missing science of consciousness*. New York: Oxford University Press.

Wilshire, B. W. (1968). *Romanticism and evolution*. New York: G. P. Putnam.

——(2005). *Get "em all, kill 'em!: Genocide, terrorism, righteous communitie*s. Lanham, MD: Lexington Books (Rowman & Littlefield).

Part Three

Integrative Learning

The Search for Meaning and Uncommon Values

Diana Chapman Walsh

> *I am convinced that...we as a nation must undergo a radical revolution of values. We must rapidly begin the shift from a "thing-oriented" society to a "person-oriented" society. When machines and computers, profit motives and property rights are considered more important than people, the giant triplets of racism, materialism and militarism are incapable of being conquered.*
>
> Martin Luther King, Jr, from a 1967 speech
> at the Riverside Church in New York

Recent trends in college student values should be of great concern to everyone. The "materialism" value (wanting to be very well off financially) has become more important to incoming first-year students, while the "existential" value (developing a meaningful philosophy of life) has faded as a driving motivation for college students. This is one of the many challenges facing those who work in higher education today. If we look beyond these challenges, we may be able to catch a glimpse of a larger context and longer view.

Although students are motivated by materialism, there is ample and growing empirical evidence that college and university students are clamoring for more help learning to manage the stresses in their everyday lives. It is evident that they need greater sophistication in thinking about how to set priorities, decide what truly matters to them, what constitutes a life well lived and how they can set out on what Jack Kornfield has called "a path with heart." The results of a survey (Astin, 2005) show that approximately 75% of college freshmen are searching for meaning and purpose and are interested in spirituality.

The "S" Word

The "S" word (spirituality) makes many people on college campuses cringe, particularly faculty. However, more and more college students are saying that, while they are not religious, they are spiritual. What do they mean by this? Actually, it is a distinction Americans have made for a long time, contrasting the formality, bureaucracy and behavioral restrictions of organized religion with the emotionality, individuality, and personal freedom of the spiritual quest. Robert Fuller estimates that as many as twenty percent of Americans are "spiritually inclined," which would make them one of the nation's largest religious faiths (if they were indeed a single faith) (Wolfe, 2001).

Robert William Fogel (2001, p. 203), the 1993 Nobel laureate in economics, argues in his new book, *The Fourth Great Awakening*, that "spiritual estrangement from mainstream society," rather than absence of necessary material goods, is "the principal characteristic of those afflicted by chronic poverty." From a policy perspective, he argues from broad historical trends that this means "material assistance" is necessary but not sufficient "to provide spiritual resources" for those most deprived of them: "the chronically poor, the alienated young, the defeated mid-lifers, and the estranged elderly." He sees the need to produce "spiritual regeneration" as the major challenge to the nation's long-standing commitment to "egalitarian progress." Spirituality is the central organizing construct in his complex analysis.

Conversely, Jon Kabat-Zinn one of the early Westerners to bring Buddhist practices to American medicine, entirely avoids using the word "spiritual," which, he says, "creates more practical problems than it solves," because of its "inaccurate, incomplete, and frequently misguided connotations." He worries about "tendencies toward self-deception, deluded thinking, grandiosity, self-inflation, and impulses toward exploitation and cruelty directed at other beings," and suggests that overblown language exacerbates such tendencies. He counsels us simply to make a regular practice of "examining who we are... questioning our view of the world and our place in it, and ...cultivating some appreciation for the fullness of each moment we are alive" (Kabat-Zinn, 1994, p. 264).

The clarification of the meaning of the terms being discussed here can be found in the Dalai Lama's *Ethics for the New Millennium*. In his refreshingly straightforward way, he offers a distinction between religion and spirituality:

> Spirituality I take to be concerned with those qualities of the human spirit– such as love and compassion, patience, tolerance, forgiveness, contentment, a sense of responsibility, a sense of harmony–which bring happiness to both self and others. While ritual and prayer, along with the questions of [faith in the claims to salvation], are directly connected to religion, these inner qualities need not be....There is thus no reason why...individual[s] should not develop them, even to a high degree, without recourse to any religious or metaphysical belief system. This is why I sometimes say that religion is something we can perhaps do without. What we cannot do without are these basic spiritual qualities. (Dalai Lama, 19, p. 22)

Whether we embrace or eschew the "S" word probably matters less than whether we agree that these are indeed qualities today's college students cannot do without—the "qualities of the human spirit" the Dalai Lama cites above, including: "love and compassion, patience, tolerance, forgiveness, contentment, a sense of responsibility, a sense of harmony—which bring happiness to both self and others."

Student Needs

Certainly the terrorist events of September 11, 2001, had an enormous and complex impact on how we can help today's college students truly prepare for challenges they will face, develop a grounded and clear sense not only of what they want to do in the world, but also who they want to be, and what difference they want to make.

For the sake of the students, then, so that they can not just survive college, but thrive and grow while there, we need to think differently about how we help them develop what social epidemiologist Aaron Antonovsky termed a "sense of coherence." In his studies of survivors of the Holocaust and other unspeakable horrors, Antonovsky identified a general orientation to life that seemed to explain why some people were able to survive these cosmic threats. The survivors generally understood life to be reasonably predictable and manageable, and when it wasn't, they had personal and social resources that helped them anticipate and cope. Predictability and manageability, then, were the first two elements of this construct, and the third—and most important—was meaningfulness. This refers to a propensity and an ability, no matter how harsh the circumstances, to find meaning in whatever life offered.

Victor Frankl describes something similar. Today's students are facing a world that too often looks unpredictable, unmanageable, and meaningless, a world that looks fragmented and incoherent. That alone is reason for us to worry. Students are ends in themselves, and we are failing them profoundly if we send them off with diplomas and nothing to orient around but earning enough money to pay off their loans and then grow wealthy. At the same time, society has increasingly urgent unmet needs of the higher education enterprise, needs that will not be met until we find better ways to attend to the meaning-making task of late adolescence. It doesn't make students a means to an end to take seriously our obligation to those larger social needs.

The first obvious impact of the events of September 11, 2001, was the way in which everyone came together to maintain the vital connections that those acts of terror intended to destroy. We all found ourselves valuing community in a visceral way, noticing and treasuring our connections more than ever. We convened to console each other and express our resolve. We witnessed stunning acts of altruism and heroism in firefighters, police, teachers, travelers, and grieving family members, ordinary people who made extraordinary moral choices. We found ourselves rediscovering the essential goodness of the human character. We realized how much we love our country and the high ideals for which it stands. We worried that we haven't been vigilant enough, careful enough, responsible enough, informed enough as inheritors and stewards of those ideals.

We also experienced a heightened clarity about our mission as educators—the task of helping young people try to make sense of confusing events that will affect their lives, events that needed to be put into historical, political, and cultural context. There was a clear and important role for the academy, as a space within which a multiplicity of views can be freely and openly explored. Protecting spaces where people could disagree seemed increasingly important as the nation closed ranks. We hoped that our scholars and teachers, and their values of free expression, might offer a healthy balance between security and liberty, between vigilance and normalcy, between patriotism and internationalism, between standing unequivocally against evil while still asking questions about how our country is viewed around the world, and why.

All of this was palpably true, and yet, after the immediate grief and coming together, we entered a second phase in which we began to split apart. There was, paradoxically, both a flatness and an edginess, almost as though only the negative energy could draw us up out of our depression. Academia came under sharp attack. Articles and editorials began to appear blaming multiculturalism for having made faculty and students "moral relativists," afraid to judge anyone, even terrorists. Questioning our nation's foreign policy became unpatriotic.

Before long, "9/11" was swept up into the commercial world of spectacle. Frank Rich captured this bitingly in his op ed. piece in *The New York Times*, "Patriotism on the Cheap."

> "9/11" is now free to be a brand, ready to do its American duty and move product. Ground Zero is at last an official tourist attraction with its own viewing stand, with vendors and lines to rival those at Disneyland. (Wave and smile for the folks back home). Barnes and Noble offers competing coffee-table books handsomely packaging the carnage of yesteryear. (Rich, 2001)

So how do we help this new generation of college students find transcendent meaning in their lives … these students who have been shaped by a bizarre world of spectacle and celebrity, and by a materialistic, self-indulgent culture for which our generation bears much responsibility? How can we structure their undergraduate college experience to be sure that they will learn what they need to know about the Dalai Lama's "qualities of the human spirit?"

If there is a crisis of morale on college campuses today, it is the worry many of us have that the pressures of technology, popular culture, the market, and consumption are moving us farther and farther not only from the traditional sources of comfort and purpose (family, religion, even state and nation) but also farther from the organizing vision behind a liberal education. So, if we want our students to set out on a lifelong path of deepening insight and wisdom, what are we to do? We face at least five challenges, five areas in which we need to both sharpen our questions and focus our energies. There are no simple answers in any of the five areas.

Core Values

We need to find better ways to communicate to students a few core values and do everything in our power to cultivate them as best we can. This requires constant and creative attention, as well as a real sense for the teachable moments, day in and day out. At least three nested categories of those core values come to mind.

First are the deepest and most basic human values that remind us, as His Holiness the Dalai Lama would say, of our responsibilities to the human family—those codified, for example, in the *Universal Declaration of Human Rights*, those inscribed in the lessons and parables of every great faith tradition and those conveyed in the teachings of many of the world's great literary and artistic works, social science investigations, and, equally, in the profoundest insights of the great natural scientists. These are the universal questions we hope our faculty members are always teaching our students to think well about.

Second, and equally important, are a few bedrock institutional values, values specific to the academy—obligations that accompany the "freedoms necessary for teaching and scholarly work," as Donald Kennedy describes them in his book, *Academic Duty* (Kennedy, 1997, p. 2). These include the faculty responsibilities around which Kennedy organizes his book: to prepare, to teach, to mentor, to serve the institution, to discover, to publish, to tell the truth, to reach beyond the walls, and to change. They also include institutional expectations of students—the responsibilities we need them to take up lest their empowerment blend into an entitlement that will not serve them well in life.

Our institutional values serve as a crucial thread binding the present to the past and the future. They are vitally important in that respect for those of us who are out talking to alums and other patrons of the institution. They are equally important to our admissions officers, part of what high school seniors are looking for from college, a sense of community, an opportunity to develop the knowledge and skills they will need to "make a difference in the world," as our mission statement and so many like it state in one way or another.

Third, every institution has its own version of the indispensable core academic values and aspirations it seeks to transmit to its students. Wellesley's academic values cohere around our honor code and our ethic of student responsibility for self-governance. They are also expressed in the motto inscribed by our founder on the seal of the college, *non ministrari sed ministrare*, engraved in the nave of the chapel, and (we hope) are inculcated at orientation in the heart of every first-year student as she arrives on the campus and begins unpacking her bags. This acculturation process is a big part of why institutions like ours sponsor orientation programs, with upper-class students as transmitters of the culture.

Students are vitally important in another way that is worth pausing to underscore. Richard Light's *Making the Most of College* (2001) distills ten years of research on the choices students themselves can make to succeed at college and ways in which faculty and administrators can, as he says, "translate good intentions into practice." The Harvard students in his study had a lot to say about diversity—how a diverse student body can greatly enhance learning, because (and this is the critical finding) "college offers a fundamentally different opportunity from most other environments. The opportunity for learning from difference arises precisely because all incoming students are likely to share certain values"—assumptions that all students have come here to work hard, apply themselves academically, strive for excellence, take their commitments seriously, and, importantly, to learn from one another.

What is crucial to understand is that the good consequences do not flow automatically from bringing people together from different backgrounds. This awareness grew out of negative experiences many of the students brought from their high school years. Positive results depend on how effectively the college builds on and strengthens "the assumption of certain shared values." The students explained that this is because communicating across difference is always risky and difficult. People will not take the risk of seeming offensive or insensitive (or worse) unless the institution has managed to set "a tone of good will." Emphasizing a few core values is a top priority, and our question is how best to do it.

Listen for the Value Conflicts

Second (and paradoxically, even as we emphasize the values we do have in common), I think we need to listen harder for the value conflicts and to engage them more deeply and more seriously. They will be the engines of institutional growth and healthy change. Often they will emerge from the students, who bring fresh perspectives as they move through our institutions faster than any of the rest of us.

How can we listen in new ways for new manifestations of emerging and changing core values that can inspire more members of the community to become involved in increasingly central ways, to move in off the margins of the community and increase their feelings of significance, as well as their actual importance to the academic enterprise? This is very difficult. As our colleges and universities become increasingly diverse, the clash over values, meaning systems, alternative epistemologies, conflicting standards of excellence, and fundamentally different worldviews can feel like a struggle for the very soul of the institution.

Margaret J. Wheatley, in *Leadership and the New Science* (Wheatley, 1992), draws on chaos theory to provide leaders in these times of rapid change some comfort. If we can communicate a few simple guiding principles or values, the system can tolerate from its members a lot of what appears to be "random, chaotic-looking meandering." An organization that is "consistent with itself and its past," she says, provides ample room for individual freedom and self-determination. But, of course, what makes the clashes over values in the academy—differences of opinion, for example, over what educated people should know, or what constitutes high-quality scholarship, or what grades are supposed to convey and accomplish—what makes those value differences seem so cataclysmic is that they call into question the very assumption that the organization is "being consistent with itself and its past." So as we emphasize the need to articulate a few polestar values, we should not delude ourselves into believing that even they will be universally shared or understood. Can we honor those values by arguing over them, attending to the ways in which they are being contested, reshaped, transformed, redefined—revitalized?

Elie Wiesel offers a vision that might guide such a process. In a speech at Wellesley College he described a moral society—or a community striving to be moral—as one that is living in dialogue, that is honoring the humanity of every member. In such a community, we are all lifelong learners, teachers, and witnesses.

Begin with the Faculty

Third, there are several reasons to begin and end with the faculty and the academic program, even as we build on the recognition that an increasingly large share of students' learning about values, and about life, takes place outside the classroom. Granting that we are unlikely to find (or forge) consensus among the faculty on how to approach this question of values, I see several reasons why it is necessary to begin there.

First is the obvious reality that the faculty are where the power is. No change of consequence will happen in the academy without the faculty's commitment to it. Important decisions inevitably represent the collective values and aspirations of the faculty. Second, our students consider classroom discussions the safest places for a full exchange of controversial ideas. When we do surveys, students say that the classroom is the place where they are most comfortable speaking their minds, the place where the "politically correct" pressures are most attenuated. And they are not going to form grounded commitments if they are afraid to express unpopular opinions. Third, the faculty and the academic program are both where the expertise resides for a critical discussion of value commitments—how we know what we think we know—and where the responsibility lies to ensure that those questions are engaged deeply and thoughtfully.

Without even raising the specter of trying to reach consensus on specific moral commitments, faculty in many courses can (and do) teach students the relative strengths and weaknesses of alternative methods for arriving at their own judgments about what most matters to them. This is the essence of critical thinking, and it is what good teachers do. There is a very large role for the faculty in the teaching of values and moral reasoning; in fact, there is little hope of doing it well without their leadership. The question is how to engage them.

Build a Community of Inquiry

Even as we begin (and end) with the faculty, we need to recognize how much of the learning about values occurs outside the classroom. This is a very robust finding in research on student learning in college, and is reinforced in Richard Light's book: *Making the Most of College.* When Light and his colleagues asked students "to think of a specific critical incident or moment that had changed them profoundly," he reports, "four-fifths of them chose a situation or event outside of the classroom." This finding confirms something we have known, namely that we teach a silent curriculum not documented in the course catalogue, that we are residential learning communities, and that the community aspect is vital.

In her book, *Cultivating Humanity*, Martha Nussbaum places this point in historical context (Nussbaum, 1997). Today's institutions of higher learning, she observes, are organized around the idea, going back to Plato and Aristotle, that we humans can free, can liberate our minds if we can develop the discipline of accepting only those beliefs that stand systematic tests of reason and of consistency and thoughtful justification. In some ways, this is the antidote to the very legitimate concerns that many faculty have that students' spiritual explorations will lead them in directions that will be anti-intellectual and/or irrational. Sorting successfully through the competing values in modern life requires, first and foremost, a method.

Hunter Lewis's book, *A Question of Values*, identifies six modes of moral reasoning (Lewis, 1990, pp. 183–184). Value systems, he says, are based on authority, logic, sense experience, emotion, intuition and "science." Focusing "on modes of believing and knowing, rather than on beliefs *per se*," he points out, "underscores how bias and subjectivity necessarily creep into any discussion of values." Education for critical thinking, then, can provide students the intellectual scaffolding they need to be clear about the frameworks out of which they are operating on any given issue. One hopes that this will enable them to free themselves from prejudice and blind ignorance, the essence, of course, of what a liberal education is all about. It is an education that involves a special kind of human interaction, a constant testing of our most cherished convictions, the ones we most take for granted, against serious and disturbing challenges in the classroom or beyond.

That kind of learning requires a community engaged in a common enterprise, an inquiring community whose members are committed above all to learning from one another everything they can about how a different experience or perspective or how a new insight, argument, or data point might forever alter their own tentative and provisional notions of what is true. Maintaining such a community makes demands on everyone: showing up and being truly present, listening openly and sympathetically to others, exposing their own thinking to critical scrutiny, taking full responsibility for their truth claims, even at the risk of embarrassment or failure, assuming good intentions on the part of others, even when they say things of which we disapprove.

Such are the obligations and duties—the ethical claims really—of a community of inquiry, holding as a collective project the ideal of a liberal education. Ultimately, these same obligations are the demands of citizenship in a democracy. At college, these are the practices that provide opportunities for students to learn, in a safe and accepting space, how to take up and defend informed positions of their own, how to know, to the extent possible, what they know; how they know it.

Be the Change We Want to See

To maintain these special communities of inquiry in these contentious times, those in leadership positions (and that includes the entire faculty) need to be self-conscious about the values we enact in our day-to-day lives. We need to be mindful of Gandhi's dictum to be the change we want to see.

The leadership from above is of the sort described in Richard Light's book. It sets expectations and a tone, provides Margaret Wheatley's "simple governing principles: guiding visions, strong values, organizational beliefs" that can liberate members of an organization to operate without many rules. To say that leadership is needed from above is not to advocate for an authoritarian structure in which the organization's values are dictated from on high. Quite the contrary, effective leadership is most effective precisely when it draws more and more people into the collective process of forging meaning and making sense of the work that aligns them in a common purpose. Just as

John Dewey believed that education for democracy ought to be organized democratically, we can say that an education about values ought to take place in an environment that is self-conscious about its own values.

Our students are very sophisticated, and they watch us closely. They see right through us when our behaviors or our institutional practices violate the values we espouse. There has to be a congruence between our inner and outer worlds. Parker Palmer has written as well on this challenge to leadership as anyone I know—on how leaders and teachers can maintain the identity and integrity they need to "project a spirit of light...on that which is 'other' than us." He points out that we all share responsibility, as he states it "for creating the external world....We can approach the world with a spirit of hope or of despair. "We have a choice," Parker says, "and in that choice we create the world that is" (Palmer, 1990). This is especially important for leaders, he says, because they, by virtue of their positions, have unusual opportunities to project onto other people shadow or light, to create worlds for others that are filled with hope or filled with despair. Leaders therefore have a special responsibility for what goes on inside themselves, "lest the act of leadership create more harm than good."

On a personal level, this means facing one's demons daily, recognizing one's self-deceptions, small and large, staying with them rather than looking away in shame or self-delusion. On an institutional level, it means bringing into one's daily work that same paradoxical commitment to being both brutally honest and lovingly forgiving of one's own and others' inevitable mistakes. When we make that commitment and stay with it as best we can, it becomes inescapably the case that if we are really doing our jobs by focusing on student learning and academic excellence, then we will be creating meaning for our students as well as for ourselves. We can't do the one without the other.

There are many forces at play in the world today that are working against that expansive vision of a liberal education. However, if we can hold on to it—each of us who is privileged to be in a position to shape, and be shaped by, hungry young minds, and hearts that are open and unfolding—if we organize our work around this expansive vision, then I believe our institutions of higher learning can continue to be oases where all of us can pause for a time and dwell within the questions that truly matter.

References

Astin, A. & Astin, H.S. (April, 2005). *The spiritual life of college students: A national study of college students' search for meaning and purpose.* Los Angeles: UCLA Higher Education Research Institute.

Dalai Lama. (1999). *Ethics for the new millennium.* New York: Riverhead Books.

Fogel, R.W. (2000). *The fourth great awakening and the future of egalitarianism.* Chicago: University of Chicago Press.

Kabat-Zinn, J. (1994). *Wherever you go there you are: Mindfulness meditation in everyday life.* New York: Hyperion.

Kennedy, D. (1997). *Academic duty.* Cambridge, MA: Harvard University Press.

Lewis, H. (1990). *A question of values.* San Francisco: Harper.

Light, R.J. (2001). *Making the most of college.* Cambridge, MA: Harvard University Press.

Nussbaum, M.C. (1997). *Cultivating humanity.* Cambridge, MA: Harvard University Press.

Palmer, P.J. (1990). *Leading from within.* Indianapolis, IN: Office for Campus Ministries.

Rich, F. (2001, January 5). Patriotism on the cheap. *The New York Times.*

Wheatley, M. J. (1992). *Leadership and the new science.* San Francisco: Berrett-Koehler.

Wolfe, A. (2001). *Moral freedom.* New York: W. W. Norton & Company.

How Do We Educate for Partnership and Peace? Putting Spirituality into Action

Riane Eisler

Until we see what we are, we cannot
take steps to become what we should be.
Charlotte Perkins Gilman

Imbuing our lives with spirituality in the sense of meaning, purpose, connection, and caring has been a central theme of my work. My purpose in this essay is not to argue that we should be more spiritual or empathic; spiritual leaders have been making this case throughout history. What concerns me here is how we can help to create the conditions that make it possible, that support rather than inhibit or distort, our great human capacity, our human yearning, for meaning, purpose, connection, and caring.

In our age of nuclear and bacteriological weaponry, the world's habitual violence is not sustainable. In recognition of the gravity of our situation, the United Nations has declared the years 2001 through 2010 the *International Decade for a Culture of Peace and Nonviolence for the Children of the World*. Now it is up to us to ask: What is a culture of peace, and what can we do to help create it? How is a more spiritually evolved or caring, less violent, more connected way of life actually possible?

Our culture tells us that violence is inevitable. The story is widely repeated, even in many spiritual traditions, that human nature is innately flawed. We hear similar stories from science, stories about selfish genes (Dawkins, 1990). In this instance, science and religion share the same premise, i.e., that human nature is problematic, dangerous, and must be controlled.

Given the historical record, it would be naïve to believe that violent behavior is not part of our genetic equipment. Humans have an astounding capacity to hurt members of their own species. However, caring, peaceableness, empathy—these dispositions and qualities are also genetically rooted; otherwise we would not be capable of cultivating them. Because all of these capacities are components in our genetic repertoire, we must push beyond the traditional "nature versus nurture" dichotomy. Genetic capabilities are not automatically expressed; our behavior patterns result from an interaction of genes and experience.

This is as true for mice as it is for humans. Gariépy et al. bred mice to be aggressive for several generations (see, for example, Gariépy, Bauer, & Cairns, 2001). The mice were reared in isolation in order to reinforce violent, aggressive behaviors. However, when these high-aggression mice were brought out of isolation upon reaching puberty (about 45 days old) and placed in rooms for periods between 45 and 69 days, many of these mice, genetically bred to be violent, became nonviolent and nonaggressive.

Of course, human behavior is much more flexible than animal behavior because so much more of our behavior is based on learning. The point here is that not even genetic predispositions are automatically triggered into action. At issue is always the interaction of experience with genes (See e.g., Eisler & Levine, 2002). For humans, experience is largely shaped by culture

Consequently, it is necessary to focus on an examination of what kinds of cultures produce experiences that facilitate or inhibit our genetic potential for caring, connection, and for spirituality—spirituality in the sense of connectivity and of awareness of our integral interconnection. For three decades, the question of what kind of beliefs, institutions, and cultural systems either support or inhibit the expression of human genetic capacities has been the central question that has animated my research.

As a scholar, understanding this issue is motivated by my own experience. I was born in Vienna and grew up at a time of massive regression to the domination model—the rise to power of the Nazis in Germany and in my native Austria. I was seven years old when the Gestapo came to drag my father away, and I witnessed then not only the expression of the cruel, insensitive, violent part of our behavioral repertoire, but I also witnessed spirituality in action. I witnessed spiritual courage. I witnessed my mother standing up to the Gestapo, standing up to cruelty and violence. She acted out of love, out of caring, out of a sense of connectedness—an act that could have cost her life, but by a miracle she was able to obtain my father's release.

We were able to escape Vienna, to escape Europe, but only, again, by a mere thread. We left Europe on one of the last ships to Cuba following a ship that has since been made famous by the film *The Voyage of the Damned*. The ship we followed was the *St. Louis*. It was a ship of a thousand Jewish refugees—women, men, children—a ship that was not admitted by the Cuban authorities, even though the refugees had purchased visas, as we had, to Cuba. It was a ship that was not admitted by any other nation in the Americas, including the United States, so all of these thousand people had to go back to Europe. Of course, most of them were killed in Nazi extermination camps. We were right behind that ship.

This experience created searing questions in my mind about the cultural systems that generate and sustain such cruelty and violence. At the same time, I have attempted to understand the profound human capacity for caring, for connectedness, and for a more spiritually evolved way of living. The world is in desperate need of a new approach if we are to avoid spiraling down into a culture of selfishness and violence. This essay provides a blueprint for such an approach.

Understanding Dominator and Partnership Cultural Dynamics

I have found that, cross-culturally and transhistorically, all cultures can be placed on a continuum anchored by two fundamental underlying possibilities for structuring social norms and institutions, from the family, education and religion, to politics and economics (Eisler, 1987). The study of what I call "relational dynamics" has made it possible to identify a system of cultural categories called the *partnership* or *respect model* and the *domination* or *dominator model*. This classification system transcends conventional categories, such as religious versus secular, right versus left, East versus West, that fail to address the kinds of relationships and behaviors supported or limited by the institutions of a given culture.

The world is all too rich with examples of dominator cultures. They can be found across the world, from Stalin's Soviet Union to Khomeini's Iran, from Afghanistan under the Taliban to Uganda under Idi Amin. They all have the same core configuration involving three main components. The first component of this configuration is rigid, top-down control in both the family and the state. Power is used to intimidate and manipulate the powerless for the benefit of those in authority. The second core component is the ranking of one half of humanity over the other half. This is an orientation that brought us into a matriarchy versus patriarchy dichotomy, which itself is a product of a dominator mentality. In the dominator mentality, there are only two alternatives: dominate or be dominated. Theoretically, it could be the female half over the male half. Historically, though, there has never been a matriarchy. (Societies where women have a more equal voice have sometimes been called matriarchies, but they are not societies where women rule men, as implied in the term matriarchy as the opposite of patriarchy.) There have been, and still are, societies oriented toward the partnership model (Eisler, 1987; 2000, 2002). But the historically prevailing pattern has involved the ranking of the male half of humanity over the female half.

The third core component of this configuration is institutionalized violence that is socially idealized and condoned and even morally sanctioned. By violence, I mean to suggest behaviors ranging from lack of empathy to outright cruelty. It is such aggressive behavior that is precisely what is needed to maintain top-down relations of domination, whether man over woman, man over man, race over race, religion over religion, or nation over nation. Ultimately such relations of domination must be maintained by fear and by force. The force component involves a system of beliefs, including a cultural construction of beliefs about human nature and spirituality, that make these kinds of behaviors and relations seem inevitable.

The key characteristics of the dominator and partnership models are outlined in the table below (Eisler, 2000):

Partnership Model	Dominator Model
Egalitarian structure with hierarchies of actualization	Authoritarian structure with hierarchies of domination
Equal valuing of females and males	Ranking of males over females
Institutionalization of mutual honoring, respect, and peaceful conflict resolution	Institutionalization of fear, violence, and abuse
High social investment in stereotypically "feminine" traits and activities, such as empathy, caring, nonviolence and caregiving	High social investment in stereotypically "masculine" traits and activities, such as the control and conquest of people and nature
Myth and stories honoring partnership	Myths and stories honoring domination

Table 1: Core configuration of the Partnership Model and Dominator Model, adapted from Riane Eisler, *The Power of Partnership* (2002).

The Middle Ages in Europe, although often portrayed as a more "spiritual" epoch, involved a strong orientation toward domination. The medieval Church was very top-down, brutally punishing dissent and repressing enemies. The core cultural structure, in many ways, resembled that of the Taliban: burning a woman alive for heresy is similar to stoning a woman to death for violating religious law. In both cases, the public display of violence is intended to maintain rankings of domination. Medieval European culture condoned violence against women and against children. Men could legally beat their wives for not obeying their orders and severe corporal punishment of children was practiced in both homes and schools. That culture also used extensive violence against any religious or political dissent, and against minority groups, such as Jews.

Fortunately, we have been moving toward the partnership end of the continuum over the past several hundred years, despite enormous resistance and periodic regressions. If we had not been moving toward the partnership end of the continuum, my work, and the larger movement toward transformation in institutions of all kinds, would not exist. Such conversations would be heresy, rather than the leading edge of change.

As a culture moves toward the partnership model, a different core configuration emerges. It is found today in some indigenous, tribal cultures such as the Muso of China, agrarian cultures such as the Minangkabau of Sumatra, and the industrialized Scandinavian societies. The northern European societies may not be ideal—there never is a pure partnership society—and every society will involve some level of violence. Nevertheless, nations such as Sweden, Norway, and Finland feature more egalitarian economic and political democracies. They have reduced the large gaps between rich and poor, gaps that are characteristic of domination-oriented societies.

These Scandinavian nations were also the first to move toward industrial democracy. They pioneered the use of teams, self-directed groups of workers that replaced assembly lines in which workers are basically cogs in the industrial machine.

In terms of the second part of the core partnership configuration, what appears in the Scandinavian societies is a much more equal partnership between the two halves of humanity, between women and men. In Sweden, Norway, Finland, and Iceland, women comprise between 35 and 45 percent of legislatures. Once that point is reached, something critical occurs for bringing spirituality into action. As the status of women rises, so does the status of those traits and activities that, in the domination mentality, are stereotypically associated with women, with femininity. These are traits of caring, nonviolence, and empathy. As a consequence, these kinds of values and activities are supported by national policies. These nations fund universal health care, elder care, childcare, and other nurturing activities—rather than, as in the dominator model, punishing and controlling people, as in policies where there's never enough money for caring for people, but always money for prisons, armaments, and wars.

When I use the term "stereotypically masculine and feminine," I want to emphasize that I mean just that, rather than implying that men and women have fixed traits. As gender roles change, this becomes obvious. Many fathers in the United States today are redefining fathering in terms of the more stereotypically feminine approach of caregiving that involves a kind of tenderness which has historically been associated with women. Caring behavior by men, in the domination model, is ridiculed as weak and feminine.

If we really think about it, most world spiritual traditions have a common emphasis on stereotypically feminine values: empathy, nonviolence, caring. Despite such espoused values, however, in societies—or in periods or in subcultures—that orient themselves to the domination model, such values will be repressed. They are plentiful in rhetoric, but scarce in reality. By contrast, societies that have moved toward the partnership end of the continuum feature caring social policies. Although such policies are often criticized as creating a bloated *welfare state*, if we look at the move of Scandinavian nations such as Norway and Sweden from poverty to prosperity, it is evident that it is precisely these policies that have brought prosperity because they support human development, including spiritual development.

To return to the third component in the core configuration, that of violence, it is not coincidental that laws prohibiting violence against children
and families have been pioneered by the Scandinavian nations. In addition, it
is not coincidental that there is a very strong men's movement in the Scandinavian world trying to disentangle masculinity or male identity from its
equation with domination, conquest, and violence that is part of the domination model, and it is not coincidental that the first peace academies have
emerged in the Scandinavian region.

This configuration is also found in some tribal societies around the
world. Societies such as the Teduray, as described by anthropologist Stuart
Schlegel (1998), have spiritual teachings about nonviolence as well as elaborate social mechanisms for the avoidance of violence and the prevention of
cycles of violence. Violence is not integral to male socialization, men are not
ranked over women, and they do not have tribal hierarchies of domination.
What they have instead are elders, both female and male, who are highly respected because of their wisdom, and who play an important role in mediat-
ing conflict.

Among the Teduray, as among the Minangkabau, spirituality is understood in a more "feminine" form, as nurturance. Caring behavior is understood as inherent in nature, including human nature, so that nurturance is part
of the male role in society (Sanday, 2002). In other words, these are societies
with a belief system that emphasizes human possibilities, that focuses on the
positive rather than the negative aspects of our very large genetic repertoire.

Constructing Partnership in Education

The task of creating more peaceful, more equitable, and more spiritually
evolved societies demands a rethinking of our fundamental cultural institutions. As a society, we must systematically consider where key intervention
points might be. Clearly, a rethinking of education is in order—a rethinking
that would extend from early childhood education through universities and
beyond. To generate sustained cultural change, far more must be done than
reforming education; nevertheless, new models of schooling can accelerate
the shift toward partnership by preparing a new generation with understanding and experience in a partnership way of being, interacting, and thinking.

Like all educational endeavors, partnership education consists of three
components: process, structure, and content. All of these elements are deeply
interconnected. The table below illustrates the contrast between partnership
and dominator models in school structures, content, and processes (Eisler,
2000).

A key element of partnership education is to show that partnership relations are possible (Eisler, 2000; Eisler & Miller, eds., 2004). This learning

should happen both at a conceptual and an experiential level. Thus, a partnership *process* in teaching and learning is an essential aspect of partnership education. Partnership process is an integrated pedagogy that honors students as whole and diverse individuals. It focuses not only on cognitive learning

The Partnership Model values and supports:	The Dominator Model values and supports:
Teacher and student knowledge and experience are valued	Teacher is the sole source of information and knowledge
Learning and teaching are integrated and multidisciplinary	Learning and teaching are artificially fragmented and compartmentalized
Curriculum, leadership, and decision making are gender balanced	Curriculum is male centered; leadership and decision making are male controlled
Multicultural reality of human experience is valued and tapped as a source of learning	One cultural worldview is the measure with which others are analyzed and evaluated
Social and physical sciences emphasize our interconnection with other people and nature	Social and physical sciences emphasize the conquest of people and nature
Mutual responsibility, empathy, and caring are highlighted and modeled	Relations based on control and manipulation are highlighted and valued

Table 2: Partnership and Dominator Education, adapted from Riane Eisler, *Tomorrow's Children* (2000).

but also on the affective dimensions of learning. It cultivates less linear, more intuitive, contextualized, and holistic ways of learning. Partnership processes model partnership relations in daily interaction, showing students that their voices will be heard, their ideas respected, and their emotional needs understood. This kind of environment promotes not only learning and personal growth for individual children, but also, on a larger scale, the shift to a less violent, more equitable and caring society.

The core elements of partnership *structure* are a democratic and egalitarian rather than an authoritarian organizational structure, gender balance rather than male dominance and emphasis on nonviolent and mutually caring and respectful relationships. When educational institutions follow this template, their structure models partnership relations and supports both partnership process and content.

There are deep interconnections between structure and process in education. Schools typically place young people in authoritarian structures that do not allow for authentic participation. Such structures do not prepare students for engagement in a democratic society; moreover, they tend to create resentment and alienation. The modern educational methods practiced in many schools often rely on negative motivations, such as fear, guilt, and shame. Such methods force children to focus primarily on competition rather than empathic cooperation, and in significant ways, they can suppress inquisitiveness.

Dominator-oriented educational structures may have suited the autocratic monarchies and feudal fiefdoms that preceded more democratic societies. They may have been appropriate for industrial assembly lines structured to conform to the dominator model, where workers were forced to be mere cogs in the industrial machine and to strictly follow orders without question. However, dominator structures are inappropriate for a democratic society that seeks to nurture the highest potentials of all its members.

In terms of our educational organizations—and all cultural institutions— we need to differentiate between *hierarchies of domination* and *hierarchies of actualization* (Eisler, 2000). Hierarchies of domination are imposed and maintained by fear. They are held in place by the power that is idealized, and even sanctified, in dominator-oriented societies: the power to inflict pain and to kill. By contrast, hierarchies of actualization are primarily based not on power over, but on power to (the power to help and to nurture others) as well as power with (the collective power to accomplish things together). In hierarchies of actualization, accountability flows not only from the bottom up but also from the top down. In other words, accountability flows in both directions.

A partnership-oriented education will help students to be better prepared to function in our postindustrial economy. Hierarchies of domination tend to produce workers who can take orders, who can find their place in an authoritarian structure. However, the focus now is on the development of young people as self-directed, creative learners who will be able to create teams, nurture collaboration, and work in more fluid, flexible configurations.

Universities have an important role in supporting the movement toward partnership in primary and secondary education. At one level, universities train the next generation of teachers. Although state requirements allow little space for experimentation, teacher training programs must be approached more creatively—and more collaboratively—than has been the traditional practice, in order to provide teachers with understanding and experience in a partnership approach. Further, universities can influence the canon, that body of great works that must be read by younger learners in order to be considered an educated person. The traditional list has been inherited from an earlier time that elevated a dominator model, and it is no coincidence that women and persons of color have been largely excluded.

When I attended university, I felt like an outsider. I later realized that this was not so much because I was a foreigner, but because I was a woman. Everything students read in those days was written by and about people who were not like me. Such an absence is based on, and perpetuates, a dominator culture. Women's absence from the curriculum tends to justify their subordinate position because it supports the false conclusion that they are inferior. It communicates the impression that women have contributed little to cultural advancement, ignoring not only the many women in art, literature, and science who were excluded from the canon but also the essential role that women's traditional roles of nurturance play in the world.

Understanding gender is critical for understanding core social dynamics. The cultural construction of the roles and relations, and the socialization for gender roles, profoundly affect everything in a social system. In a dominator-oriented culture, children grow up with a cognitive and emotional orientation that one kind of person is put on this earth to be served and the other one is put on this earth to serve, that one person is supposed to dominate and is superior and the other person is supposed to be dominated and be inferior. This view is then generalized to all differences, whether of race, religion, or ethnicity, producing in-group/out-group mentalities. Building a culture of peace must involve a systemic examination of how young people are socialized, in school and outside.

In terms of educational *content*, schools tend to reinforce concepts and ideas that belong to a dominator tradition. The construction of evolution is a telling example. The way that evolution is taught, whether it is in high school or in universities or in television documentaries, places the emphasis on precisely those behaviors that are appropriate for relations of domination and submission. The other side of the evolution story is not told. Evolution has also supported the development of nurturance. By the grace of evolution, we humans receive biochemical rewards, neuropeptides that give us enormous pleasure, not only when we are cared for, but also when we care for another. The pleasure of caring is a common human experience, yet it has been omitted from the evolutionary story.

Young people need to be told about that part of our evolutionary story—the story of what I call "*meaningful evolution*" (Eisler, 2000). Young people are empowered when they know that our strivings for love, beauty, and justice are rooted in human evolution. When young people understand that these strivings are at the core of our humanity, they can imbue their lives with greater meaning. Most importantly, they can more consciously and caringly participate in the great adventure of the evolution of the planet.

I have chosen the phrase *meaningful evolution* to describe a view of evolution in which we can find a larger sense of purpose. This view differs sharply from fundamentalist religious interpretations that totally ignore scientific findings. However, it also differs from theories presented as neo-Darwinian, that ignore what Darwin himself emphasized: that factors other than random variation and natural selection come into play at the human level of evolution, as evolution theorist David Loye points out in his book *Darwin's Lost Theory of Love* (Loye, 1999). This notion of meaningful evolution highlights that what we do in this lifetime is meaningful because it advances the evolution of our species and fulfills our responsibilities on this planet.

Meaningful evolution transcends the conventional polarity between spirituality and science, grounding spirituality in evolution. It identifies for us as a species a meaningful relationship to life and the wonder of the universe. It takes into account key evolutionary developments such as the evolution of consciousness, creativity, and love. By offering a more inclusive story of evolution—one that does not ignore the fact that love and creativity are just as grounded in evolution as violence and destructiveness—it also supports what I have called spiritual courage: putting love into action, even when it means going against established dominator norms.

Our teaching of science requires a more balanced narrative, a narrative that illuminates an evolution toward a more spiritually evolved, caring way of being. Reptiles such as the rainbow lizard are notorious for being uncaring to their offspring: They eat them if the little lizards don't scurry off into the underbrush after they hatch. However, in mammals, caring becomes an essential aspect of parent-offspring relations. Unlike most reptiles, baby mammals cannot simply walk off and survive on their own when they are born. They require food, protection from predators, and guidance in learning survival skills. For humans, caring is absolutely vital—infants actually die without emotional care.

A long period of care is critical for a child's development. Human babies do not have fully developed brains when they are born. If they did, they would not be able to fit through the birth canal. So the human brain must instead continue to develop outside the mother's womb after the baby is born, particularly during the first year, but also for many years after. Many of the brain's neural pathways are, in critical respects, laid down after birth. This means that, for humans, nurture is just as critical as nature, if not more so.

A partnership-oriented curriculum is important to balance the messages of domination that students receive in the classrooms and through the media. This is true in the social sciences as well as the natural sciences. The field of history, for example, is organized along a dominator logic, with an emphasis on "great men," warfare, and territorial acquisition.

From a partnership perspective, there is a powerful series of social movements that challenge entrenched traditions of domination. These include the movement for individual rights and liberty, the women's rights movement—challenging the power of men to rule over the women and children in the castles of their homes, the abolitionist movement, the civil rights movement, and the indigenous rights movement. Each of these movements challenges relations of domination that place one group as superior to another. The environmental movement challenges another tradition of domination, the *conquest of nature*.

Appreciating the dynamics and successes of social movements is essential to a more balanced education. Examples of liberation struggles can help students feel more hopeful and less cynical about their power to create change and their connection with a long struggle for equality.

In every discipline, traditions of domination need to be critically examined and brought into balance with partnership-oriented ideas and experiences. Doing so is a powerful means of bringing spirituality into action.

The Long Journey to Partnership

Many people feel disheartened, fearing that the progressive social movements have failed. From my perspective, however, it is clear that dominator regressions are part of a dynamic process where backlashes against the movement toward partnership reconstruct, in both old and new forms, the kinds of social structures, beliefs, and behaviors that support and strengthen dominator elements in our cultures.

It is instructive that, whether in Europe under Hitler and Stalin, or in the Mideast and Asia under Khomeini and the Taliban, periods of regressions have been times when there is a push to force women back into their "traditional roles" in male-dominated families where children are severely punished for any failure to obey orders, no matter how arbitrary or unjust. We are today experiencing such a regressive movement in many regions of the world, including the United States. Although far from the genocide of a Hitler or Stalin, here so-called religious fundamentalist leaders fan fear and hate, advocate a move back to more authoritarian and male-dominated families and schools, and support public policies in which there is always enough government funding for armies and prisons (weaponry, coercion, and punishment) but not for caring for children or the elderly (empathic caregiving).

How can we avoid these backlashes? My research shows that they will continue unless we take advantage of the dislocations of the shift from an industrial to a postindustrial economy to build the foundations on which a less violent, more equitable, and more human system of relations can rest. These foundations include partnership relations in childcare, gender roles, economics, spirituality, and—overarching all of these —formal and informal education.

I have identified four key interventions for accelerating the movement toward partnership. The first is the formation of national and international alliances to work for an end to violence against children and women. The Spiritual Alliance to Stop Intimate Violence (www.saiv.net) is such an alliance. The second is a concerted global campaign for gender equity, encompassing issues ranging from raising the status, rights, and opportunities of women to increasing the availability of community-supported family planning. The third is the development of new economic rules and institutions that recognize and reward the socially essential work of caregiving. The fourth is a conscious effort to shift education—formal and informal—toward partnership process, content, and structure.

At this point in our cultural evolution, when the rapid change from industrial to postindustrial society is destabilizing many entrenched beliefs and institutions, we have the opportunity to bring our cultural evolution more in line with the evolutionary thrust in our species toward our highest human potentials—including our powerful need and capacity for love. In fact, we humans have, from the beginning, been unconscious cocreators of our evolution. Both our culture and much of our physical environment are human creations. However, to take advantage of the tremendous opportunity offered by our unsettled time, we have to become conscious cocreators of a partnership future.

First, we need a clear understanding of the partnership and dominator models. Second, we need to identify the most effective interventions that, through changes in beliefs and behaviors, can interrupt the replication of the dominator elements of our culture. Third, we need to develop new social and economic inventions that promote partnership relations. These ultimately are the aims of partnership education.

References

Dawkins, R. (1990). *The selfish gene.* New York: Oxford University Press.

Eisler, R. (1987). The chalice and the blade: Our history, our future. San Francisco: Harper.

——(2000). *Tomorrow's children: A blueprint for partnership education in the 21ˢᵗ century.* Boulder, CO: Westview Press.

——(2002). *The power of partnership: Seven relationships that will change your life.* Novato, CA: New World Library.

——(work in progress). *Redefining destiny.*

Eisler, R. & Levine, D.S. (2002). Nurture, nature, and caring: We are not prisoners of our genes. *Brain and Mind, 3,* 9–52.

Eisler, R. & Miller, R., eds. (2004). *Educating for a culture of peace.* Portsmouth, NH: Heine-mann.

Gariépy, J. L., Bauer, D. J., Cairns, R. B. (2001). Selective breeding for differential aggression in mice provides evidence for heterochrony in social behaviours. *Animal Behaviour, 61,* 933–947.

Loye, D. (1999). *Darwin's lost theory of love.* New York: iUniverse (www.iuniverse.com).

Sanday, P.R. (2002). *Women at the center: Life in a modern matriarchy.* Ithaca, NY: Cornell University Press.

Schlegel, S. (1998). *Wisdom from a rainforest: The spiritual journey of an anthropologist.* Athens: University of Georgia Press.

Emotional Intelligence

Daniel Goleman

*Anyone can become angry—that is
easy. But to be angry with the right
person, to the right degree, at the
right time, for the right purpose, and
in the right way— that is not easy.*
Aristotle
The Nicomachean Ethics

*It is with the heart that one sees
rightly; what is essential is invisible
to the eye.*
Antoine de Saint-Exupéry
The Little Prince

What is the relationship between leadership and emotional intelligence—and with contemplative practice? What is the significance of this intelligence for all of us? And what, after all, is the essence of leadership?

As a case in point, imagine with me for a moment a scene that occurred on the morning of September 11, 2001, on the 50th floor of the World Trade Center. Six men are on an elevator going up. In that elevator are five men in three-piece suits and another man—not in a suit, but holding a bucket of soapy water and a squeegee on a pole. He is there to wash the windows. Suddenly, an enormous explosion extinguishes the lights and sets the elevator swinging like a pendulum. The men on the elevator are all unaware that they have only 100 minutes before the building is going to collapse. Who, in that moment of panic, uncertainty, and apprehension, emerges as a leader? The window washer. He realizes that if they all work together they can pry open the door and use the pole of the squeegee to hold it open. However, once they pry open the door, they find themselves staring at a wall with a huge number 50 on it. They are on an express elevator with no stops at the 50th floor!

Then the window washer has another realization to help with the next step. What they are facing is drywall. There is a metal binder on the squeegee, which can be used to scrape through drywall if the rubber part is removed. After scraping and scraping together, they manage to break through three layers of drywall, creating a one-foot square area under a sink in a bathroom on the 50th floor. After crawling through they come face to face with an astonished fireman, who thought he had led everyone to safety and is amazed to see these men appear. They managed to get down and lived to tell the story.

The leader in this situation could have been any one of us with the presence of mind to take the lead. The window washer with the squeegee was a spontaneous leader: He saw a human predicament and took responsibility in that moment to change things for the better. In this sense, all of us can be leaders, given the opportunity.

What do we need from leaders today? What do we need for ourselves? We face a new reality, not only because the economy has downturns; not even because we are potential targets of terrorism. However, these forces in combination face us with the stark fact that, in a real sense, the battlefield is our own minds. What terrorists seek is to create fear—to put people into a state of terror. In response, the first step in that inner battle of psychological warfare must be regaining control of our own minds. In this battle our main weapon is emotional intelligence.

The Significance of Emotional Intelligence

What is emotional intelligence? We owe the term to two psychologists, Peter Salovey at Yale and Jack Mayer at the University of New Hampshire (Mayer & Salovey, 1990). In 1990 they first proposed that there is a capacity called "emotional intelligence." Essentially, the notion of "emotional intelligence" refers to how well we sense and handle our emotions and those of others. It determines, to a large extent, how well we can manage our lives and our relationships.

In my book *Primal Leadership* (Goleman, 2002) I develop the idea that the fundamental task of leadership is an emotional one. To make that case, let me first give more background on the nature and role of emotional intelligence.

According to Howard Gardner, IQ predicts only about 4%–10% of career success (Gardner, 1993). In social science such a percentage is considered significant, but leaves 90% or more attributable to other factors such as luck or family connections. A goodly amount of career success is certainly due to emotional intelligence.

And here is the remarkable discovery. How well you will eventually do over the course of your career may have little to do with how well you do at a university or college. The intellectual hurdles we jump through in a university are threshold abilities. They are what gets us onto a particular career path. In order to be a nurse, an engineer, or an accountant, we need to have a certain kind of schooling, and we have to pass certain kinds of tests. However, once people are in a given career, their IQ or their academic performance becomes less important as a predictor of who will stand out in that career—and most especially, who will emerge as a leader in the field. What becomes paramount are the attributes of emotional intelligence.

I know this from data first collected by my major professor at Harvard, David McClelland. In 1973, McClelland published an article in *American Psychologist* which was quite radical at the time (McClelland, 1973). He concluded that in selecting the best person for a job, less attention needs to be paid to a candidate's grade point average, intelligence, or personality profile, than to what is now called "competence modeling," i.e., looking within an organization at people in a given job who have been outstanding performers, compared to others in the same job who are just average performers. By carefully analyzing the competencies found in the star performers and lacking in those who are mediocre, it is possible to identify the specific strengths that account for the superior performance and then select the applicants with these characteristics.

This idea was radical then, but the use of competence models is now standard operating procedure in world-class organizations. In my book *Working With Emotional Intelligence*, I was able to do a content analysis of about 500 of these model organizations—including schools, hospitals, and corporations. I found that the ingredients that set the stars apart from the average are largely based on emotional intelligence. These factors are roughly twice as important as those based on intellect or technical skill alone. Most significantly, when it comes to leadership, emotional intelligence forms the basis for 80 to 90 percent of the competencies that distinguish the best from the worst.

Of course, purely cognitive abilities are essential for leadership, too. One of the key cognitive competencies for leadership is "big picture" or systems thinking—the ability to understand, for example, what difference a change over here is going to make for another part of the system over there, or for events in the future. This ability leads to a strategic sense of where we should go, i.e., to articulating a vision. However, once a leader has that vision of the future, he or she needs to inspire, guide, motivate, persuade, and handle myriad relationships effectively in order to fulfill the vision. The leader acts as the soul of the group, the person who creates, refines, and articulates the spirit.

The Neural Basis of Intelligence

The brain evolved from the bottom up: the emotional centers, which are now midbrain, were the first part of the central nervous system to learn the essentials for survival. From an evolutionary perspective, emotions are the mind's way of making us pay attention and giving us an immediate action plan for survival. From the emotional centers grew the neocortex, the thinking brain. In the design of the brain, feelings have priority over thought, because it has been our emotions that have helped us survive.

However, this leads to problems in modern life, because the survival mechanism from our earlier evolution is now confronted with a reality it is not designed to handle, the reality of a very complex society. So the emotional brain reacts to events that are only symbolically real as if they were physical threats. In this response, a key structure is called the *amygdala,* where emotional memories are stored—and apparently a node for the circuits where much of our emotional repertoire resides (LeDoux, 1992).

The *amygdala* is also the trigger point for the "fight, flight or freeze" response. We have brains designed with a hair-trigger response for perceived emergencies through the *amygdala.* This organ is positioned in a privileged way in the brain, with a one neuron-long connection to the thalamus, the part of the brain where all sensory input goes before it is translated into the language of the brain and disseminated throughout. This one neuron-long connection, discovered by Joseph LeDoux at New York University, allows a scan of everything happening to us to see if a similar event occurred in the past (LeDoux, 1992). The *amygdala* is able, if it senses a threat, to engage the rest of the brain and take it over. Because the *amygdala* learns much of its repertoire in childhood, it therefore tends to react rather childishly, with childish impulses. Another problem is that the part of the brain initiating emotional impulse is separate from the part of the brain regulating emotion (Ekman & Davidson, 1994). This separation creates the possibility of the regulatory center's becoming overwhelmed and unable to perform its function. The result is an "*amygdala* highjack," which you can recognize in situations where you have an immediate and powerful emotional reaction—but after the dust settles you regret what you said or did. This impulse goes from the emotional center up to the prefrontal area, which is the brain's executive center. The pre-frontal area gets information from other parts of the brain and that gives you the opportunity to make a more effective response than the *amygdala* impulse alone.

Emotional intelligence, then, largely deals with abilities based in the circuitry running from the *amygdala* and other emotional centers to the prefrontal cortex. This makes emotional intelligence quite distinct neurologically from purely neocortical abilities, which we draw upon in order to master academic content or technical skills. In other words, the IQ abilities, from an anatomical point of view, are clearly distinct from emotional intelligence.

Emotional Intelligence and Contemplative Practice

Now I want to connect the information about the brain and emotional intelligence to contemplative practice and suggest specific ways in which contemplative practice can strengthen the four elements of emotional intelligence.

Self-Awareness

The first aspect of emotional intelligence is self-awareness—knowing what you are feeling as you are feeling it. Of course we may think it self-evident that we always know what we feel—but the truth is we usually do not. While there is a stream of mood that runs parallel to the stream of thought, typically we spend most of our day lost in thought. We are thinking about the next assignment, the next paper, what to have for lunch, and on and on. We are continually preoccupied with our thoughts, and typically only notice the stream of feeling as emotions build up and call our attention to them. Why should it matter that we have the capacity to attune to a feeling in an ongoing way? It turns out to be extremely important as a pilot through life.

Research by Matt Lieberman at UCLA on intuition—on knowing more than we can say—suggests that the basal ganglia, which are connected to the *amygdala* and to other parts of the brain as well, collect decision rules from our experiences as we go through life (Lieberman, 2000). This is how our life wisdom grows—whenever there is a lesson to be learned, this is the part of the brain where learning takes place—but completely outside our conscious awareness. Because this wisdom is beyond the thinking brain, we know more than we can say in words. To access this wisdom, we have to be able to tune in to our gut feeling.

If we rush through life, lost in our thoughts, we will never pause for the necessary moment of reflection. This is one power of contemplative practice. With a regular contemplative practice—or even a practice that may not be formal contemplation, but is time alone when you reflect on what is going on inside—we give ourselves a better chance to hear that small murmur within, the voice of wisdom.

There is a corollary to the saying of Socrates, that the unexamined life is not worth living: if we are going to live an unexamined life, we should not inflict it on the rest of the world. In order to know whether our actions are in keeping with our own sense of meaning, priority, and value, we need to tune in to that inner sense of whether it feels right or not. For that is how the brain and the mind, moment to moment, let us know whether we are on the right path.

This capacity to stay in touch with our own truth, our sense of rightness, makes possible a key leadership quality: authenticity. The authentic leader remains true to his or her values and sense of meaning. That allows a leader to speak to others from the heart, with a ring of authenticity.

Self-Mastery and Presence

The foundational capacity of emotional intelligence is knowing our emotions—self-awareness—a capacity that makes possible the second: the ability to handle our disturbing emotions effectively. Aristotle expressed the dilemma of emotional self-mastery very well in his Nichomachean Ethics: Anyone can get angry—but to get angry with the right person in the right way, at the right time, and for the right reason, is not so easy.

Some of the most telling research on managing emotions and what it means for our ability to function, was done by Philip Peake, who is now at Smith College, when he was at Stanford working with Walter Mischel (Peake, Mischel, & Shoda, 1990). Four-year-olds in pre-school at Stanford—children of professors and graduate students—were brought in to a room one by one and seated at a small table with a big, juicy marshmallow on it. Then they were told, "You can have that marshmallow right now—but if you can wait until I get back from running an errand, you can have two marshmallows." The experimenter then leaves the room.

About a third of the kids can't wait—they just grab that marshmallow and gobble it down on the spot. Another third wait the seven or eight minutes until the experimenter comes back and they get the two treats (the rest were somewhere in between those who grabbed and those who waited the full time). The children were then tracked down some fourteen years later, when they were about to graduate from high school. When the two groups were compared—those who grabbed and those who waited the full amount of time—some startling differences emerged. Those who waited, compared to those who grabbed immediately, were more composed under stress, got along better with their friends and peers, and were better able to keep their eye on a goal and defer gratification. The kids who sought immediate gratification, eating the marshmallow right away, were just the opposite: more prone to falling apart under stress, getting along less well with others, and were less able to delay gratification in pursuit of their goals. However, the most stunning finding was completely unexpected. Those who waited, compared to those who grabbed, had a 210-point advantage on their SAT scores. Why should something as simple as waiting for a marshmallow predict how well you are going to do on the SAT?

My interpretation has to do with how the brain is structured. A child full of emotional impulses has a mind pumping out preoccupying thoughts, which are experienced as intruding into that child's attention. The capacity for attention is limited. To the extent such thoughts occupy attention, they limit what's left for other things—the assignment I'm reading, what the teacher is saying. They diminish a child's attentional capacity.

Whether at school, at university, or at work the individual who is continually preoccupied by thoughts will thereby not be able to pay as much attention—whether to the lessons being taught or to the work that has to be done. If you are anxious about something, it becomes harder to stop thinking about it, and so more difficult to focus your attention on the task at hand.

This can create a vicious cycle: If you are poor at handling distressing emotions, it will interfere with your performance—which in itself can create more distress.

One of the oldest principles in psychology, the Yerkes-Dodson Law, shows that the relationship between performance and stress is an upside down U (Goleman, 2002). If you are bored and daydreaming, your involvement is too low, and you do poorly. However, if you have a deadline, it creates a "good stress" that focuses you, so your performance improves. In the best case, your interest and motivation are high, your abilities match the challenge, and you can get into the flow state where performance is peak. However, as the challenge overreaches your abilities—say you have ten deadlines you just can't handle—then you shade over into the zone that generates debilitating stress, and you are overwhelmed.

What this means in terms of handling emotions brings us back to that circuitry between the prefrontal cortex and the *amygdala*. If you are in a state where emotions are allowed to get out of control, where you are susceptible to *amygdala* highjack, you can't handle your emotions. The implication for leadership: leaders must first get their own emotions in hand to stay calm in crisis.

What does this have to do with contemplative practice? To answer that, I have to give some scientific background. According to research by Richard Davidson at the University of Wisconsin, when we are upset, when we are losing it, what is happening in the brain involves high activity in the circuits that converge on the *amygdala*. These circuits also drive a high level of activity in the right prefrontal area (Davidson, Jackson & Kalin, 2000). When we are feeling mellow and upbeat about what we are doing, the *amygdala* is quiet as is the right prefrontal cortex—but the left prefrontal cortex is very active. The left prefrontal cortex seems to be a part of the brain that controls the *amygdala*, and facilitates positive emotion. Each of us has a characteristic ratio of right-to-left prefrontal activation. If far to the right, a person is in the negative mood range and may have a high risk of clinical depression or anxiety disorder. If far to the left, the person more often feels positive moods— energized, optimistic, flexible.

Jon Kabat-Zinn has been involved in research at the University of Wisconsin at Madison with Richard Davidson (Davidson, et al., 2003). They brought a mindfulness program into a biotechnology company and offered it to workers under tremendous pressure to do their work very quickly. When offered an opportunity to learn mindfulness practice, many of the biotechnology workers were enthusiastic because they thought that perhaps this would help them handle the stress better. The researchers found that ten weeks of mindfulness practice caused a shift in the workers from right prefrontal activation toward the left, i.e., from a tendency toward negative emotional states to positive ones. With this shift, the participants adopted a different attitude to their stressful situations. They reported they were enjoying their work. They were better able to control their distress and so reach a more positive mood range through mindfulness meditation. When it comes to managing emotions—an essential leadership ability—contemplative practice seemingly does this in a very powerful way at the level of the brain. In terms of leadership, the ability to keep your mind calm and clear facilitates presence, being focused on what is happening in the moment. For a leader, this focus means you can be more present to the people you are dealing with and more connected.

Empathy

The third element of emotional intelligence is empathy—perspective-taking, as well as the ability to sense what other people are feeling, without their telling us in words. Of course, people have other ways of telling us: through their tone of voice or facial expression. Empathy is extremely important because it is the basis of caring, altruism, and compassion. If we are to feel for someone, we must first feel with them, i.e., understanding the way in which they are suffering.

It is very disturbing to see what happens in young babies who have been neglected, compared with well-loved toddlers. If a little friend has fallen down and is crying, a well-loved toddler will go over and try to make that friend feel better. However, with toddlers who have been abused or neglected by age two or three, we see something very different. They will go over to the other child who is crying and start yelling at them; if they don't stop crying they might start hitting them. They seem not to be developing what usually emerges very clearly at that time of life—the capacity of empathy.

In times of tension, when people are anxious, empathy—in the sense of seeing others clearly—can be one of the victims. A son of a friend of mine, who lives in Philadelphia but attends the University of Nevada, was going back to school just a few days after the events of September 11. He ended up on one of the first flights out from Philadelphia to Nevada. He is of multiracial parentage and was traveling first-class because of upgrades passed on to him by his mother. The plane had not yet taken off. He was quietly reading a Chinese novel with a cover picture of a woman with a long pigtail and some Chinese characters, when he noticed there was some kind of hub-bub going on.

A flight attendant had concluded that the novel he was reading was in Arabic and that he looked as though he could have been from the Middle East—and that, because he was wearing funny looking pants with a lot of pockets, he was somehow suspicious. So the plane could not take off before police came on and questioned him. It was, of course, a misperception, but there was a lot of that going in the tense days after September 11, 2001. The reason is that when we are anxious, when we are fearful, the *amygdala* over-powers the rest of the brain, and we start to take shortcuts in the mind, rely-ing on stereotypes.

What does this have to do with contemplative practice? Much research suggests that people engaging in contemplative practice become more em-pathic, more able to appreciate what other people see from their perspective. Once again contemplative practice seems to boost aspects of emotional intel-ligence that matter for leadership.

If a leader is to communicate effectively, she must be able to empathize, to understand the perspective of others. That allows her to fine-tune her own message so that it comes not just from her heart but speaks to that of others.

I remember talking with Reverend Calvin Butts, who has a large church in Harlem, about the need for empathy in leaders. He said that when he se-lects those who will be groomed to lead their own congregation, he looks for "the heart of a preacher" —people who genuinely care about other people.

Resonance

The fourth aspect of emotional intelligence is managing relationships with another person. This hinges on being able to handle emotions in rela-tionships. I remember something that happened to me in Manhattan many years ago on a hot muggy day—the kind of day in New York when everyone feels a bit irritable. I was certainly feeling that way as I waited for a bus and was surprised when the driver said, in a friendly tone as I got on, "How're you doin?" As we continued up Madison Avenue, I was pleasantly surprised to realize that this bus driver was carrying on a conversation with everyone on the bus! He carried on an ongoing dialogue: "Oh, looking for suits? The store up on the right is having a great sale on suits; you should check it out. Have you seen the exhibit at the Museum of Natural History?" He was en-gaging every person on the bus. As people got off the bus he'd say, "So long, it's been great having you," and everyone responded, "Yeah, it's been great being on this bus." That man was an urban saint. He was passing good feel-ings on to everyone on the bus. He was using his role to affect the internal state of other people. Emotions are an open loop system. The limbic system, the emotional system of the brain, is perhaps the only biological system de-signed to be regulated by other people as well as by ourselves. Emotions are meant to be contagious—one person can help another calm down, for exam-ple; think of a mother soothing her crying infant.

Emotions are contagious. Consider an experiment that involves two strangers who come into a room, fill out a mood checklist, then sit in silence looking at each other for two or three minutes (Sullins, 1991). They fill out the checklist again afterward. It turns out that the person most emotionally expressive in the dyad passes his or her emotional state on to the other person in two or three minutes of silence.

These experiments lead to an interesting implication for leadership: in order to affect a person in the best way, we need to first handle our own emotions. In organizational life, for example, and perhaps in the university, when you ask people to identify the most effective leaders, the best communicators, the best listeners, they point to people who are able to manage their own emotions, who can set aside their own concerns and preoccupations. Those are the people who can really be present here and now for the other person.

When an abrasive, difficult person with strong opinions engages in a discussion with someone else about a topic on which they really disagree, and they become reactive with each other, the situation spirals out of control as you can well imagine (Goleman, 2004). They become increasingly more agitated over the course of the discussion. However, if the other person stays composed, does not become reactive but is able to manage emotions and be engaged, then the upset, abrasive person can be moved into a positive state. That was basically what the bus driver was doing for people on the bus—and it is something that we all can do for each other.

Again it turns out that contemplative practice facilitates this ability, because it lets us be authentic, present to others, and empathic—all of which allows resonance, connecting heart-to-heart with others. Resonant leaders are on the same wavelength as those they lead. In fact, research with thousands of executives and those they work for shows that those who lead with such resonance get the best results.

Bad News, Good News

Let me conclude with some bad news and then some good news. The bad news is that, on average, emotional intelligence has been on the decline in America for two decades (Achenbach & Howell, 1989). The first evidence came from a study of two random cohorts of American children, chosen to represent the entire U.S. population. It found that between the mid-1970s and the late 1980s, American children declined across the board on measures of behavior reflecting emotional intelligence abilities. On average, they were more lonely and depressed, anxious and disobedient, and so on—they declined on 42 such measures, and went up on none. More recent data suggest that such abilities are coming back, but not to the level they were in that first assessment, in the early 1970s (T. Achenbach, 2002).

This means that schools, businesses, and other organizations need to pay more attention to helping young people develop and strengthen these skills—and that's the good news: all of these abilities are learned. I am an advocate for teaching emotional intelligence skills to children from earliest grades through high school because it has a positive impact on their ability to achieve academically. Studies by the Consortium for Academic, Social, and Emotional Learning at the University of Illinois show that these skills help reduce substance abuse, violence in the schools, drop-outs, and unwanted pregnancies, each of which may be seen as due to a deficit in emotional intelligence. A good source of information for educators and those interested in school programs is the Web site www.casel.org

This kind of education takes into account neuroplasticity, the fact that the brain can change at any point and continues to be reshaped throughout life by repeated experiences. For example, the switch from right prefrontal dominance to the left in those practicing mindfulness mediation is an example of neuroplasticity—of a change in the brain through repeated experience.

When it comes to cultivating strengths in emotional intelligence, such learning needs to be experiential to be effective. The cognitive centers learn through an associative mode, where simply reading about something is enough. However, emotional intelligence involves the emotional centers of the brain, which learn best through other modalities: through modeling, through practice, through rehearsal, through enacting these skills in life and doing it repeatedly. Furthermore, if you keep trying the new, better way over and over, as life situations present opportunities to practice, you can reach a point where they become automatic. That means the brain has changed, strengthening the circuitry supporting the new habit. That kind of learning can last a lifetime.

It was Gandhi who said that, as human beings, our greatness lies not so much in our ability to remake the world, but in our ability to remake ourselves.

This essay was produced from the transcript of a talk at the University of Massachusetts Amherst, November 2001.

References

Achenbach, T. (2002, January). Personal communication, University of Vermont.

Achenbach, T. & Howell, C. (1989). Are America's children's problems getting worse? a 13-year comparison. *Journal of the American Academy of Child and Adolescent Psychiatry.*

Davidson, R. J. et. al. (2003). Alterations in brain and immune function produced by mindfulness meditation. *Psychosomatic Medicine*, 65, 564–570.

Davidson, R. J., Jackson, D. C., & Kalin, N. (2000). Emotion, plasticity, context, and regulation: Perspectives from affective neuroscience. *Psychological Bulletin,* 126, 6, 890–906.

Ekman, P. & Davidson, R. (Eds.). (1994). *Questions about emotion.* New York: Oxford University Press.

Gardner, H. (Ed.). (1993). *Multiple intelligences: The theory in practice.* New York: Basic Books.

Goleman, D. (2002). *Primal leadership.* Boston: Harvard Business School Press.

——(2004). *Destructive emotions.* New York: Bantam Books.

Goleman, D., Boyatzis, R. & McKee, A. (2002). *Primal leadership: Realizing the power of emotional intelligence.* Boston: Harvard Business School Press.

LeDoux, J. (1992). Emotion and the limbic system concept. *Concepts in Neuroscience*, 2.

Lieberman, M. (2000). Intuition: A social cognitive neuroscience approach, *Psychological Bulletin*, 126, 109–137.

Mayer, J. D. & Salovey, P. (1990). Emotional intelligence, *Imagination, Cognition, and Personality* 9, pp.185–211.

McClelland, D. (1973). Testing for competence rather than intelligence, *American Psychologist* 46.

Peake, P. K., Mischel, W. & Shoda, Y. (1990). Predicting adolescent cognitive and self-regulatory competencies from preschool delay of gratification. *Developmental Psychology*, *26* (6), 978–986.

Sullins, E. (1991, April). *Personality and Social Psychology Bulletin.*

Part Four

Integrative Living and Action

Wherever You Go, There You Are:
Living Your Life as If It Really Matters

Jon Kabat-Zinn

> *Quick now, here, now, always —*
> *A condition of complete simplicity*
> *(Costing not less than everything)*
> T.S. Eliot, Four Quartets

In 1966, I was a 22-year-old graduate student at MIT. The Vietnam War was building up, and although I loved science in general and molecular biology in particular, which was what I was studying, I was unsure of exactly what I was doing there. Walking the interminable hallways one day, I remember feeling particularly depressed and out of sorts. In that mood, my eyes casually wandered the various bulletin boards overflowing with notices and posters. One in particular jumped out at me: "The Three Pillars of Zen: Talk by Philip Kapleau" (Kapleau, 1967). I had no idea what Zen was or who Kapleau was. It turns out he had been invited to speak by Huston Smith, a professor of philosophy and religion at MIT in those days. I had no idea who Huston Smith was either. For some mysterious reason, I decided to go. It turned out that only five other people showed up out of all of MIT. I did not know it then, but that talk would have a profound effect on my life trajectory.

Kapleau spoke personally about his experiences as a journalist covering the Nuremberg War Crimes Tribunal, then going to Japan and sitting in an unheated Zen monastery in the middle of winter. I vividly recall his recounting that, although the conditions were spartan and a lot of the time it felt like torture to sit for interminable hours in the meditation hall, his long-standing stomach ulcers cleared up after about six months. He described what was involved in Zen meditation and the core spirit behind Zen: one of utter wakefulness and presence. He challenged us to inquire as to whether we were truly awake in our lives. I knew I was not, and the approach seemed credible and devoid of a lot of mumbo jumbo. It was basically about paying attention, pure and simple.

The large stream of contemplative disciplines, or consciousness disciplines (Walsh, 1980), of which Zen and mindfulness are two major and interweaving tributaries, is attuned and directed to the practical and systematic cultivation of wakefulness and clarity of mind and heart. We might ask, because we have had little experience of it in our formal education, "Is it possible for us to learn to tune our human instrument, the mind and the body, in such a way that we remain awake? Are we in fact awake, ever? How often are we fully present? Anywhere?"

To me, these were and remain illuminating and challenging questions. It does not take much self-observation to see that we can be on automatic pilot virtually all the time. You can easily check it out for yourself. See how much of the time you are actually fully here and how much of the time there is a kind of internal fragmentation, with part of your mind here and another part somewhere else. Such fragmentation is as old as civilization itself. This condition is even more prevalent now, with our addictive propensity for multitasking, fed by the seductions of the digital era we have so recently entered. While talking with somebody on the phone, we may now find our eyes scanning our e-mails and even writing new ones. There is a way in which the technology actually lulls us into a more somnambulant automaticity, even as it serves us by its convenience, efficiency, and power.

To counter this trend, to embark on a quest for nonfragmentation, is not trivial work. It involves cultivating intimacy with our own interiority, a willingness to inquire into what it truly means to be human. It is a great adventure, which involves trusting in our own capacity for inquiry, for clear seeing, for waking up and getting out of our own way. It could be said that it is actually the hardest work on the planet, and perhaps the most urgent.

Dimensions of Knowing

I do not mean to suggest that mindfulness is the answer to all of life's problems. There is no answer for all of life's problems. However, there are a lot of questions worth asking and worthy of deep inquiry. Mindfulness, if cultivated through practice, can reveal additional dimensions within experience that often remain completely hidden, opaque to us, or that we tend to neglect and ignore even if we do know about them intellectually. The reason we do not develop these interior dimensions of experience, including the universe of lived experience unfolding in the present moment, is that it simply has not been part of our culture. The large numbers of people showing up at talks, compared to the turnout for Kapleau in 1966, is an indication of a huge sea change in our society, what I like to think of as a collective "rotation in consciousness" based on our individual yearnings for something more complete than what we are immersed in much of the time.

We are beginning to acknowledge that there may be different ways of knowing phenomena and that each may have complete or partial validity within its own sphere of inquiry. In quantum physics they speak about the phenomenon of complementarity—an electron, for instance, or another elementary particle, has properties that sometimes look like a wave and sometimes look like a particle, depending on how you design the experimental apparatus (Feinberg, 1977). In reality, an electron is neither just a wave nor just a particle. You cannot really say what it is in any given moment because the act of observing has itself an influence on the electron. You would have to avoid looking in order for it to be what it is, but in that moment, its properties are no longer known. This says something about the nature of reality and about our interacting and interfacing with it. Reality on any level continues to elude all attempts to define its deepest nature, whether we are talking about superstrings or the brain and emotions. There are always new ways of perceiving and thinking that allow our understanding to go deeper. So experientially, when we begin to pay attention to how we actually see and learn and feel—the very fact that we are paying attention is transformative and allows us to tap into multiple dimensions of our being that might otherwise go unnoticed and unused for our entire lives.

Physicist Brian Greene, in his book, *The Elegant Universe*, informs us uninitiated souls that the universe may very well have eleven dimensions rather than four (Greene, 1999). The theory postulates that, at the moment of the Big Bang when everything came out of nothing (although how that happened is beyond explaining, apparently), eleven dimensions appeared but 7 of them failed to "unfurl." They are still locked into the fundamental nature of matter on an unthinkably small scale.

If the cosmologists can stretch our imagination to that degree, I think it is only fair that we be permitted, by analogy, to think of ourselves as having multiple hidden dimensions as well, many of which have not yet unfurled. How much of the time is our vision and understanding of things colored by the lenses of our previous conditioning and belief systems? At times, it is difficult for us to experience freedom or spontaneity because we tend to be so constrained in our perceptions by our own ideas and opinions. These may keep us from growing in certain dimensions and from even entering other dimensions of our being and our potential at all.

Universities are beginning to acknowledge that there are multiple intelligences, including emotional intelligence, and that the faculty and administrators need to accommodate people's different learning styles, keeping in mind that one may not be "superior" to another. They are simply multiple channels, different ways of knowing. One of the challenges of being human is to learn how to tune to the various channels or dimensions of experience that are available to us so that when we need to bring one kind of intelligence to bear on a particular situation, we do not go numb in that very moment. Unfortunately, though, we often do go numb because of our past conditioning. For example, so much energy can go into thinking that thinking itself can dominate our reality. We literally become disembodied—especially in those dark moments when everything seems to fall apart in our lives. Many of the currents within universities are now actually speaking to embodiment—to bringing the body back in. Take, for example, a university class called "Sacred Indian Dance." This is a form of meditation, an art, a science in its own right, and a complementary way of knowing to which not everyone will be drawn. However, the fact that the class is offered is important, even if only five students sign up for it.

Similarly, not everyone will be drawn to meditation, especially if you think of meditation as sitting still like a statue in a museum. In fact, if you think about it for a moment, meditation is a radical and most unusual act. To actually stop is in itself a radical act, particularly in this era (by radical I mean an act that is deeply rooted and fundamental). Meditation ultimately is an act of love—an affirmation of nonseparation and connectedness, of belonging, and of awareness. In the act of opening to multiple channels or dimensions of experience, without any agenda and without doing anything, we give ourselves over to them in ways that catalyze true learning, true growth, and true healing of the wounds we may be carrying yet may not even acknowledge to ourselves. Most of us do not get by on this planet without some scarring, emotional as well as physical. To heal involves recognizing and reclaiming what the physicist David Bohm calls our wholeness (Bohm, 1980) reclaiming those other dimensions of being and of knowing that have yet to unfurl in us. Healing involves coming to terms with things as they are in the only time we ever have… to see, or learn, or grow, or love, that is, this moment, the present moment, what we so facilely call "now." It asks us to transform, to actually reconstitute ourselves, to undergo what you might think of as a "molecular rearrangement" to a way of being that releases our potential to be fully human. We are being rearranged anyway. What do you think eating is? What do you think breathing is? What do you think learning is? An extremely important part of this work is collaborating with these natural biological capacities by grounding our awareness in embodied experience (Varela, Thompson, & Rosch, 1991).

An operational definition of mindfulness meditation is paying attention on purpose in the present moment, nonjudgmentally. Through kindness and self-compassion, we remove our thought and opinion glasses and suspend judgment intentionally. Attention and intention are at the absolute core of all contemplative, reflective practice. Many of the great insights in science arose when individual scientists dropped their thinking minds for a moment and somehow gave themselves over to not knowing.

Now, meditation is not just about calmness. Sometimes it is about being really tense and terrified and in huge amounts of pain, or overwhelmed with sadness, confusion, lack of confidence, or by feelings of unworthiness. These mind states and body states are part and parcel of the human condition. We may think that, if only I were a good meditator, all of these problems would fall away. That is not what meditation is, although it is a common misconception. Another misconception is that, if I meditate, my mind will go blank, and I will not have any thoughts. Instead, meditation is about developing a certain kind of relationship to our thoughts and to thinking, and to our feeling states, allowing them to be seen and recognized as events that appear, linger for a time, and then disappear in the field of awareness. In fact, what we call the field of awareness is itself a huge mystery. Awareness, sentience, consciousness, whatever we choose to call it, is a huge mystery, even to cognitive neuroscience. That we can be awake and aware, even partially, is an almost incomprehensible dimension of our humanity. However, it is undeniable that we can and do manifest awareness to one degree or another from moment to moment, and it is precisely here, in the examined qualities of awareness itself, where these new degrees of freedom in our lives reside.

The vice chancellor of a major public university told me recently that much of the time she finds herself standing in the middle of chaos. Now it is one thing to be standing in the middle of chaos and be caught up in it, quite another to be able to embrace that chaos and not feel it all has to be fixed or brought under tight control. There is no way of "fixing" chaos, because it is embedded in the nature of reality. Not everything is predictable. Real world events are for the most part nonlinear. You do not get to control the whole show. You are lucky even to influence your body for five seconds. However, you do get to work with it and to dance with it if you are willing to do a certain kind of work, what we might call interior work. This is the challenge of the contemplative disciplines, the willingness to show up in the first place, and to engage, to step in, to do the dance, to inquire, to ask, "Who is dancing? Who is here? Who is thinking?" These are profound meditative practices. It is the deepest work we can do on the planet—at least as deep and as valid as any other exploration. It does not preclude following your creative passions and calling. You can cultivate mindfulness on any path you wind up following. It takes no extra time, only remembering. Your experience of it, and frequently whatever comes of it, will be the better for your having brought the full spectrum of your awareness to it, step-by-step, moment-by-moment, in an easy, noncontrived way.

Talk of contemplative frameworks and ways of being and knowing, and even some contemplative practices are now making their way into the university. It feels like something of a groundswell. This is not a case of one person getting an idea and trying to impose it on everybody. Instead it is about something missing in our lives, perhaps only a subtle longing to affirm and actually realize (in the sense of make real) our wholeness. We do not have to be fixed, nor are we fundamentally broken, no matter what is going on in our lives. On the contrary, we were and are always whole. One has only to look at the lives of Stephen Hawkins or Christopher Reeve as examples of this, of mobilizing the full range of one's capacities, even under extremely adverse conditions, and working with what is.

We are whole, even if we are missing an arm or a leg or a breast. We are still whole. That is the nature of being alive. However, to know it and to embody it in the face of all our conditioning and automaticity and the enormity of what happens in life is a lot of work, what you might call the work of transformative interiority. Poets engage in this kind of work—not just yogis and meditators, and regular people we will never hear of, who live with and transcend their limitations every day. Great artists and great scientists also visit this territory. Some may even take up permanent residency. The virtues of silence and awareness and wise acceptance (very different from passive resignation) have been recognized by Western culture from its very origins, although few history courses are taught from this perspective. However, one gets the sense that Sappho, Socrates, Aristotle, and Plato were great contemplatives, as were Pythagoras, Newton, Archimedes, and Maxwell.

Poetry and Contemplation

You could say Emily Dickinson was a contemplative as well. Outwardly, she was a recluse and rarely left her house. Through her poetry, however, we have a glimpse of the territories she traveled, illuminating and revealing for us a world far beyond the merely autobiographical, as all great poets do. Perhaps she had to stay in her house to write such poems (Dickinson, 1961):

Me from Myself—to banish—
Had I Art
Impregnable my Fortress
Unto All Heart—

But since Myself—assault Me
How have I peace
Except by subjugating
Consciousness?

And since We're mutual Monarch
How this be
Except by Abdication—
Me—of Me?

Have you ever had the feeling that you were being torn apart by different interior voices competing for who you actually are today and what you are going to do? These voices are often conflicted, not always so happy. In trying to protect ourselves from love and the ravages of the world, a lot of us may have abdicated parts of ourselves, perhaps even for decades. Part of it may be due to peer pressure. We are afraid to reveal aspects of ourselves for fear of nonacceptance. This shutting off from parts of ourselves can take place even in our own minds. Then we say, "I don't want to go there." Every time we draw a line in the mind and think we cannot possibly go beyond that demarcation, we create a prison, a boundary, a dimension that does not unfurl, that does not allow us to inquire into wholeness because we are bound up, fettered by our own fear habit and our avoidance habit. You may not yet be learning such matters in school, except perhaps in a few courses with a few courageous teachers. You are not going to learn this from books either, although books can assist you in the learning. This is a place where the learning comes from inside and from your own willingness to commit to being true to yourself—not forgetting your sovereignty, nor abdicating it. Education should be the honoring of your sovereignty, what the Buddhists call your true nature, by drawing forth what you already are, what is already here. The word *education* is from the Latin *educare*, to draw forth—drawing forth and igniting passion for what is real. Unfortunately, formal education too often follows the inoculation model—loading information into students and then requiring them to disgorge it on tests, more often than not inadvertently immunizing them for life against any further interest in the subject.

The full actuality of things lies beyond our ability to describe it through words alone. That is why mathematicians prefer the pristine purity of abstraction and proof and an economy of words. However, what is most important and mysterious in the lived experience of our lives as they unfold, can be pointed to through the skillful use of words. It is in the pointing and then in the actual looking to what is being pointed at that the beauty and adventure lie and are recreated for us anew through our experiencing of the poem. The words are mere scaffolding, pointing beyond themselves, which explains why poets can be such powerful allies in this work.

The great Spanish poet, Juan Ramón Jiménez, winner of the Nobel Prize in Literature, has a poem on the same theme as Emily Dickinson's (Jiménez, 1995):

> *I am not I.*
> *I am this one*
> *Walking beside me whom I do not see.*
> *Whom at times I manage to visit,*
> *And whom at other times I forget;*
> *The one who remains silent when I talk,*
> *The one who forgives sweet, when I hate,*
> *The one who takes a walk where I am not,*
> *The one who will remain standing when I die.*

Derek Walcott, a Caribbean poet and Nobel Laureate writes in *Love after Love* (Walcott, 1986):

> *The time will come*
> *when, with elation,*
> *you will greet yourself arriving*

at your own door, in your own mirror,
and each will smile at the other's welcome,

and say, sit here. Eat.
You will love again the stranger who was your self.
Give wine. Give bread. Give back your heart
to itself, to the stranger who has loved you

all your life, whom you ignored
for another, who knows you by heart.
Take down the love letters from the bookshelf,

the photographs, the desperate notes,
peel your own image from the mirror.
Sit. Feast on your life.

These poems, if we really listen to them, can function as actual doorways into contemplative practice. They are orthogonal or complementary ways of knowing, of being embodied, of recognizing yourself at your own door, in your own mirror. "The time will come," the poem begins, but when will that time be if you are zooming through your life on autopilot? You might go along for thirty or forty years, then all of a sudden wonder, "Where have I been? How did I ever get here?"

Alan Lightman, a physicist and writer, recently published a novel called *The Diagnosis* (Lightman, 2000) about a businessman who works in Boston and lives in the suburbs. He gets on the T in the morning rush hour with hordes of people in their three-piece suits with cell phones, people just like him. Somewhere between stops on the subway line he travels every morning, he forgets who he is and where he is going. It is a terrifying narrative, hauntingly revealing something palpably diagnostic of our age. We are at high risk of being entrained, hypnotized into a consensus trance—and of losing both sight of and a feel for who and what we actually are. This is what Dickinson and Jiménez and Walcott are alluding to. These are Western poets inquiring into this deepest of questions, who we actually are, and taking note of how easily we betray the stranger who is our own self. They are pointing to what Buddhists might call our "true nature," with the same energy and enthusiasm physicists might bring to probing deeply into the nature of the atom, or the quark, or superstrings.

The Mindfulness-Based Stress Reduction Clinic

I would like to give a brief description of our work at the Stress Reduction Clinic at the University of Massachusetts Medical Center in Worcester (Kabat-Zinn, 1990). Founded in 1979, it is the oldest and largest mind/body clinic in the country. To date, over 15,000 people have completed the eight-week outpatient training program in mindfulness meditation and its applications to stress, pain, illness, and the conduct of our everyday lives. The motivation behind it was to bring meditation right into the heart of mainstream medicine and health care and see if it would not be of some added benefit in the relief of suffering. So many people fall through the cracks of the health care system, more accurately a disease-care system, and so many are profoundly dissatisfied with how they are treated, and with their outcomes. Much of this dissatisfaction is linked to not feeling seen or heard, or feeling that one's concerns have not been adequately met and attended to.

The idea behind the stress reduction clinic was to set it up as a net that could catch people falling through the cracks in the health care system and challenge them to do something for themselves, that no one else could possibly do for them, including their doctors, as a complement to whatever other more traditional treatments they might be receiving. Such a safety net and outright challenge might be an extraordinary boon for these patients, an opportunity to do something for themselves, to engage, to participate, to tap into deep inner resources they might not even know they had for learning, for growing, for healing, and for transformation across the lifespan. Moreover, it would also be a boon to physicians, an additional but unique resource in the hospital where they could send patients who were not responding fully to their treatments or in need of additional attention.

We all recognize that, amazing as modern medicine is, and it is truly amazing in many respects, it also has real limits in any given moment. What is more, there are few cures in medicine, especially for chronic diseases, so we are often left short of our expectations to recover completely from injury or illness. It is also true that the book has not yet been written on what human beings are capable of if we learn how to tap into the inner resources just mentioned. In this regard, we make a strong differentiation between "curing" and "healing." While there may not be many outright cures in medicine, healing —a deep coming to terms with things as they are—is always a possibility and a potentially profound transformation of both body and mind. Clearly, and for many reasons, not the least of which is going to be cost, the medicine of the twenty-first century is going to be a much more participatory medicine in which we will become more active agents in both the decision making and in learning how to take better care of ourselves preventively, and as a complement to the care and treatments we receive from our health care teams. Whether it is colon cancer, breast cancer, or chronic back pain, anxiety disorder, hypertension, or irritable bowel syndrome, if a person is willing to work, we are willing to work with them. I am referring to the work of getting to know ourselves better, of becoming more embodied, of learning how to attend to what is most important via the vehicle of training in moment-to-moment, nonjudgmental awareness, namely mindfulness. This is the limitless work of becoming intimate with our own interiority. However, to maximize the number of people who could relate to it, and because on the deepest of levels our stress reflects the uncertainty and anguish of the human condition, as well as our biological and psychological capacity for creative adaptation to changing conditions, from the beginning we simply called this interior work "stress reduction."

I recently was asked to give a talk at Spaulding Rehabilitation Hospital in a symposium on complementary and alternative practices in rehabilitation medicine. Before I gave it, I looked up the word "rehabilitation" in a big dictionary. In turns out that it does not just mean to re-enable. The deep meaning of the word is "to learn to live inside again," from an even deeper Indo-European root (*ghabe*) meaning "giving and receiving" (Kabat-Zinn, 2002). With these connotations, rehabilitation becomes a fairly accurate description of what happens in the stress reduction clinic. If a person finds him or herself in need of cardiac, pulmonary, or physical rehabilitation, it is never just a matter of getting back on one's feet, but also of learning to live inside one's body as it is now, in the present moment, with things exactly as they are, and then working with the situation, giving yourself over to it, and receiving what it has to teach and trusting the process moment by moment. From that kind of discipline, which will include all the attendant difficulties, such as the physical pain and emotional anguish that can plague us in such times, we nevertheless bring to the present moment a gentle spaciousness of awareness as best we can. We come gradually to stabilize that awareness through practice and rest within it, less caught perhaps in the stream of discursive thinking, taking note of whatever arises, and thereby growing into the fullness of ourselves and what is possible. That is what the practice of meditative awareness, of mindfulness, invites us to engage in.

It may even be fair to say that, in a fundamental way, perhaps most of us need to learn to live inside again, not just within what we think of as the body, but within the seamless unity of mind and heart, perhaps over and over again, perhaps even with every breath. Perhaps we are starving for, longing for, needing desperately to give ourselves over to the actuality of our experience with a high degree of intimacy and sensitivity, moment by moment, and receive what our very lives have to teach us if we can be there (which is always here), awake within their unfolding.

We tell people before they start in the stress reduction clinic that from our point of view, "as long as you are breathing, there is more right with you than wrong with you, no matter what is wrong with you" (Kabat-Zinn, 1990). Our orientation is to pour energy into what is already right with you, and let the rest of the health care system take care of what is wrong. How to begin? By coming to our senses, all of them, including the mind, which the Buddhists regard as another sense. We start by paying attention to our moment-to-moment experience of hearing, seeing, tasting, touching, smelling, knowing, in the body, within the breath, and over and over again when we forget or get caught up in the stream of thinking, or hijacked by unhelpful emotional reactions that compound our suffering.

The present moment is always now, and now is the place we do not inhabit when we are on autopilot. "When I graduate... when I get married... when I retire, then..." But the only moment we are ever alive is in this moment, and so the challenge for our patients is whether they are willing to work with us in the here and now, to learn to "re-inhabit" the actuality of their situation as it is, not as we expected or hoped it to be, and to take this on as the huge adventure it is, because we still do not know how it will unfold. There is now a powerful and widespread demand among what are called "health care consumers" for what some people call complementary and alternative practices in medicine, and I and many others prefer to call an *integrative medicine*, one that goes far beyond merely replacing an allopathic approach with an alternative one, but rather a complete evidence-based integration of allopathic and nontraditional ways of understanding and treating disease and dis-ease. At the University of Massachusetts Amherst, and elsewhere, faculty and other educational leaders are beginning to speak of *integrative education* and are even envisioning the *integrative university* (Scott, 2000). It is all based on the understanding of the multidimensionality of being and of ways of knowing (Zajonc, 2000). This is not some "new age" phrase. These different and complementary ways of knowing must be held up to the deepest levels of human scrutiny and, if found lacking, then they should be discarded. However, if they are found to be of value, then we need to embrace them. If we cannot immediately find a realistic mechanism to explain their effects, perhaps we should not be entirely surprised because we do not even know what a thought is in the realm of cognitive science and neurophysiology, or how light of a certain wavelength falling on the retina transforms into an experience of what we call "blue."

In addition to the formal research studies we conduct through the stress reduction clinic, we also ask our patients more informally about their experiences. We usually ask if they feel they got anything out of the program, and if "yes," what? Typically, one of the first things many people say, is "the breathing." This is interesting, considering that they were breathing before they took the program. I think what they mean is that they got in touch with their breathing and discovered that it could be an ally in their coming back to themselves, and opening up new and previously hidden dimensions of embodied experience. They also quite often say things like, "I discovered that I am not my thoughts; I am not my illness; I am not my disease; I am not the ideas that I have about myself."

These discoveries suggest that at some deep level, the practice of mindfulness within the context of Mindfulness-Based Stress Reduction (MBSR) is indeed transformational, and liberating. However, liberating from what? The Buddhists would say it is liberation from core impulses, habits, and conditioning that imprison us and that continually give rise to mind states of greed, of hatred, and of delusion or ignorance which, unexamined, keep us from waking up to new degrees of freedom that are always available to us in our lives if we stop ignoring what is right under our noses, so to speak.

If we really start paying a degree of systematic attention to what is on our minds, we will notice that very often the mind is trying to get something we don't have, whether it is a car, a house, a relationship, an advanced degree—the list is endless. It is so easy to fall into thinking, "If I just have this, I will be complete. If I live there, I will be happier." However, whatever our attainments, we discover that there is no end to wanting. A more liberative and mindful strategy might be to live our lives from moment to moment and then, when we get what we want—whether it is a car, love, or a Ph.D. —at least we will be there for all of it when it arrives, and along the way to it as well, which is a completely different experience from putting our life on hold until we have it. Can you feel the difference?

Transformation is Now

Sometime we are consumed by hatred—of all the things we are trying to keep away from or keep away from us out of fear. We run from everything that causes anxiety. We can be completely preoccupied if not obsessed with what we do not like about our bodies, our relationships, our parents, and about our teachers. We are left off-balance by such fears and how they work on us. When we start to examine what is on our minds, we see right away that a lot of it is delusional; that our thoughts are, for the most part, highly inaccurate. When we begin to pay attention and liberate ourselves through awareness in even the smallest of ways, even for one moment, from our greed, hatred and delusion, when we have an impulse to grab for something, but we become aware of it before we do and we purposefully do not pursue it reflexively, maybe even just for fun to see what would happen, an extraordinary balance between giving and receiving may arise in that very moment, and with it, a completely nonconceptual knowing of another dimension of experience can emerge, right here and now.

It could be called equanimity, or standing in your life as if it really mattered, feeling like you do not need one more thing to be complete. This is not implying that you have to become a recluse or a renunciant. It simply means that in that moment, you are free of your own imprisoning desire. That is a huge step. In fact, you are free of your own fear. That is not saying that you will not have any more desires or fear, even in the very next moment. Rather, it is an acknowledgment to yourself that it is all right to have fear and desires. Everybody has fear. Everybody has desires. The questions are: Can we work with these mind states when they arise? Can we recognize them for what they are and embrace whatever presents itself in awareness? Can we dance with it? That is both the skill and the calling of contemplative practice.

Transformational contemplative practices constitute one of the most profound and, at the same time, poorly understood emergences in human society in the past 10,000 years. We are just now in the incubatory stages of their globalization. As a species, we have not quite figured out yet how to deal with the incredible precocity of the human organism and human intelligence and its capabilities for shaping our environment, both for good and for ill. Moreover, we have not quite figured out how to keep the greed, hatred, and delusion at least sufficiently in check so that we will not think we have to be perpetually at war to live in peace, so that we will not pollute the playpen irrevocably for our grandchildren and their grandchildren. If we really want to think about the power and the beauty of being human, perhaps it is time for us to become planetary adults and fully realize our potential by coming to our senses, appreciating the interior landscape as well as shaping with greater wisdom our relationship to the outer one, including other people, customs, and ways of living that are strange or even aversive to us. The stakes are huge because we could lose ourselves, not just as individuals but also as a society, as families and as human beings. If there is going to be a transformation, let it be a liberative transformation to greater wisdom and a plurality of complementary ways of knowing. Let it be based on kindness and compassion, developing out of our own ongoing work on ourselves as individuals and as a society to cultivate and refine our capacity for awareness and for true inner as well as outer freedom.

In this regard, the interface between science and the humanities is particularly important and relevant at this juncture, due in part to the extraordinary scientific discoveries and advances in engineering that are now taking place in the fields of computers, neural networks, artificial intelligence, robotics, nanotechnology, human cloning, and the molecular biology of aging. This is fascinating science. However, as these fields progress, and they are progressing at an incredibly rapid rate, they raise important ethical questions that have to be adequately met and addressed in widespread conversations, because these technologies have the potential to transform the very biology of our species before we have even come to a full interior understanding of its potential (Joy, 2000; Kurzweil, 1999). Much of this innovative science and technology is developed within or in partnership with universities. If we are not paying attention to the human aspect, and if universities do not begin to take responsibility for participating and contributing to such an inquiry, at the very least opening up widespread conversation about these issues, and about integrative ways of bringing together different ways of knowing, it would be a major repudiation of our responsibilities as scientists and scholars, and as human beings.

Therefore, the intangible gifts to culture and humanity that come out of the arts, poetry, scholarship, out of the healing arts and the contemplative traditions and what they have to teach us are now more relevant and important than ever. They need to assertively take their places in this conversation. They remind us that we can stand secure in our humanness, in our insecurity about the ever-changing nature of reality. They remind us that we can embrace, even celebrate what is imperfect about us and in need, we think, of perfecting. Perhaps we are perfect as we are, including our imperfections, with our inborn capacity to pay attention, and thus to learn and grow. Certainly we are perfectly what we are. When we make a commitment to become familiar and intimate with the life of the mind, that way of knowing, way of being, that way of seeing becomes a veritable doorway into waking up, a way of giving yourself back to yourself, of standing in your life as if it really mattered, chaotic or not in any moment. To experience the full spectrum of our experience while we have the chance would not only be a gift of wholeness and healing to ourselves, but would be transformative of our institutions, of our families, of our ways of being, and of our ways of knowing.

Conclusion

I will end with a favorite passage from Albert Einstein. I saw it in *The New York Times* on the 25th anniversary of his death (1980). He wrote it in response to a rabbi who had written explaining that he had sought in vain to comfort his nineteen-year-old daughter over the death of her sixteen-year-old sister, "a sinless, beautiful 16-year old child." Einstein responded:

> A human being is a part of the whole called by us "Universe," a part limited in time and space. He experiences himself, his thoughts and feelings as something separated from the rest—a kind of optical delusion of his consciousness. This delusion is a kind of prison for us, restricting us to our personal desires, and to affection for a few persons nearest to us. Our task is to free ourselves from this prison by widening our circle of compassion to embrace all living creatures and the whole of nature in its beauty. Nobody is able to achieve this completely, but the striving for such achievement is in itself a part of liberation and a foundation for inner security.

I find it revealing that Einstein, whose insights virtually single-handedly transformed our scientific notions of time and space, and matter and energy, is pointing to the illusory nature of our perception that we are apart from the whole rather than part of it. His wisdom in this passage embodies as much that of the contemplative yogi as it does the great physicist. He is willing to speak of compassion, liberation, and inner security. In every country, in every culture, in every age there have been people who have delved deeply into the nature of reality, have contributed immeasurably to the wealth of our understanding of ourselves as human beings. Together, their individual and collective efforts constitute important contributions to our understanding of the mystery of the universe. We may not all be blessed with the insights of an Einstein, or an Emily Dickinson, but we are all blessed with the insights that are available to us, if we are willing to show up and do the work that is ours to do. These issues, and this work, merit conversation and exploration, inwardly and outwardly, in every university.

This essay was produced from the transcript of the talk in the Five College Series on the Contemplative Mind and Higher Education, titled, "Wherever You Go: Living Your Life as if It Really Mattered" at the University of Massachusetts Amherst, March 15, 2001.

References

Bohm, D. (1980). *Wholeness and the implicate order*. London: Routledge & Kegan.

Dickinson, E. (1961). *Me from myself – to banish*. In T. H. Johnson (Ed.), Final Harvest: *Emily Dickinson's poems*. Boston: Little Brown. (Original work published 1890).

Einstein, A. (1972). The Einstein papers: Man of many parts long involved in the cause of peace. *The New York Times*. March 29, p. 22.

Eliot, T. S. (1943). *Four quartets*. New York: Harcourt Brace.

Feinberg, G. (1977). *What is the world made of? Atoms, leptons, quarks, and other tantalizing particles*. Garden City, NY: Anchor, Doubleday.

Greene, B. (1999). *The elegant universe*. New York: Norton.

Jiménez, J. R. (1995). I am not I. In R. Bly (Ed.), *The soul is here for its own joy: Sacred poems from many cultures*. New York: Harper Collins.

Joy, B. (April, 2000). Why the future doesn't need us. *Wired Magazine*, 238–262.

Kabat-Zinn, J. (1990). *Full catastrophe living: Using the wisdom of your body and mind to face stress, pain and illness*. New York: Delta.

——(2002). Mindfulness: The heart of rehabilitation. In E. Leskowitz (Ed.), *Complementary and alternative medicine in rehabilitation*. St. Louis, MO: Churchill Livingstone.

Kapleau, P. (1967). *The three pillars of Zen: Teaching, practice, enlightenment*. Boston: Beacon.

Kurzweil, R. (1999). *The age of spiritual machines*. New York: Viking.

Lightman, A. (2000). *The diagnosis*. New York: Pantheon.

Scott, D. K. (2000). Spirituality in an integrative age. In V. H. Kazanjian & P. L. Laurence (Eds.), *Education as transformation: Religious pluralism, spirituality, and a new vision for higher education in America*. New York: Peter Lang.

Varela, F., Thompson, E., & Rosch, R. (1991). *The embodied mind*. Cambridge, MA: MIT Press.

Walcott, D. (1968). *Derek Walcott collected poems 1948–1984*. New York: Farrar, Straus, Giroux.

Walsh, R. N. (1980). The consciousness disciplines and the behavioral sciences: Questions of comparison and assessment. *American Journal of Psychiatry*, 137, 663–673.

Zajonc, A. (2000). Molding the self and the common cognitive sources of science and religion. In V. H. Kazanjian & P. L. Laurence (Eds.), *Education as transformation: Religious pluralism, spirituality, and a new vision for higher education in America*. New York: Peter Lang.

On Being a Human at Law

Steven Keeva

> *The way we spend our days is the way we spend our lives.*
> *Annie Dillard*

Near the beginning of the Academy Award-nominated film *In the Bedroom*, Natalie, a character played by the actress Marissa Tomei, rolls about on a sun-dappled Maine hillside with her young lover, Frank. Every detail in the frame somehow speaks to the pleasure they take in each other's company and conveys a sense that they are exactly where they want to be. At one point, her face refulgent, Natalie smiles and releases five single-syllable words into the embracing sky. "I can feel my life," she says.

These words astounded me—such stark simplicity in the service of naming what it is we all want: to really feel what it means to be alive. In fact, I have taken to quoting Natalie in speeches I give to lawyers across the country. When I do, the reaction is arresting: The room becomes quieter; then as I ask if they, in their law practices, are able to feel their lives, there comes a palpable sense of sadness and loss.

It is probably safe to say that regardless of our occupations, most of us only rarely experience our lives in this special way. It is not as though there is a conspiracy to deny us such moments, but rather we tend to be too distracted to notice them as they pass. It is little wonder. We live in a culture that mitigates against our natural capacity to feel our lives. The density of information that ceaselessly bathes and/or assaults us makes it more challenging than ever to feel what is delicate and evanescent, as is so much of what makes life meaningful. Add to this the fact that, as the social critic Thomas de Zengotita has written, we live in a world that "virtualizes" everything (de Zengotita, 2000). This means, to paraphrase de Zengotita, we become numb to the world around us and come to experience nature, for example, as "nature," and the singularity of our subjective experience as merely "feelings." In such a culture, it is powerful indeed when the quotation marks are ripped away and unmediated experience triumphs, as it did for Natalie in that lovely movie scene.

However, let us return to the sadness in those lawyer-filled rooms. What is it about? My sense is that it reflects a shared but hardly ever acknowledged awareness that the culture of the legal profession is uniquely inimical to a sense of presence in one's own life. The perceived need to be constantly on guard, to cover one's flanks, second guess the opposition and have all the answers all the time detracts mightily from establishing any connection with the inner life—the source from which the joy of being emanates.

It is no surprise then that when the words spirituality and law are uttered in close proximity, it is all but inevitable that someone within earshot will point out that lawyers constitute an oxymoron. What is surprising, however, is how rarely it is a lawyer who makes such a comment. The truth is that for all the unhappiness that plagues the profession, lawyers seem to understand intuitively that the two concepts are—or should be—linked, even if they do not know what is required of them in order to experience the connection. Clearly, some people in our society see lawyers as the enemy. What is more troubling to me is that so many lawyers see themselves—that is, their professional selves—as the enemy of their own sense of balance and well-being.

For some time now the American legal profession has been in the throes of a spiritual crisis, one that has often been trivialized as merely a lack of civility within the bar. The latter is certainly a symptom, but deeper issues have largely been ignored. One reason for this omission, I believe, is a prevailing fear that investigating the spiritual dimensions of life in the law might compromise the laser-like, reductionist, lawyerly way of thinking that both the legal academy and the profession deem to be not only fundamental, but also sufficient. In *Transforming Practice* (Keeva, 1999), I describe the issue this way:

> Such gifts as emotional intelligence, compassion, and warmth have little if any standing in the current legal culture. And in a legal academy that extols the economic analysis of legal outcomes while giving almost no consideration to the law's—and law practice's—psychological and emotional effects, students fall under the spell of a legal map that is at odds, in both its narrowness and its lack of mystery and feeling, with life as they lived it prior to law school. In no time flat, intellectual rigor has become their true north, and a mountain range of reason has replaced their old landscapes of feeling, convictions and beliefs.

In fact, there is persuasive evidence that spirituality enhances, rather than detracts from, analytical thinking by providing a context within which creative, life-enhancing meanings can emerge (Keeva, 1999).

A metaphor I like to use to describe this obsession with "thinking like a lawyer" comes from Saki Santorelli, Director of the Center for Mindfulness in Medicine, Healthcare, and Society at the University of Massachusetts Medical School. "The linear, discursive mind has come loose from its moorings—its proper place," he has written. "We have built a boat and mistaken it for the sea. Yet beyond the labels of patient or practitioner (read "client" and "lawyer") we are all in the same boat thirsting for the same living water" (Santorelli, 1999).

If the legal profession tends to mistake its boat for the ocean, by marginalizing all that is beyond its limited contents, perhaps it makes sense to extend the metaphor and suggest that these days the craft is listing, taking on water, and causing a kind of professional seasickness. The evidence is there in a growing body of literature that describes practitioners who suffer from depression at higher levels than members of any other profession, as well as an extraordinarily high incidence of substance abuse, divorce and emotional dysfunction (Heinz et al., 1999; Schiltz, 1999).

Lawyers today are dying to feel whole. But that yearning can be difficult to satisfy while working in ways that do little or nothing to enhance one's own, or one's clients' sense of wholeness. For lawyers to really feel their lives, they need to spend time in the larger ocean, open to all that cannot be held in or experienced by the linear, discursive mind.

For some time now I have explored the role that spirituality can, and increasingly does, play in lawyers' lives. For this chapter, I define spirituality—perhaps a bit clumsily—as that inner part of us where we are sensitive to the deepest, most nuanced levels of meaning in our lives. It supports, contextualizes, and humanizes all that we do, as it moves us toward greater authenticity and more integrated lives. It is the foundation of the legal work of Mohandas K. Gandhi, who was a lawyer by training and came to see, as he put it, that "the true function of a lawyer was to unite parties riven asunder"—that is, to heal (Gandhi, 1954, p. 168).

Lawyers are overwhelmingly outer-directed people—that is to say, lawyers tend to neglect the inner life of mind and spirit, even as they ache for ways to experience themselves more deeply through their work. One wise observer, having described the body of law as "the tissue of the outer life," had this to say about the plight of lawyers: "It's a sad thing, but because they work with the law all the time, they tend to live above the surface, alone" (Lehman, 1997).

Living this way—particularly in view of the relentless demands on most lawyers' time—tends to thwart the yearning for integration and wholeness. Indeed, practicing law can be a remarkably disintegrative pursuit, one that would almost certainly make the possibility of feeling one's life while at work seem laughably unrealistic to most practitioners.

Forms of Alienation

Although the causes of lawyer unhappiness and alienation are rather complex, the symptoms are clear enough. What I refer to as the "Seven Types of Separation" is a characterization of the predominant ways in which lawyers experience themselves as cut off from the world around them and from themselves (for further elaboration, see Keeva, 1999, p. 14). Having first appeared in my book, *Transforming Practices*, in slightly different form, it has been widely reprinted or excerpted in legal publications—an indication, I believe, of a deep yearning for recognition of what underlies the current unhappiness in the profession.

Seven Types of Separation

***Separation from oneself*:** Having been acculturated to a profession in which adversarial tactics have proliferated beyond litigation into areas that used to be free from such rancor, lawyers lose touch with the more subtle expressions and yearnings of their hearts and minds and come to feel fragmented and often unhealthy. This sense of separation is often measured in the distance they have come from who they once were: sensitive, caring, creative people. Feeling lost, many look to money to create at least a semblance of integration (the surface integration of a cohesive lifestyle), but ultimately a feeling of wholeness is elusive. Lawyers who experience this kind of separation tend to feel trapped between others' perceptions of their success, on the one hand, and their own experience of spiritual emptiness, on the other.

Separation from clients: Too often, lawyers sense that there are roles to play that preclude real human-to-human contact with clients. (This can be particularly uncomfortable when clients are suffering, as they so often are when they seek a lawyer's help.) This situation creates a hole at the heart of the relationship, the place where authentic human contact ought to be, frequently leaving both parties dissatisfied.

Separation from the law firm: No longer particularly cohesive, law firms are more bottom-line oriented than ever. They tend to support disintegration by failing to emphasize the importance of personal growth and career development for partners, associates, and staff, and by rewarding people only for that which can be measured in dollars and cents. These demands can create a great deal of anxiety in lawyers who can come to feel like Hollywood actors who are only considered as good as their last roles. When it is all about winning, there is a long way to fall.

Separation from friends and family: The stresses of a law practice create a great deal of inner turmoil. An inability to express what is going on internally causes a painful sense of separation from the people about whom one cares most. Some lawyers speak of living in a separate world from the rest of their family, a state of affairs that adds tremendous conflict to an already stressful professional life. Sadly, the seeds of this kind of separation are often sown in law school.

Separation from life as people live it: Integration is also reflected in a sense of being different, of living apart from "normal" people. Besieged by public antipathy toward their profession, many lawyers feel misunderstood, bewildered, scorned. Many describe the problem as a double whammy: not only are they hurt by widespread disapprobation, but often they themselves have a hard time finding much to like about what they do for a living.

Separation from the law as an expression of self in the world: Being separated from law as a lawyer may mean for a lawyer to be separated from the very purpose of one's life. While it might have once seemed as if the law were the ideal vehicle for achieving that purpose (to help people, to advance the cause of justice, to foster economic development, or whatever), many lawyers have resigned themselves to disappointment in the face of a professional reality that does not seem to support their personal goals. The feeling, either implicit or expressed, is typically articulated this way: I didn't go to law school to do this!

Separation from the larger profession: This final form is a sense of disenfranchisement, of feeling alienated, from a profession that has gone astray and does little to promote more balanced lives or assuage, or even to acknowledge, lawyers' feelings of separation. The message to lawyers is clear: you're on your own.

Upon further reflection, I would add one other kind of separation to this list, one not included on my original version, but which, I have become convinced, is quite significant. This is a sense of generally being out of rhythm with both the natural and human worlds. To a great extent this is a problem throughout our society, in which we have forsaken the notion that a healthy, well-adjusted life requires a balance between work and rest. For lawyers, however, this is doubly vexing for one particular reason: the prevalence of hourly billing. There is something especially twisted about such an arrangement in the way it so badly equates time with money and thereby creates an incentive for not resting at all.

The Inner Journey

Despite the lack of integration and a very real professional malaise, experience tells me that most lawyers have not yet given up hope of finding a better way to be, and know themselves, as lawyers.

Clearly, this assessment has something to do with professional identity and the fact that most lawyers define their roles in a rather limited way. In a recent conversation that brought this home for me, a nationally known author and speaker, having recently addressed a law firm for the first time, described to me something he found to be particularly curious. "I spoke to these lawyers as members of a helping profession," he said, "because I thought that's what they were." However, he soon realized, that was not how they saw themselves. "Apparently, I surprised them by talking to them that way," he recalled. "And I was surprised that they were surprised. At first, they seemed confused, but then I could tell that they were starting to like the idea" (Kundtz, 1998).

It is amazing but true: lawyers often do not realize that they can help people as people—that is, on the human level—rather than merely as ambulatory clusters of legal issues. (In this way they tend to resemble physicians who cannot see the patient for the symptoms.) I see this phenomenon when I talk to lawyers about the notion of law as a healing profession, that by looking through a healing lens, so to speak, they can learn to recognize opportunities to help in truly significant ways. They can come to see too that, just as in medicine, there is a profound difference between curing and healing. Curing involves simply fixing the legal problem—selling the business, writing the contract, getting the divorce, or whatever—while healing is about helping the client become whole again (Keeva, 1999, pp. 105–106).

When clients go to see lawyers, more often than not they carry with them some combination of fear, confusion, and anger. After all, something has gone wrong in their lives, often something quite traumatic. Recognizing this, respecting it, and trying to help heal those feelings—often simply by listening deeply, without judgment—can be profoundly satisfying, both for the client and the lawyer. In fact, in a profession where zero-sum mindsets are the norm, and all value accrues to winning, the inner life can be a saving grace by providing sources of meaning and value that are not determined by the outer culture (Keeva, 2001). Lawyers who appreciate this reality are likely to cultivate vibrant inner lives. They make room in their lives for practices that deepen their spirituality by enhancing their awareness, focusing their attention, and revealing their bottom-line connectedness with other people. As a result, lawyers come to appreciate their own, their clients' and even their opponents' common humanity, realizing that in the realm of spirituality, categories such as winning and losing are not particularly relevant.

John McShane is a well-known criminal and family law practitioner in Dallas who often takes clients on the basis that he will work toward a healing result. "I know for certain that by bringing an ethic of care and a healing orientation to a case, I have made a difference in clients' lives, regardless of the legal outcome," he says (Keeva, 2000). He is clear about the value of this work, regardless of how many traditional lawyers might raise their eyebrows when he talks about it. "People sometimes say, 'My God, why would a client hire someone with this touchy-feely approach to the law?,' " he says. "The answer is, it makes sense. It resonates with that deep universal need for healing." I would add that that need is as compelling for the lawyer as it is for the client.

The idea that law can, and indeed should, be practiced as a healing profession is slowly catching on in the legal world. In fact, the first institution to be solely dedicated to advancing the concept—The John E. Fetzer International Centre for Healing and the Law—recently opened its doors in western Michigan and Washington, D.C., in 2002. Its mission is unabashedly spiritual, though nondenominational, in that it conceives of healing as a fundamentally spiritual process that can be both cultivated (an inner process) and learned (more outer and skill focused). It requires both an ability to bring forth inner wisdom and intuition, and to act in the world to serve others by listening deeply and understanding that all parties to conflict truly are whole, multifaceted beings.

The Centre was conceived as a place for education and contemplation, a place where lawyers, judges, educators, and students can share their experiences and insights about the roots and responsibilities of the legal profession and thereby reinvigorate their professional lives. Through educational, publishing, and advocacy efforts, the Centre hopes to pioneer a new vision of legal professionals in our society, one rooted in the reconciling and counseling nature of the law, rather than the adversarial model. I have had the opportunity to speak to groups of lawyers about the Centre's mission and have always found among them keen interest and, mixed with some skepticism, a great deal of hope for its success.

Feeling Alive in the Law

For some lawyers, and their numbers are growing, law practice is hardly synonymous with alienation from self and others. In fact, it is a way into feeling their lives as authentic expressions of who they are. Consider a story about Rick, a Michigan trial lawyer who does mostly personal injury work, and whose spirituality informs his law practice and his life. Rick is so present to his clients' needs and to his own passion for helping them that I tend to think that if Marissa Tomei's Natalie were ever to become a lawyer, Rick is the kind she would become. Here is an example of how he relates to clients or would-be clients (Halpert, 1999).

About a year ago, a couple—I'll call them the Holts—came to see Rick after a crisis upended their lives. Their teenage daughter, like her recently deceased twin, had lived her entire life suffering from a rare, degenerative muscular disease; then, she had been sexually assaulted in her bed at the nursing home where she lived.

Mr. Holt, beside himself with rage and grief, felt that someone had to pay for the horror that befell his daughter. He wanted to sue the home. Mrs. Holt did not. Up until the incident, she pointed out, the care they had provided was exemplary, and they had not hesitated to report the crime. After an hour of listening and asking questions, Rick told the Holts that they had an excellent case. In fact, he said, his considerable experience in litigating such matters told him that they were likely to recover at least a million dollars. "But," he added, "I don't think you should bring the claim." They were stunned. Understanding the math and knowing roughly what Rick stood to lose if they prevailed in the case (and knowing what people say about lawyers), they asked him why he felt the way he did.

First, he told them, they were relatively young, and once their daughter died—which was likely to be soon—they still had time to enjoy their lives. Protracted litigation would make that impossible for some time. Second, they would have to move their daughter to another facility. Because the closest one that offered comparable care was three hours away, it would put a terrible strain on the family.

Finally, he told them what he thought was the most important reason: "It's clear to me that what has kept the two of you sane over the years is your relationship," he said. "But you disagree on how to approach this. If you pursue a lawsuit, there's a good chance it will tear your marriage apart."

Offering to abide by their wishes, Rick asked only that they take some time to reflect, then get back to him the following week. The Holts had spoken of their religious faith, and Rick suggested that they consult with their minister. What Rick stood to "lose" if the Holts took his advice was around $300,000, his take in the event of a million-dollar court judgment or a settlement. The Holts called the following Monday to tell Rick they had decided not to sue the home.

Rick's practice abounds with such stories, and he has recently begun to do innovative work with the use of apology—something most lawyers avoid assiduously, fearing that it might be seen as an admission of guilt or liability (Halpert, n.d.).

For Rick, however, the question that really matters is, "Will it help my client to heal if the person responsible for her injury apologizes for hurting her?" If, in consultation with his client, he determines that it likely will, Rick seeks ways to address any fears or concerns that might stand in the way of the interaction, almost always clearing the way for this simple human interaction that has, from time immemorial, been an essential ingredient in the healing process.

It seems to me that Rick understands certain things that other lawyers would do well to consider. It is clear to him, for example, that legal issues do not have lives of their own; they arrive on the backs and in the lives of human beings who need to be heard and understood before their legal situation can be properly addressed. He knows that love is a more powerful force than self-interest, anger, or vengeance, and that it is crucial to grasp its role in clients' lives, and to allow it a place in his own professional life. Rick understands too that everything starts with seeing people whole, and that when one listens deeply and with commitment, so that people feel truly understood, one is helping them to act with integrity.

For Rick, it all comes down to this: "When you're emotionally intimate with a person going through a terrible time and you can make a difference, there's incredible joy in that. That's the joy that to me makes being a lawyer today worth it" (Keeva, 1999, p. 128). Rick spent a great deal of time searching for a way to practice law that minimizes the gap between who he is as a human being and what he does as a lawyer. By doing so, he has found a way to feel his life through his work.

Another Kind of Practice

Deep and nonjudgmental listening; seeing the client as a whole, multifaceted person; offering caring, respectful attention to what the client deems important—these are the very things people seek from spiritual counsel. Lawyers may be lay persons, but like doctors and the clergy they must come to understand that their mere presence can have a salutary or a negative effect on the clients they see. Research tells us that when people feel heard they become calmer; their blood pressure drops, as it does for the listener as well (Lynch, 1998). We also know that the mere presence of a physician has a measurable impact on patients' healing. There is no reason this should not be true for lawyers as well.

Spiritual practice is a time-tested way to become open to what the practice of law can really be. Just as there is growing interest in—I would say a spiritual pull toward—healing and the law, so too is there a growing awareness that contemplative practices can deepen the experience of practicing law even in the face of a tumultuous workaday reality.

In the last few years, the law schools at Yale, Columbia, and Harvard universities, as well as a number of lesser known institutions, have offered programs that expose students to the benefits of meditation and mindfulness. (See www.contemplativemind.org for reports on contemplative law retreats.)

These practices, as well as prayer, focused time in nature, journaling, and other activities have been found to help counterbalance adversarial and zero-sum mindsets by enhancing self-awareness and thereby illuminating a wide spectrum of possibilities that do not appear in the traditional lawyer's mental "boat."

The practice of mindfulness—that is, paying attention in the moment, moment to moment, and without judgment, to one's mind and body as well as to the outer world—has proved to be of particular interest to lawyers. Evidence of this includes programs held at law firms and others designed specifically for lawyers (and sometimes judges) at remote locations, as well as a program held at Harvard Law School entitled "Mindfulness in Law and ADR" on March 8, 2002, and web cast at http://www.pon.harvard.edu/news/ 2002/riskin_mindfulness.php3.

One reason for this would seem to be its portability—that is, it is a practice that can be done at any time of day in any location, at work or at rest, alone or with others. In other words, it does not require extra time or necessarily impose on the pursuit of billable hours (although the practice is significantly enhanced by regular meditation).

A second reason for the growing interest among lawyers in mindfulness practice is its investigative nature, an aspect with which many people who choose a career in the law seem to be comfortable. Rather than requiring particular beliefs or even a willingness to suspend disbelief, it asks simply that one observe one's body and mind in order to see what is really there in the present moment, moment to moment. Where is your mind right now? Are you present, or are you worrying about this afternoon's hearing? Are you aware of your breath? Are you identifying with any particular thoughts or feelings? If so, can you feel any sensations rising out of this attachment? What happens when you simply notice the way your mind jumps about from obligation to obligation, fear to fear, dissatisfaction to pleasant reminiscence?

We turn to spiritual practice for a variety of reasons, among them a desire for greater clarity, presence and insight in our lives. Mindfulness practices—those that emphasize the power of being awake to the moment without identifying with the thoughts and feelings that can color experience— produce benefits that include the following:

Quieting the mind: This common goal of spiritual practice is particularly important because it provides an opening through which creativity and wisdom can arise. Neither can blossom when the mind is absorbed in incessant chatter, mindless reactivity, and unexamined habitual thinking. When lawyers learn to meditate, they are often shocked at the relentless cascade of thoughts that reveals itself once they become quiet and direct their attention inward. "The difficult thing," says a lawyer who teaches meditation at a Boston law firm, "is to convince them that noticing this is a good thing" (Heargreaves-Heald, 2002) because it is the first step toward attaining inner quiet.

Moving beyond limiting mindsets: Mindfulness creates the possibility of seeing beyond mindsets that cause suffering for lawyers and law students alike (zero-sum thinking, for example). Mindful awareness is beneficial not only for the client and the case, but for the lawyer as well, who comes to feel the satisfaction that comes from being in control of his faculties and able to express himself in the desired mode, rather than reactively amid a thicket of expectations, artificial structures, and overlays.

Enhancing relationships: In the area of lawyer-client relationships, research reveals a kind of Gordian Knot (Keeva, 2002). On one hand, studies have made quite clear that clients crave supportive, productive human relationships with good lawyers; on the other, they reveal that lawyers feel isolated from supportive, productive human relationships. How does one reconcile these realities? Clearly, something is amiss on the level of awareness that relates to a sense of diminished potential for truly satisfying relationships. By expanding the field of awareness—one of the primary purposes of contemplative practices—opportunities for better lawyer-client relationships often become clearer.

Boosting energy: The lawyers I know who have the greatest capacity for work—work typically done with both passion and compassion—are those with regular contemplative practices. The literature on meditation is full of stories about people whose practices drastically boosted their personal energy and reduced their need for sleep. It may have something to do with what author and meditation teacher Jack Kornfield refers to as "stopping the war within." By promoting nonjudgmental observation, meditation gradually reveals the disruptive and divisive role judgment can play in all aspects of life. War, whether internal or on an actual battlefield, is depleting. Peace is energizing (Kornfield, 1993, p. 22).

Enhancing discernment: Lawyers operate in a world of judgment and continual commentary, constantly arriving at opinions (whether internal or verbally) as facts emerge. Unfortunately, this can have a corrosive affect on one's ability to see reality as it is, unfettered by neat categories and designations. Diverting this energy into discernment—a mental activity that seeks clarity and understanding rather than rote categorization—opens new avenues of investigation and an expanded field of inquiry, while avoiding the corrosive nature of judgment.

Reducing reactivity: A number of spiritual traditions emphasize the value of taking the stance of a witness to one's own experience. If a person can imagine that one's awareness is like the sky, in which thoughts, feelings, and sensations come and go like the clouds, then one can choose when it is appropriate to act on any one of them, or simply to watch them drift by. This is immensely freeing for lawyers who regularly find themselves reflexively lured into unproductive discussions or arguments. Mindfulness reveals options.

The Contemplative Counselor

I often ask lawyers a question that most find surprising: if your minister, rabbi, or other clergy person were to tell you that he or she needed some time to reflect in silence and get clear and balanced so that he or she could better help members of his or her congregation, would you find that strange? Inevitably, the answer is "no." In fact, I am often told that it would seem strange if he or she did not want to do that.

Then I ask them why they do not give themselves time for reflection. After all, in a fundamental way they are in the same position as that clergyperson. People come to them for succor in difficult times, knowing that they are privy to an arcane body of knowledge and a language all their own. Being in such a position, clients may be somewhat skeptical or anxious, but they also hope to be well cared for. Although lawyers may tend to overlook it, clients have, on some level, a therapeutic expectation of them. (The fact that they often fail to meet this expectation has a lot to do with their standing in society today.)

The legal profession at its roots truly is a healing/helping profession. Moreover, if one knows where to look, it is possible to find nodes of healing intention expressed through the law in private firms large and small, legal aid clinics, public defenders' and prosecutors' offices and in-house legal departments, among other places. Succeeding in this realm, however, and finding the joy that it offers, requires an inward turn, a way of focusing close attention to one's habitual thought processes and learning what gets in the way of being present for oneself and for one's clients.

In the Cathedral

The following quotes represent a composite drawn from several programs I conducted in 2001 and 2002.

I propose an exercise to a group of lawyers. Pretend, I tell them, that your office is one of the following: a workshop, a house of worship, a foundry, a dance studio, a psychotherapist's office, a garden, or an artist's atelier. Now stop for a few minutes and imagine yourself there, in whatever kind of "office" you have chosen. Close your eyes and visualize the place. Survey it, walk around it, breathe in its air.

Next, try to notice how you feel there. Has anything changed in your sense of yourself or your relationship to your surroundings? Take some time to really "be" there. Then, breathe deeply a few times, relax, and try to bring a client to mind—a particular client, perhaps one you have seen recently, whose presence you can easily summon.

Into this creative place, this worshipful place, this place that honors craft and growth, comes this particular client, bringing with her the same legal "problem" she brought recently. Has anything changed? If so, what is it? In your mind's eye, observe your interaction once again. What does this fresh context reveal to you about what might be possible in your work? Does the interaction feel different in some way?

"I saw my client at my yoga studio," says one person who clearly felt sufficiently unconstrained to choose her own venue. "It was quiet, simple and spare. And when I sat down with this particular woman, who was quite upset about a number of things in her life, I felt quiet and centered inside. I became acutely aware of her as a physical being, one with a great deal of tension, particularly in her neck. Then I listened as she said things that went right past me the last time I saw her."

"I got a bit grandiose and found myself practicing law in a cathedral," said another participant. "And suddenly everything in the room was filled with meaning. It wasn't totally clear to me what the meaning was, but I could feel the presence of meaning and felt certain it would be revealed over time. I also saw my client—a man who can be very difficult—as a child of God, or of the universe or whatever. I was able to watch him and listen to him without getting caught up in my own judgments about who he is. I didn't judge myself either because it was clear to me that I have as much connection to divinity as he has. What was really great was that it occurred to me that, like a clergyman, I, as a lawyer, have a choice about how I want to deal with people. I can choose to be open and trusting instead of punctilious and closed off. I can have faith in the client's own wisdom about what result would make him feel most complete and satisfied, or I can give him the benefit of my 'superior' legal wisdom. I learned quite a bit in just a handful of minutes."

The exercise is an eye-opener, a simple way of bringing awareness of alternative ways of being and processing information. Suddenly it becomes clear that the overlays we put on our experience—or let others place there—are arbitrary and do not necessarily fit our needs. This, too, is a kind of mindfulness practice, one of becoming aware of the possibilities inherent in adopting new metaphors for, or angles of approach to, your work, and how they can reveal the beauty and possibility in what has always been there.

References

de Zengotita, T. (2000). The numbing of the American mind: Culture as anesthetic. *Harper's Magazine* 304:38.

Fischer, L. (Ed.). (2003). *The essential Ghandian anthology of his writing on his life, work and ideas.* New York: Vintage Books.

Gandhi, M. K. (1954). *The story of my experiments with truth: Gandhi's Autobiography.* Washington, DC: Public Affairs Press.

Halpert, R. (May, 1999). Interview for "The toughest nice firm around." *ABA Journal* 85.

——(n.d.) Q & A: On apology. http://www.transformingpractices.com/ qa/ qa8 apology.html.

Heargreaves-Heald, H. (2000). Private communication.

Heinz, J. P. et al. (1999). Lawyers and their discontents: Findings from a survey of the Chicago bar. *Indiana Law Review 74,* 735.

Keeva, S. (2000). Passionate practitioner. *ABA Journal 86,* p. 57. Keeva, S. (2001). Finding satisfaction: Zapping the zero-sum demon. *Law Practice Management Magazine, 27* (5), 65.

——(Spring, 2002). Practicing from the inside out. *Harvard Negotiation Law Review,* 97–107.

Kornfield, J. (1993). *A path with heart: A guide through the perils and promises of spiritual life.* New York: Bantam Books.

Kundtz, D. (1998). Personal interview.

Lehman, R. (1997). Interview with then-president of Fetzer Institute, Kalamazoo, Michigan.

Lynch, J. J. (1985). *The language of the heart: The body's response to human dialogue.* New York: Basic Books; Baltimore: Bancroft Press.

Santorelli, S. (1999). *Heal thy self: Lessons on mindfulness and medicine.* New York: Bell Tower.

Schiltz, P. (1999). On being a happy, healthy and ethical member of an unhappy, unhealthy and unethical profession. *Vanderbilt Law Review, 52,* 871.

Spirituality in Business and Life: Asking the Right Questions

Peter Senge

Why are you so unhappy?
Why are we so unhappy?
Because everything you do
and ninety-nine percent of what you think
is for yourself.
And there isn't one.
                    Wu Wei, Twelfth Century

For many years, I worked with a diverse network of people in organizations. For the most part, I consciously avoided the word spirituality. In business there was no difficulty at all in using the word spirit—that was not a problematic word. Like any word, it resonates better with some than others, but it raised fewer concerns. Most people in thinking about concrete experiences in an organization will respond right away when asked if they have ever been part of a team with any spirit. They know what it means, and they can anchor it directly in what they experience. However, somehow the word spirituality creates ambiguity and concerns. In our culture, we put an emphasis on nouns; we like to make nouns out of dynamic processes. So I suggest a caution: in our culture, particularly our media-oriented culture, this tendency to create nouns takes phenomena which are living, growing, transient— which is to say, life—and makes them into things. This is a problem. I have seen one fad after another after another move through our business community and our society. There is this voice in the back of my head, saying, "Gee, I wonder if three or four years down the road, we will say, we have done spirituality; now what's next?" This is what happens with fads.

Knowing that reality, I could not help wondering why our work has had such an impact. I am not sure it has to do with the inherent qualities or merits of the work. There are many people doing work that has great merit. It is a little bit shocking to see how many people say, "Yes, I read this book, and my organization uses it; we study it." I have thought a lot about this over the years. Why has this work gone beyond a fad? I think there is a very simple explanation consistent with my experience. If anything is really powerful as a deep current in our present-day society, it is the very simple awareness that there is something wrong with our way of living. It is not complicated. Children see this very quickly, and I often see that teenagers also understand. Something is really amiss; we sense it.

For example, when the first book in the series, *The Fifth Discipline*, was published in 1990, I was most curious about how people would take the subject of dialogue. I thought it was the least proven of any of the ideas there because most of the ideas, tools, and methods that we discussed had been in use for many years. However, dialogue was something that crept in at the end, yet seemed so important that we had to include it. Since that time, many dialogue groups have begun and many people have integrated the practice of "check-in" or some sort of dialogic technique into their regular work sessions.

Philosophical Issues

Recently I visited a school system in the West. In many school systems, extraordinary changes are happening because people are actually letting children get together and talk—really talk. Then the adults start listening and eventually hear what is going on. Once these dialogic practices get started, they almost never stop, even if the form changes. People move to different jobs, leave one company or organization and go to another. However, they almost always look for some way to restart the practice. It has become very apparent to me that in some sense the simple reality is we are looking for a better way to live.

How curious that we would come to a point where we need to rediscover meaning. It shows how far we have drifted as a people. For most cultures— indeed for most of history—there has not been a lot of confusion about meaning. We are clear that what binds the culture together is this common search and continual questioning. What am I here for? What's going on? Who am I? How do I fit in? What is the story? Some of you have probably read Thomas Berry, who has been the president of the Teilhard de Chardin society for many years. He began writing several years ago about very powerful themes, including the loss of our story (Berry, 1988, 1999; Swimme & Berry, 1992). We have no story. In the Judeo-Christian Western world, there was a story that held things together for a long time, at least for some people, but that story no longer works, even for that group of people. We have lost our story and come to a point where we need to rediscover meaning and meaningfulness.

Recently a colleague shared with me that he was still wondering and still struggling with our fundamental question—about working in public institutions and engaging in dialogue about meaning with people who may feel that nothing is wrong, that the institutions are working fine, that the separation of their souls or their vocation from their teaching or their work is healthy. For them, it seems so easy just to go home and watch TV and not worry about these matters. He had relatives, friends, and professors with this attitude, but he did not know how to talk with them, because they did not share the yearning for connection that he felt and the kind of questions he had. We fail to share questions. We fail to know what questions to ask to cross that gap. He was looking for some reflection on how we can engage within our institutions in dialogue about spirituality outside of our usual groups.

The questioner seemed to be saying, "I need more language to use; I need to have something I can talk with people about; I need to have some way that I can take the message out; I need to have something I can take out into the world as my message, as a way of communicating with people. Maybe these people do not care, or maybe they do—I have to find out. Is that reasonable?" The questioner was not asking how to approach people in an evangelical way. He was asking how to help people come to share in a question that he feels strongly about, how to transform something together. There are so many faculty and so many staff in universities who take little interest in this topic. However, we want to be engaged in transformation; so how do we engage them in these questions, when it is everything that matters?

I have never met anybody who does not think that life is important. So I want to use the statement as a springboard. Of course, all of us have our favorite, "I am not a proselytizer!" speech, but there is another part of us ready to go to the death for a cause that the world needs to fix. When the opportunity presents itself for people to relate work and life, they almost never pass up that opportunity—as long as it is available in a safe manner. This is a simplistic statement, and perhaps self-evident, but when given the opportunity we are all extraordinarily curious about our lives, how we live these lives and why.

Now the problem for most of us is that our work is disconnected from our lives. Our way of organizing work—our way of creating roles, responsibilities, tasks, and so on—separates us from our work not just because we have no interest in the subject. We are all aware that choices are made in our lives. We can cover that up—denial is a very powerful force in the present culture. There are many colluding forces we deny. We can really carry on this story: it really wasn't me; I was forced into it; my father wanted me to do this work, or my mother; but at some level, we cannot accept it. At some level we know we have made choices. However, we are really curious. We wonder, given the choices, what is happening today, and whether my life reflects my choices? I have had the opportunity to work for about fifteen years with people on this question: What is my mission for my life? I have found everyone is deeply interested in these questions.

The word company, we often believe, means business and profit. The purpose of business is business, to make money. Companies everywhere have mission statements, vision statements, little cards people have in their pockets. However, if you talk to 98% of people, in any field, they will tell you directly—without even looking at the mission statement—the purpose of the company is to make money. In today's jargon, the purpose of the company is to maximize return on the shareholder's investment. The word company has a French root, the same root as the word companion, and it really means a sharing of bread. The oldest word in Swedish for company means nourishment for life. The oldest word in Chinese, the oldest symbol, roughly translated means, life's work. Now isn't that interesting? Company is a gathering of people doing something together. What could be more essential for our lives than what we are doing? We have lots of lofty rhetoric, lots of great ideals. However, we should recognize that the core territory is this universal question: What am I doing?

As I think about the word spirit or spirituality, I immediately think about its multiple meanings, and one that often gets lost is, "What am I doing?" If you think about someone who really has moved you as a person, someone whom you would regard as having depth, a spiritual quality, what that person does is a key dimension of his or her distinctiveness. Something about the way the person's life was focused and how his or her energies were directed was in line with something that was quite integral or essential to that individual. For me, work has been an extraordinary opportunity to deal with these questions. All of us have the central concern about using our lives well. Obviously, it would be easy to overstate this point and not recognize very powerful cultural counterforces pulling in the opposite direction. As I mentioned, there is a belief in our culture that the purpose of a business is to make money. This perspective is almost universal. There is also a story about us as individuals that says what we really care about in life is ourselves. What we care about is how much money we make, and how much power we have.

It would be naïve to discuss these issues and ignore the fact that we live in a cultural stream. We are all products of history. We stand in it; it surrounds us; it is us; it moves through us. In fact, that cultural history speaks loudly and clearly, at least over the last hundred years or more. According to our cultural story, the ultimate goal is to get ahead of others. Students enter MBA programs and immediately start to ask, "How am I going to get the right job that will let me climb to the top in the next decade?"

Practical Issues

Now I shall shift from the philosophical to the concrete and raise the question of what are we doing practically. We know we have huge problems in the way we live, not only at a personal level but also at a collective level. Perhaps a lot of people would not agree, particularly in this country. Americans are among the least aware on the subject of the deeply problematic nature of our way of living collectively.

I attended a meeting in India several years ago with people from all around the world for a three-day dialogue. The group was diverse with about a third of the participants from business, a third from nongovernmental agencies, and a third from government. We discussed what was going on in the world—the "call of the times" was the question. I was a little bit surprised, because as Americans we live with an illusion that the whole world is trying to catch up with us, but of course when you meet people from other countries the perspective is very different. They do not necessarily want to live like Americans. While they seek material advance, they have grave misgivings about the materialistic culture we live in and the sacrifices it requires in terms of time, genuine human relations, and real security.

There are extraordinary problems in their countries—the social problems, the environmental problems, the intractability of the issues. Things are not the way they should be. And, given the current global interdependence, we are part of these problems. Unless we change our way of living, the prospect ahead is not very encouraging. There must be a spiritual revolution, as the only possible way we can imagine all of these issues actually changing. We need either to change what we are doing or do it with the kind of passion and conviction that we know we can bring to it. Without this, no new policies will be developed, and no drastic change in organizations will occur. Perhaps I am naïve about this, but I actually find that around the world, even in this country, when people have a chance to slow down and think about it, they are deeply concerned about the way we live. There is no complacency or belief that everything is going as well as the media would suggest. People complain about not having enough time. Most people are aware that the time to talk with friends has all but vanished, that lunches have disappeared from our work settings, and that socializing does not occur much anymore. People are also very aware that the poor are getting poorer and the rich are getting richer in most parts of the world. According to the World Bank, the bottom quartile of the population, in terms of income share, has lost ground. About a quarter of the people have only a little more than one percent of the world income, versus about twice that 25 years ago. The same phenomenon is going on right here at home.

So how do I connect where I live, where I am, and what I do, to my sense of this larger whole? That is a huge question. Very few people or organizations are willing to talk about the problem, but some are. In 1997, at Stanford, John Brown, who is the Chair and CEO of British Petroleum, gave a remarkable speech. Up to that time, few oil executives ever spoke publicly about environmental issues like climate change. The subject was not discussible in public. He said, "Look, we'd really be fooling ourselves if we continue to pretend there's nothing going on with the climate in the world. No one knows conclusively, but if we wait until the scientific evidence is absolutely conclusive, we'll have waited much too long to do anything." It was a historic speech—almost as if the CEO of a tobacco company stood up and said, "Let's face it, we all know smoking kills." Remarkable things are starting to happen where people are finding ways to connect these big issues with themselves.

Educational Issues

We know that our educational system is an unmitigated disaster. How many shootings do we need to know that something is really not working? Focusing on standardized test scores is not going to make the difference. We have a system of education that is an anachronism for the kind of world in which we live. It was invented in the middle of the nineteenth century, and it was patterned after an assembly line. How do you move up? You go through grade 1, grade 2, grade 3, grade 4, grade 5. Where did that come from? We got it from modeling the schools after an assembly line to create a uniform product known as the "educated person" who could work on an assembly line. We should not be surprised that the system fails and that our only solution to the problem is to try to turn up the speed a little more. We see the results of this kind of disarray all around us; therefore the real question is how to connect these problems with what we do.

The challenge is not simply solving the problems of education. Rather we must ask ourselves about the way we go about daily life. What do I connect with and when and how? Do I pay proper attention? Can I become more aware of this deeper issue of how we live? What is the nature of living?

Today we might say that science is the religion of this age, and that scientists are very much like the high priests or the shamans of another age. One of the extraordinary people to be part of our global Society of Learning community is Humberto Maturana, a very famous biologist well known for his biological theory of cognition—a pioneering way of thinking about how a biological entity like a human being or a plant makes sense of its world. While there are a lot of theories out there, none of them are really grounded in experimental biology. What makes Maturana especially interesting is that he is an extraordinary human being. As a Chilean, he stayed in Chile through all the political turmoil in the 1970s and 1980s, and he stayed at some considerable risk. He is a real hero. He can barely go anyplace in Chile without people coming up to greet him on the street. Many of his books are about living. That should not be so surprising, when you think about it. However, very few biologists actually write about living from a human perspective. What are the implications of our understanding of living systems for how we live? Not too many biologists have taken up that question. However, he has, and his extraordinary perspective speaks very deeply to all of us struggling with our concern for a world no longer dominated by the industrial age and reductionism, and this quest for absolute truth.

When we were children and learned chemistry, biology, or physics in school, no one mentioned that this was a story that a group of people in Cambridge developed seventy-five years ago. Instead, they told us how it worked. This is a cell, and this is how it is put together, and this is a cell wall, the nucleus, and so on. Science is always presented to young children as a story of the truth. When people comment that science may be the religion of our age, I believe they have a point. We put science on a pedestal with the unique cultural role of telling everyone the truth—a role that business certainly does not have. Even so, anyone who has anything to do with science knows otherwise. Science can feel like a very personal, very interpersonal, even very political, endeavor.

In the school system in Corvallis, Oregon, a group of us, including Maturana, spent a morning with the students. This is one of the schools that actually understands that the key to the future involves a postindustrial system of education with children in the center rather than the adults. This school lets the students talk and helps the adults listen. After listening, Humberto said, "When one human being tries to tell another human being what's really going on, don't you see what's really happening here? Don't you see what they're really up to? When one human being tells another human being what's going on, what they're actually doing is making a demand for obedience or submission."

Perhaps some of the roots of our problems of living together come from how we teach children. Perhaps once we bring young people into this world of absolutes by saying, let me tell you what's really going on, we bring them out of the world of society, out of the world of living with one another. As Maturana points out, from a biological perspective, one biological entity can never claim any access to reality. It is not biologically possible. Your mind does not see a plant. Our language and our culture tell us that our eyes see a plant. However, what actually happens at a biological level is much more complicated than that. Something, which we can never describe in absolute terms, is out there interacting with something inside us, leading to an experience that Maturana describes beautifully as bringing forth a reality. This is the only way biologically to make sense of cognition. In other words, each and every one of us at every instance, at every moment of our existence, is bringing forth a reality. Moreover, if we could only understand that, we might be able to live with one another. We may have to stop saying: "This is what is really going on." We need to rediscover our curiosity. According to Maturana, when someone has said something that does not make sense, the question is always about the reality within which that statement makes sense.

The question is never about what is wrong with the speaker. Doesn't she see what's really going on?

Our education system is violent. I say these words with great caution, because I do not mean to criticize teachers. I hope they appreciate what I mean in the context of what I just said about communicating with one another from this vantage point of "I can tell you about reality," as opposed to informing you about the thinking and appreciation and coherence-making that a group of people have made about some situations which may be of some use to you as you are living your life.

I have experienced dozens of dialogue sessions with children. I have heard eloquence again and again. We only have one ground rule when we go into a school with adults present: the adults must not talk, because then they will take over. The teachers will click into teacher mode right away. So the ground rule is, for the first hour no adults may speak. If the session lasts two hours, the adults may speak during the second hour. Children usually agree to that right away. I have yet to hear these sessions end without some teacher commenting on how eloquent these children are. Teachers are amazed at the thoughtfulness, at the concern they have about important issues. Really the only surprise is why they are surprised.

Spiritual Practice

So what is spiritual practice? Maybe the key issue is how to live with one another and with all the things around us. Obviously meditation and cultivation are important, whatever your contemplative practices. If you lack a contemplative practice, get it. Find what is right for you. Do not waste your time. Because it seems to me that the opportunity is staring us in the face. Wherever we are, whatever we are doing, we still face the question: How do we live with one another? How many times do we listen to one another? How many times do we not listen for the reality in which that statement makes sense as opposed to listening for what is wrong? How do we connect it to who we are?

Speed seems antithetical to space for reflection. Indeed speed is a huge issue for everybody. No one has time to do the things they want to do with twenty-four hours of e-mail seven days a week, or voicemail, and so on. There is an organizational part of this with which the business world is really struggling. It boils down to an extraordinary misunderstanding at some level. People are trying to run organizations that are more adaptive, flexible, capable of adjusting to a dynamic world. However, we will not get there by running around like a bunch of chickens with our heads cut off. To become more flexible and adaptive requires more awareness, and more awareness actually requires slowing down. In disciplines of all sorts, whether jazz music or tai chi, if we aspire to become more capable of improvisation, of being able to move with what is present in the moment, then we have to expand our capacity to be aware of what is present in the moment. This level of awareness is not reached by becoming frantic. We sometimes confuse being frenetic with being adaptive, which leads to the deep confusion in the business world.

The key to the future in the business world will be electronic communication, although at present it is a problem for all of us. It really is not a problem. Just stop and think for a minute: your life has always had more information then you can possibly take advantage of. When you drive by the library, do you feel compelled to go in and read all the books? Do you have to read all the e-mail? Now obviously there are also questions of relationship—because I sent you an e-mail, and I will be hurt if you fail to respond. Well, that comes in establishing the boundaries relationships require. All relationships have boundaries. So if we do not respond to all the e-mail, we have to negotiate that with one another. The new question concerns living together. As living systems, we have biological capacities. We are not solely biological, but we are partly biological. We have capacities. So to me, the practical question is a personal one. First, I keep asking myself, what do I want to do and how much time do I want to spend on my e-mail, or my voicemail, and then I negotiate with my network of relationships whether I can do that in a way consonant with the relationships I want to maintain. In addition, we must question our practices to expand awareness. Strangely enough, in a speeded up world, meditation may become a survival skill. It is a joke. Meditation is not a survival skill, but until we can quiet ourselves, we cannot deal with being frenetic. The question always deals with becoming aware without getting caught up. It has critical implications for us.

I was in conversation not that long ago with the Director of the Shambhala Retreat Center in Nova Scotia. We were joking that, in the business world, meditation has become discussible now because it gained legitimate entry as stress reduction. He said, when we introduce people to meditation, we tell them it is about stress intensification because it opens us to what is going on. We begin to realize that there is a lot going on. Without practices of some sort, I think our capacities to be aware in turbulent and uncertain settings are really more of the challenge and we find how to build those capacities.

There is a problem with spirituality in companies which concerns how spirituality might improve the management of our companies. In that sense spirituality could be a mechanism to make more money! Spirituality could be used to make people feel comfortable with the fact that, although working well, they do not understand what the real goal of their company is.

I also have real problems talking about spirituality in companies. If the larger context does not change, spirituality becomes yet another technique to keep doing what we have always been doing. I guarantee that within three years, we will be saying, "We have tried spirituality and now what else are we going to try?" However, it is not really difficult to talk about these issues, if we talk about you or me doing whatever we are doing. We can develop a discipline of reflection and inquiry about our motives. What does it mean for me? Is it really what I want to be doing in my life? If not, what can we do to change it? This line of inquiry is accessible to all of us, which does not imply we can change right now. We all have constraints in our lives. In fact, constraints may keep us doing something we do not want to do, but seldom have I seen a situation without some latitude.

Then there is the question of the purpose of a business. I actually think a lot of people are starting to raise that question so that we stop telling ourselves the dominant story of the last fifty to seventy-five years, particularly in business schools and consulting firms, that the purpose of the business is to maximize the return on investment, which is surely an idiotic view today. In the world there is a surplus of financial capital. It's true! The global financial markets have an extraordinary surplus of financial capital. We are trying to maximize a resource that is already in excess supply. There are a billion or two billion people in the world underemployed—no work, no meaningful employment. So, we have this strange world where we are destroying natural resources, habitat, species, while gradually starting to pay the price that will be evident in your insurance premiums next year. Losses within the property liability insurance industry have been rising to historic levels in recent years. We are all starting to pay the price for instability in the global climate. At that level, the CEO might not be able to initiate change but a group of people in conversations cutting across organizational boundaries will change the focus of the purpose of the business.

Remarkably there are businesses in the world today which are really serious about starting to manage what they call the triple bottom line of how an organization pays equal attention to financial, social, and environmental impacts. We have to be successful in all of those, because if not we will not be viable and be undeserving of financial investment.

A real shift is occurring. We really should be driving cars that get 200 miles to the gallon, which is absolutely feasible. I believe that in twenty years it could happen, even in ten years. However, there must be a real shift in how people think about the Ford Motor Company or British Petroleum. One person cannot do that alone. It will take a critical mass of people, including enough people in positions of authority.

What can each of us do as individuals to bring spirituality into our work? First, do not go preach about it—foster conversations. Ask yourself in conversations with people around you, why are we doing what we do? Are we doing it the way we want to be doing it? Do we want to go to meetings? If not, why don't we change the meetings? There is already plenty we can do right here at home. There is another level of questions about the institution as a whole, the context. Both are equally important. Of course this comes back to systems of education, and so on. We all participate in all of these. Do you want to know why the Ford Motor Company does not have 200 mile-per-gallon cars? Because they do not believe we care enough. They have very little evidence that people care. So, we are all locked into these systems.

The ultimate irony of the systemic perspective is that it concerns each and every one of us as individuals. The ways we think and act create our system of commerce, which cannot be changed by any one person. The Chairman of Ford Motor Company, cannot change it. Believe me, he is totally powerless by himself. However, on all these levels it can be changed, but we have to decide. We have to choose that we want to live a different way and then decide what we are going to do today and tomorrow. Perhaps in this way, we will bring spirituality to the workplace.

This essay was produced from the transcript of a presentation by the author at the Conference, Going Public: Spirituality in Higher Education and the Workplace, University of Massachusetts Amherst, June 2000.

References

Berry, T. (1988). *The dream of earth*. San Francisco: Sierra Club Books.
———(1999). *The great work*. New York: Random House.
Swimme, B., & Berry, T. (1992). *The universe story*. San Francisco: Harper.

Ways of Questioning That Can Transform Organizations—and People

Mark Kriger

When you fuse all past and present
fools and sages, sky into earth,
and everything else, you will see
how these questions have helped us.
David Rothenberg

Human systems grow toward what they
persistently ask questions about.
David Cooperrider and Diana Whitney

There is currently a deep crisis in human affairs. It is occurring at virtually all levels of human scale from the individual to the organizational to the societal. The symptoms of the crisis are numerous. At the societal level we just have to turn on any news program to observe the breakdown of social structures, not only in the Middle East, in Africa, in Central Asia, and in South America, but also in Western Europe and North America. Most people have no idea how to intervene in the complexity of breakdowns that appear in the daily news (Owen, 1991; Handy, 1994).

At the organizational level one has to ask most people in the workplace what sense of meaning, purpose, and, ultimately, joy they derive from their work. At the individual level one simply has to observe the lack of enthusiasm with which many people go about their daily activities (Rosenberg, 2001). Something clearly has to change, but the pervasiveness and complexity of the transformation that is being called for seems nearly intractable.

Fritjof Capra (1997), a theoretical physicist by training, stated the dynamics of the above very succinctly in *The Web of Life: A New Understanding of Living Systems*:

> The more we study the major problems of our time, the more we come to realize that they cannot be understood in isolation. They are systemic problems, which means they are interconnected and interdependent. (p. 5)

He goes on to say:

> There are solutions to the major problems of our time, some of them even simple. But they require a radical shift in our perceptions, our thinking, our values …(However) the recognition that a profound change of perception and thinking is needed, if we are to survive, has not yet reached most of our corporate leaders, either, or the administrators and professors or our large universities. (p. 6)

Given the depth of the problems one is compelled to ask, "Why is this?"

The central thesis of this essay is that, by asking appropriate and well-timed questions, we direct inquiry to differing domains of voice and levels of being. The questions we ask reflect who we are and who we aspire to be. Close attention to questioning reveals the type and depth of transformation taking place or potentially taking place in ourselves—and in the institutions we inhabit. Without questioning and actively inquiring we are likely to fall asleep to our True Nature at the deepest level, which is ever present and creatively evolving in its manifestation.

Taking a Step Back

As a starting point, think of the way questions arise frequently and spontaneously from children. Most of us, as children, asked lots of questions such as:

- Why is the sky blue? (Questions about facts)
- Is there a God? (Transcendental questions)
- Why am I here? (Questions of intent and purpose)

As far back as I can remember I asked questions—lots of questions. Most of my teachers, beginning in kindergarten, tended to be uncomfortable with my asking nearly unceasing, and largely unanswerable, questions. It is only now that I am beginning to ask: "Why were they so uncomfortable?" At another level: "Why have I refused to let go of my questions? Where have all these questions led me?" Finally: "What am I learning?" The most fundamental question that few people ask with any real deep, consistent interest is: "Who am I?" As we shall see, it is probably the most important question one can ask because it has the power to transform fundamentally the depth and the quality of our consciousness. These questions come from what Paul Lawrence and Nitin Nohria (2002) of Harvard University call the "drive to learn," which they argue is deeply seated within human evolution.

The following story about questions nicely portrays the above:

My father once told me a story about his childhood in the 1920s. He was walking on the beach with his father when he began to wonder about the color of the sky. "Why is the sky blue?" he asked my grandfather. Grandpa replied, "Well, son, I don't really know." My father looked up at the sky as they continued their walk. Half an hour later, my father began to wonder about the clouds. "Gee, Pop," he asked my grandfather, "What makes the clouds so white and fluffy?" "I'm not really sure," my grandfather told him. As they walked farther down the shore, the tide began to come in. This, too, prompted my father's curiosity, so he asked, "What makes the tides come and go?" "I can't really tell you," answered the old man, "but I'm glad you're asking these questions. Keep on asking questions, my boy. If you don't ask questions, you'll never learn anything." (Friedman, 1996, p. 245)

When we become adults, these earlier questions often attenuate and lose their importance to more practical issues. New questions take their place:

- What should I do next in my life?
- How can I get along better with my spouse?
- Is there a way to get paid for what I really would like to do?

As Kabat-Zinn (1994) so directly and simply points out, "Wherever you go, there you are." You can never go anyplace in each moment except to where you are in the present. However, very early in life we begin to develop the power to think and to imagine ourselves in situations other than where we happen to be. Education in primary, secondary school and in institutions of higher learning, aims to facilitate the exploration of fundamental areas of learning while deepening the skills and competencies that allow people to find gainful employment. Over time the asking of the most fundamental questions tends to attenuate as the mundane events of each successive phase in the life cycle of being a person take on urgency and press us toward the practicalities of finding a job, seeking a spouse or life partner, balancing career or job with family, and the inevitable challenges of making one's way through life. Once we become embedded in the web of life issues, most people find it increasingly difficult to step back from incessant thinking and imagining to be fully present to what is immediately around and within us. What can individuals or organizations do to counteract this deadening tendency?

Toward More Conscious Questioning:
A Personal Journey

Over the years I have been fortunate to have had a number of good teachers: in philosophy, computer science, religion, history, strategic management, psychology, and leadership. The best teachers, I discovered, did not teach me by trying to impart to me their *knowledge*, as one would inject a patient with a vaccine. Instead, they encouraged me to ask good questions and to learn from the process of striving to address those questions. Most importantly, they shared some of the passion and commitment with which they were pursuing and learning from their own personal journeys.

Some years ago, in the early 1970s, I was riding in a car in London with an author and writer of about twenty books on Zen Buddhism, named Paul

Reps. He was approximately 80 years old at the time, but he had the curiosity and openness of a young boy of about ten. He was looking with amazement out of the automobile window at the sights of London. All of a sudden he looked with interest up toward the sky and with great intensity asked, "Did you see that?!" I quickly responded, "What?" Three decades later I still remember his reply, "Look at the way the lines of those buildings are intersecting with the sky!"

With one powerful but simple question Reps made me realize that *looking at* versus deeply *seeing* are two very different processes. Looking is to grasp at with the senses; seeing is a form of *direct knowing*. By means of his way of perceiving things, coupled with a well-timed question and subsequent answer, he transformed the way I perceive the shapes of buildings and the sights of a city forever. Thus, the power of a well-framed and well-worded question is to bring about a shift in perception and, ultimately, to increase one's knowledge. However, what do we mean by knowledge?

Most people, when asked if knowledge is inherently valuable to have, will tend to respond, "Of course." Many, however, do not recognize that knowledge can be gained in two very different ways. The first leads to a pyramidal resource-oriented view of the world, where you believe that the more you have of it, the closer you are to knowing things as they are. This aspect of knowledge is additive and allows researchers and scientists to build theories about the way things are that can be subsequently tested. Through cycles of theory building and hypothesis testing successively more elegant and complete edifices of knowledge can be built, leading to larger and larger bodies of knowledge and predictability about the world as we know it. The pyramidal approach to knowledge is one of the cornerstones of higher education, especially in the Western world.

The second approach to knowledge assumes that knowing something tends to limit the likelihood we will cultivate a beginner's mind (Suzuki, 1970), which is ever inquisitive and open to seeing the world around us and within us in new ways. This beginner's mind was what Reps was able to cultivate in others through his well-timed and very pointed questions.

Millions of books have been written to shed light on different areas and aspects of knowledge. However, if we believe that reading any book or essay, including this one, is going to solve the most significant problems we face, we fall into the trap of a false worldview: thinking that codifiable knowledge alone, without deep experience and burning questions, will result in the deeper levels of learning. A good book often impels us to see the world in new ways and to ask a few good questions that direct our inner search and inform our actions and decisions in the world. It is the art and power of engaging one's inner self in the process of good questions that we shall focus on next. In essence, an appropriate question can become the generative element for engaging the inner self.

Questions as Drivers of Learning and Inquiry

Why are questions such powerful tools for both gathering information and for motivating individuals and social units, such as organizations, to change? Why do effective leaders and managers sometimes consciously, but often only unconsciously, ask good questions? How can you as a leader or as a student of leadership ask better questions, which will help you through times of constant change? Indeed, what are questions?

Questions are first and foremost a way of directing attention to some issue or subject of interest. They can be used to direct the attention of another individual or the attention of oneself, the person asking the question. Thus, a question can be either outwardly or inwardly directed. Embedded in any question is often a request: either for information, for knowledge, for action, or for someone's perception or interest to become centered on the question or on the object of the question. However, it is important to recognize that a question, like a two-edged sword, can be used either to create or to control. The intended outcome cannot be determined by the question itself, but needs to be understood within its context. This, in turn, is communicated by the emphasis, tone, and nonverbal signals which accompany the question.

Henry Mintzberg, a noted theorist of organizations and management, states: "The choice of which (managerial) roles to emphasize must reflect the current situation. The manager's job is a dynamic one, requiring constant adjustment to meet the needs of the moment" (Mintzberg, 1973, p. 182). Similarly, the process of questioning will be most effective when it reflects the current situation. Any theory of question-asking must at its root be dynamic because asking the right question in the right way and at the right time with the right emphasis is situation dependent. Thus, time, person, place, setting, medium (e.g., face-to-face, letter, telephone, formal meeting, and so on), emotional tone, content, and the length of the question are all variables to be contended with and factored in (Kriger, 1989).

In effect, questions act as trigger events in themselves and result in the creation of action agendas that address the issue(s) at hand. How a question serves to be salient in reordering organizational priorities is related to the growing area of organizational epistemology (Leonard-Barton, 1995; Nonaka & Takeuchi, 1995; von Krogh & Roos, 1995; Boisot, 1998; and Choo, 1998). At its root, organizational knowledge is created by the questions which people ask. Whether a question is taken seriously, followed up by key actors, and then used to direct the store of future organizational knowledge, is a process that is uncertain and complex.

Subjective, Intersubjective, and Objective Points of View

Any question or inquiry process has a specific point of view: the subjective or first-person singular (I), the intersubjective (we), and the third person or apparently objective point of view (it). Each inquiry mode has its own tests for validity and what constitutes truth or truthfulness (Wilber, 2000).

Universities and schools of higher education tend to structure most learning to take place from the third-person point of view, where the correspondence of propositions to external reality is the espoused domain of interest. So the study of the planets, plants, animals, chemical reactions, the brain, and ecosystems are conducted with the intent of uncovering the facts. Then, the scientific method is used to generate and test theories that explain the relationship between the observed facts. New information and facts are subsequently collected to test the theories resulting in cycles of what is known as first-order learning (Argyris, 1990). However, there is much more to learning than just generating and testing theories to explain facts.

Six Levels of Inquiry in Action

We can expand our understanding of learning from the level of facts to include six territories of experience. Each territory features a corresponding level of inquiry that, in turn, can be used to create progressively more developmentally advanced modes of questioning process (Fisher, Rooke, & Torbert, 2000) (see Figure 1).[1]

Figure 1 could be drawn in a number of ways. Indeed, each successive level of inquiry, as we proceed from left to right, contains within it the previous levels (i.e., each level is a holon, a whole that is a part of other wholes). For example, a whole atom is part of a whole molecule which, in turn, is part of a whole cell, which is part of a whole organism.

Level I: Assessing-Analyzing

Most of us learned in our primary and secondary schooling to analyze and assess things for their information content and then recapitulate or repeat what we have learned for others, specifically the teacher (see Figure 1, cell in lower left corner). In turn, the teacher then assesses what we have learned in

---

[1] According to Fisher, et al. (2000) there are four territories of experience (outcomes, action, planning, and intentionality) with four corresponding modes of inquiry (which they label assessing, performing, strategizing, and visioning). We have re-labeled "performing" as "incremental action": and to these four territories of experience have added two levels, "pure doing" and "pure being" explained below.

order to determine whether we have absorbed the appropriate facts, information, and knowledge. This type of learning is rather like being a sponge, with the learner being largely passive.

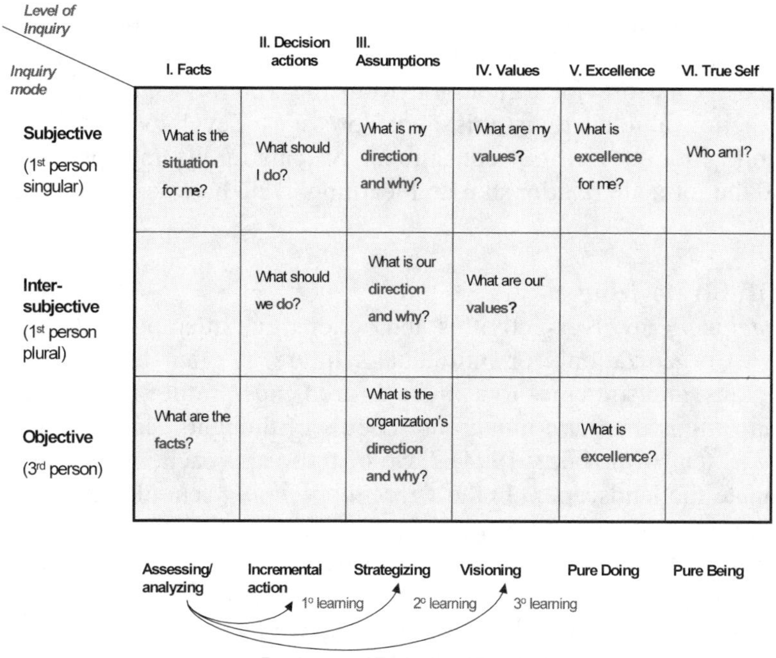

Inquiry mode \ Level of Inquiry	I. Facts	II. Decision actions	III. Assumptions	IV. Values	V. Excellence	VI. True Self
Subjective (1st person singular)	What is the situation for me?	What should I do?	What is my direction and why?	What are my values?	What is excellence for me?	Who am I?
Inter-subjective (1st person plural)		What should we do?	What is our direction and why?	What are our values?		
Objective (3rd person)	What are the facts?		What is the organization's direction and why?		What is excellence?	

Assessing/ analyzing	Incremental action	Strategizing	Visioning	Pure Doing	Pure Being

1° learning   2° learning   3° learning

Developmental Territories of Experience

Figure 1. Developmental Questioning.

The knowledge acquired in this way tends to be third-person in nature and verifiable by others. Hence, it is often considered higher and more important by the academy than subjective or intersubjective knowledge, especially knowledge about the self. This latter type of knowledge is not easily or directly verifiable by a third party, such as a teacher. As a result, most educational systems are guilty of committing what could be considered a social crime of sorts: they rarely teach the kind of knowledge that tends to be unique and the most relevant and valuable to the individual. Instead they emphasize fact-based knowledge. This approach typically becomes the primary mode for inquiry as we move into adult life.

Level II: Incremental Action

The sage never tries to store things up.
The more he does for others, the more he has.
The more he gives to others, the greater his abundance
(Lao Tzu, 1972)

Normally, the educational system does not teach students at any level how to take action, with the exception of professional schools such as medicine, law and business. It is largely assumed that if you acquire knowledge it will naturally come to inform and shape the way subsequent action takes place. This incremental mode of learning is largely tacit in nature and is linked to the domain of skills, behavior, patterns of activity and deeds.

There are many levels on which incremental action can be based, as is evidenced by the previous quotation from the *Tao Te Ching*. The type of selfless action alluded to in this quote presages Levels V and VI in our framework. In any event our educational systems rarely train people to understand the intimate relationship and learning cycle between knowledge and action.

Level III: Strategizing

Strategizing involves activities and actions that attempt to shape or determine an organization's or individual's future. It often involves creating tactics, plans, and strategies to achieve desired ends. In the strategy literature on organizations there are numerous schools of thought, according to some, as many as ten (Mintzberg, 1994). Two of these approaches to strategy tend to dominate the landscape: (1) the *strategic planning* school, which is based on assumptions of rationality and (2) the *incrementalism* school, which is based on the assumption that strategies emerge over time as managers continuously consider alternative courses of action and adapt incrementally to unfolding circumstances within the competitive environment.

The latter school is more suited to situations where prediction is difficult, if not impossible, due to the rate of change and turbulence in the environment. The planning approach is proposed and followed where predictability is easier to achieve. Increasingly, however, it is seen to have some real shortcomings, especially given the tendency toward inflexibility once the plan is in place (Courtney, 2001).

One simple but generally accepted definition of strategy from the incrementalist school is a pattern in a stream of decisions (Mintzberg, 1994). From this definition there can be both intended strategies, which result in decisions made with conscious planning and foresight, as well as realized strategies that were initially unintended but emerged as events changed. Strategies can thus be the result of intended plans or can emerge incrementally out a pattern of decisions, which was not initially intended but comes about by virtue of responses to highly unpredictable environmental conditions. Today's fast-moving information and Internet-mediated global economy seems to tilt strategizing in this direction. Strategic planning, on the other hand, is used to create some degree of predictability where possible in the short term in less turbulent environments.

Strategic decision processes in organizations are often perceived in hindsight to be the result of rational or *boundedly-rational* processes,[2] when in fact, they tend to emerge over time in consort with changing conditions. Thus, the degree of intention can be highly variable in strategizing. The challenge, especially for organizational leaders, is to create *second-order learning*.

With second-order learning, organizational members engage in inquiry processes to examine and question the assumptions underlying first-order learning, (that is, the cycles within the organization of information gathering, analyzing, and incremental action leading to further information gathering, analyzing, and so on). Second-order learning involves inquiring into the nature of the cognitive, behavioral, and emotional processes as well as the assumptions that govern an organization's overall direction (Argyris, 1990). This is, in part, accomplished by asking, "Why and how are we attempting to direct the organization in a particular direction over the longer term?" Similar ideas can also be applied to the level of the individual in activities such as career strategizing and planning. The subject of strategizing is a still rapidly evolving and complex area (Johnson & Melin, 2003).

Level IV: Visioning

Visioning involves the ability to create long-term images of some future state, either personally as an individual or collectively as a group or organization. This is a *transcognitive territory of intention* in which a person or group is consciously wishing and wanting to create a particular circumstance or set of circumstances which they consider ideal. As such, it requires one to develop intentionality, intuitions, purposes, and attention to hold mentally and eventually to realize the ideal being envisioned. It is only in the last ten to fifteen years that organizations have begun intentionally to create processes to develop and execute long-term vision and that systematic research has begun to be conducted on the subject (Larwood, Falbe, Kriger & Miesing, 1995; Schaefer & Voors, 1996). Visioning can result in *third-order learning*, where the overall intent and values that lie at the root of incremental action and strategizing are examined and submitted to inquiry. Here the organization or the individual engages in questions such as: "What are my values and my inner intent?" Due to the subtlety of such questions, it is often necessary to approach third-order learning with the help of outsiders who can help to surface and question the real intent.

However, visioning is not without a *dark side*. Recently, an increasing number of organizational consultants have come to advocate visioning as the

---

[2] *Boundedly rational* decision processes are ones in which individuals search for solutions to problems where the search terminates with a solution which is "good enough" rather than the optimum. (March & Simon, 1958; March 1994)

solution to an organization's problems. The process by which a vision is developed and communicated is often more important for its successful implementation than the content of the vision itself. For instance, if the vision is not credible and widely shared by the members of the organization, it is likely to result in resistance or, at best, mere compliance, rather than true commitment (Lipton, 1996). This is in part because visioning is based on values that are usually unique and highly personal. Thus, the *fit* between individual and organizational values, as well as management's willingness to *walk the talk*, are both crucial for creating deep commitment to the vision. In other words, incremental action (Level II) and strategizing (Level III) need to be consistent with the vision (Level IV).

Level V: Pure Doing

The essence of pure doing, the fifth level of developmental inquiry is well illustrated by the following: "If I am not for myself, who then will be for me? If I am only for myself, what am I? And if not now, when?" (Taylor, 1994). There comes a time in our life journey when we are drawn to be consciously the very beauty and truth which we have been previously unconsciously seeking in each moment, wherever we are (Kabat-Zinn, 1994). Ideally this pure doing involves that which we hold most precious and is to be lived in each moment. The Sufis call this being a son of the moment. It is a process where one is continually listening into the moment in a kind of unceasing choiceless awareness and active inquiry that enables the individual to perceive events directly as they arise. Ghalib, a Turkish Sufi mystic of the nineteenth century, stated:

> *This world is nothing more than*
> *Beauty's chance to show Herself.*
> *And what are we? -*
> *Nothing more than Beauty's chance to see Herself.*
> *For if Beauty were not seeking Herself*
> *we would not exist.*
> (Star, 1991, p. 129)

In the organizational literature one of the most popular management books of the twentieth century was entitled, *In Search of Excellence* (Peters & Waterman, 1982). The book focused on a set of twenty-five companies that were believed at the time to embody *excellence*; however, within five years most of the companies on the list no longer met the authors' original criteria for excellence. Nonetheless, a nerve was touched that resulted in the sale of over five million copies! One of the reasons that over 10,000 subsequent business books on leadership and managerial excellence came onto the market over the next two decades[3] is that leaders and managers in organizations felt drawn to the call to understand how to embody or create long-term excellence in their organizations. For many the motivation is for purely economic reasons, but for others the motivation comes from a deeply felt inner need to perform their vocation at the highest level. Often such pure doing of leadership is conducted quietly and is invisible to most others in the organization (Badaracco, 2002).

The following brief incident nicely illustrates the asking of a question from this level of deeper wisdom and what we call *pure doing*. Mother Teresa was invited to speak for an hour to a gathering of managers. She ascended the stage and then, after a time of silence, asked: "Do you know your employees? Do you love your employees?" She then sat down, having finished her speech. The same questions asked by someone else, with a different inner intent, with a different sense of timing and level of moral development, would probably have had a very different effect on the audience. The managers present were challenged to think and to act in a very different way than they had previously. If they were listening from a place of deeper inner being, they may have had access to a state of inner stillness and experienced directly what Mother Teresa was attempting to invoke through her brief but powerful use of inquiry.[4]

Level VI: Pure Being

The level of *pure being* that constitutes Level VI is not easy to describe. The *Tao Te Ching*, the ancient book of Chinese wisdom, comes about as close in words that one can come:

> *Look and it can't be seen*
> *Listen and it can't be heard*
> *Reach and it can't be grasped . . .*
> *Form that includes all forms*
> *Image without an image*
> *Subtle beyond all conception.*
> *Approach it and there is no beginning,*
> *Follow it and there is no end,*
> *You can't know it, but you can be it.*
> (Lao Tzu, 1988, Chapter XV)

In the domain of pure being, the deepest level of inquiry—self-inquiry—reveals the Divine Self knowing Itself through Itself ('Arabi, 1975). Within the nondualist Hindu tradition of *advaita,* this is the state called *Self-*

---

[3] For a small sample of some of the better books see: Torbert, 1987; Quinn, 1988; Senge, 1990; Block, 1993; Kouzes & Posner, 1995; Daft & Lengel, 1998; Goleman et al., 2002.

[4] This story was orally related to the author by Frank Elter, a manager in Telenor, the national telecom of Norway.

realization. In the words of Ramana Maharshi, one of India's greatest sages of all time: "We talk loosely of Self-realization, for lack of a better term. But how can one realize that which alone is real? All we need to do is to give up our habit of regarding as real that which is unreal. All religious practices are meant solely to help us do this" (Venkataramiah, 1994, p. 47).

Examining Figure 1 more closely, note that it contains some brief examples of the six levels of inquiry from a developmental perspective. Not all the cells have been filled in, so readers can fill in questions for their own situations. Figure 2, to further anchor the above discussion, shows where most domains of developmental questioning (higher education, organizational vision, personal identity, organizational culture and self-realization) tend to occur across the 3x6 domain of the six territories of experience and differing inquiry modes.

As illustrated in Figure 2, most formal education does not help individuals learn how to develop and inquire about their own personal identity except tangentially, to the extent that teachers engage in role modeling, nor does it teach how to enter a contemplative path that can lead, usually after much inner effort and work, to self-realization. A deep challenge facing formal higher education institutions is how to create an openness to the final three modes of experience (visioning, pure doing, and pure being), which are progressively more spiritual in nature, without imposing any particular religious viewpoint on students.

With all of the levels it is only possible to impart a practical knowledge about them if one has come to master the particular level of inquiry oneself. This poses a real challenge, and opportunity, to teachers to continue to grow and to develop into a direct personal understanding of the deeper inquiry processes consisting of visioning, pure doing and pure being. This opportunity-challenge is summarized in Figure 2, where the question is how to design educational processes and structures that facilitate the more contemplative modes of inquiry that reside towards the right-hand side of the Figure. Remember that each higher level of developmental experience contains each of the lower levels.

A story in a book by Joseph Goldstein, used to illustrate two of the six wholesome actions in Buddhism, respect and service, demonstrates the holonic property of selfless or pure doing (Goldstein, 2002). One day the Buddha came to visit a number of monks who were living together in a wooded park. The Buddha said, "I hope, Anuruddha, [addressing one of the monks] that you are all living in accord, with mutual appreciation, without disputing, blending like milk and water, viewing each other with kindly eyes." Anuruddha replied that they were. The Buddha then asked the key question: "But, Anuruddha, how do you live thus?" (Here we get to the core of our own living in accord and harmony through a profoundly simple message that comes down to us through 2500 years of human society.) Anuruddha answered:

> Venerable sir, as to that, I think thus: "It is a gain for me, it is a great gain for me, that I am living with such companions in the holy life." I maintain bodily, verbal and mental acts of loving kindness toward these venerable ones, both openly and privately. ...I consider: "Why should I not set aside what I wish to do and do what these venerable ones wish to do. We are different in body, venerable sir, but one in mind." (Goldstein, 2002, pp. 79–80)

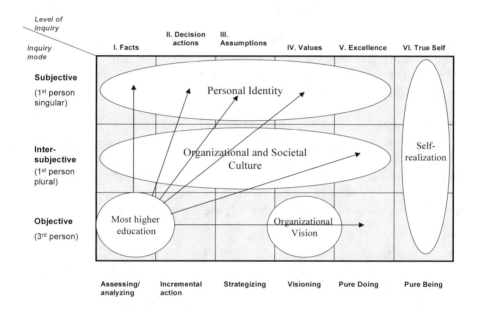

Figure 2. The Challenge for Higher Education.

The preceding story illustrates a level of leadership that is unfortunately rarely seen in today's world. It also illustrates how *pure doing* (Level V) contains within it the other levels of experience: *visioning* (Level IV)— Anuruddha sharing how the monks' values create a situation in which their lived ideals allow them to be together in harmony, on through to Level I, where Anuruddha is *analyzing* for the Buddha how he lives with the others in his community.

Control to Creativity: From I-It to I-Thou Relationships

Martin Buber, the Jewish theologian, distinguishes between two primary types of relationships, I-It and I-Thou. These terms apply not only to relationships between people but also to relationships with objects, oneself, and the Divine (Buber, 1958). It is important to recognize that I, you, and it can take on differing qualities, depending on the feeling and intent of the relationship. For example, you can become an object, an it, depending upon my relationship with you. When this occurs, we enter into an I-It relationship where you collapse from the dynamic unfolding ever-present being which you are into a static object or means toward some end created in my mind and by my intention, conscious or otherwise.

Alternatively, you can become and be for me and others a Thou and we can enter into an I-Thou relationship. There are a number of questions about the shift from control to creativity that can be asked. If one lives in a world where questions are used primarily as control mechanisms (which is generally the case in most organizational settings), resulting in primarily I-It relationships, what are the questions that can prompt examination of that paradigm and ultimately shift society to a more humanity-enhancing paradigm of I-Thou (Kriger & Malan, 1993)?

The following questions are offered as a way of looking at a set of metalevel issues involving the topic of transformational questioning in the shift from *I-It* to *I-Thou*. In a broad sense these questions arise out of this author's experience and belief that our current organizations and institutions tend to overemphasize the control element on the control-creativity spectrum. In this process they move our institutions towards the lower left-hand side of Figure 1.

- If one finds oneself in an organization where questions are generally used as control mechanisms resulting in mostly *I-It* relationships, what are the questions one can use to prompt the examination of the underlying paradigm of control in the organization?

- How do individuals know when and whether their questions are generative rather than controlling?

- When the intent behind a question is to create (be generative), but the receiver perceives the question as a means of control, and I-It in its form, is the question still generative? (For example, in the earlier example of driving through London with Paul Reps, if Reps' question had been received by the author in a different way and had perceived him to be trying to play a trick or to control, would the question still be considered transformative?)

- If the intent of a question is to control but the receiver is able to process it on a metalevel, does it then become a creative force and, hence, transformative for the individual?

(For example, in questions with implied erroneous assumptions such as "Have you stopped beating your wife?", the individual is usually caught within the incorrect framing that assumes the commission of a negative behavior. Such questions usually result in anger or, at a minimum, annoyance. Alternatively, if the receiver of such a question is mindful, then they can bring about a transformational sequence such as: 1) an initial inner pause, 2) a noticing and noting of one's feelings, 3) a letting go of feelings of defensiveness, and, finally, 4) a creative response such as posing a question back to the questioner that surfaces or makes discussable the implied assumption.)

Often it is the question, not the answer, that is important, i.e., the inquiry process that is prompted by the question. How do we teach people to disengage from their usual problem-solving mode (finding the answer) to engage in reflective inquiry and third-order learning (visioning)?

Concluding Reflections

There is no real shortage of information and knowledge in today's highly conflicted, global information economy. What is really needed is wisdom: especially the wisdom to know which questions to ask, when and how to ask them and to whom. This essay has attempted to develop some ways of thinking about the asking of fundamental timely questions that can guide transformation and renewal at varying levels of scale from the individual and organizational levels to the societal. It is set forth as one means by which people can more capably direct their own as well as organizational attention and action.

If individuals, organizations, and societies are to transform themselves and be effective in the long term, especially in highly turbulent conditions, they must find ways to intentionally channel ongoing forces of instability. One means for attaining this is to design modes of questioning which create adaptive learning, and transformation cycles designed to fit the level of turbulence in the environment. Such questioning processes are especially important in today's world where the need to create meaning as well as the drive to learn and to innovate are infusing all levels of human scale.

In essence, there are two complementary approaches to the issue of questioning processes. The first, as exemplified by recent evolutionary theorists, sees questions as a product of four innate drives that have developed over many thousands of years of human biological evolution: 1) to defend, 2) to acquire, 3) to learn, and 4) to bond (Lawrence & Nohria, 2002). The second approach, as exemplified by the perennial philosophy and spiritual traditions that lie at the root of each of the world's religious traditions, sees questioning processes as reflections of the search for inner wisdom and resultant meaning in human beings who are capable of self-awareness, self-knowledge and, ultimately, self-realization (Smith, 1991).

> Yesterday at dawn my Friend said, "How long will this unconsciousness go on?
> You fill yourself with the sharp pain of love, rather than fulfillment."
> I said, "But I can't get to You! You are the whole dark night, and I am a single can-
> dle. My life is upside down because of You!"
> The Friend replied, "I am your deepest Being. Quit talking about wanting me!"
> I said, "Then what is this restlessness?"
> The Friend: "Does the drop stay still in the ocean? Move with the entirety, and with
> the particular. Be the moisture in an oyster that helps to form one pearl."
> (Rumi, 1997, pp. 90–91)

This essay is dedicated to Huston Smith, who started me on the journey with his writing and mentoring, and to David McClelland, whose role model has kept me going as a teacher and researcher all these years. I also wish to thank Frank Elter for his assistance in creating the figures for this paper, Ken Friedman for permission to use the story about his father, and Mal Rudner, Darlene Shura and Donna Varner for their extensive comments and wondrous set of questions, which moved the manuscript to greater depth, clarity and insight.

References

'Arabi, I. (1975). *The wisdom of the prophets* (*Fusus al-Hikam*) (T. Burckhardt, Trans.). Gloucestershire, England: Beshara Publications.

Argyris, C. (1990). *Overcoming organizational defenses:Facilitating organizational learning.* Upper Saddle River, NJ: Prentice Hall.

Badaracco, Jr., J. L. (2002). *Leading quietly: An unorthodox guide to doing the right thing.* Boston: Harvard Business School Press.

Block, P. (1993). *Stewardship: Choosing service over self-interest.* San Francisco: Berrett-Koehler Publishers.

Boisot, M. (1998). *Knowledge assets: Securing competitive advantage in the information economy.* New York: Oxford University Press.

Buber, M. (1958). *I and thou.* New York: Charles Scribner & Sons.

Capra, F. (1997). *The web of life: A new understanding of living systems.* New York: Doubleday.

Choo, C.W. (1998). *The knowing organization.* New York: Oxford University Press.

Courtney, H. (2001). *20/20 foresight: Crafting strategy in an uncertain world.* Boston: Harvard Business School Press.

Daft, R. L., & Lengel, R.H. (1998). *Fusion leadership: Unlocking the subtle forces that change people and organizations.* San Francisco: Berrett-Koehler Publishers.

Fisher, D., Rooke, D. & Torbert, W. (2000). *Personal and organizational transformations through action inquiry.* Boston: Edge Work Press.

Friedman, K. (1996). Individual knowledge in the information society. In J. Olaisen, E. Munch-Pedersen, & P. Wilson, (Eds.). *Information Science: From the development of the discipline to social interaction.* Oslo: Scandinavian University Press.

Goldstein, J. (2002). *One Dharma: The emerging western Buddhism.* San Francisco: Harper.

Goleman, D., Boyatzis, R., & McKee, A. (2002). *Primal leadership: Realizing the power of emotional intelligence.* Boston, MA: Harvard Business School.

Handy, C. (1994). *The age of paradox.* Boston: Harvard Business School Press.

Johnson, G., Whittington, R. & Melin, L. 2003. Micro strategy and strategizing: Towards an activity-based view. *Journal of Management Studies* 40 (1), 3–22.

Kabat-Zinn, J. (1994). *Wherever you go, there you are.* New York: Hyperion.

Kouzes, J. M., & Posner, B. Z. (1995*). The leadership challenge: How to keep getting extraordinary things done in organizations.* San Francisco: Jossey-Bass Publishers.

Kriger, M. P. (1989). The art and power of asking questions. *The Organizational Behavior Teaching Review*, 14(1), 131–142.

Kriger, M. P., & Malan, L. C. (1993). Shifting paradigms: The valuing of personal knowledge, wisdom, and other invisible processes in organizations. *Journal of Management Inquiry* 2 (4), 391–398.

Lao Tzu. (1972). *Tao Te Ching. 1972* (G. Feng and J. English, Trans.). New York: Vintage Books.

Lao Tzu. (1988). *Tao Te Ching: A new English version* (S. Mitchell, Trans.). New York: Harper & Row.

Larwood, L., Falbe, C., Kriger, M. P., & Miesing, P. (1995). Structure and meaning of organizational vision. *Academy of Management Journal*, 38(3), 740–769.

Lawrence, P., & Nohria, N. (2002). *Driven: How human nature shapes our choices.* San Francisco: Jossey-Bass.

Leonard-Barton, D. (1995). *Wellsprings of knowledge: Building and sustaining the sources of information.* Boston: Harvard Business School Press.

Lipton, M. (1996). Demystifying the development of an organizational vision. *Sloan Management Review*, Summer, 83–92.

March, J.G. (1994). *A primer on decision making: How decisions happen.* New York: The Free Press.

March, J.G., & Simon, H.A. (1958). *Organizations.* New York: McGraw-Hill.

Mintzberg, H. (1973). *The nature of managerial work.* New York: Harper & Row Publishers.

———(1994). *The rise and fall of strategic planning.* New York: The Free Press.

Nonaka, I., & Takeuchi, H. (1995). *The knowledge-creating company: How Japanese companies create the dynamics of innovation.* New York: Oxford University Press.

Owen, H. (1991). *Riding the tiger: Doing business in a transforming world.* Potomac, MD: Abbott Publishing.

Peters, T., & Waterman, A. (1982). *In search of excellence: Lessons from America's best-run companies.* New York: Harper & Row Publishers.

Prigogine, I., & Stengers, I. (1984). *Order out of chaos: Man's new dialogue with nature.* New York: Bantam Books.

Quinn, R. E. (1988). *Beyond rational management: Mastering the paradoxes and competing demands of high performance.* San Francisco: Jossey-Bass.

Rosenberg, L. (2001). *Living in the light of death: On the art of being truly alive.* Boston: Shambhala Publications, Inc.

Rumi, M. J. (1997). *The illustrated Rumi* (C. Barks, Trans.). New York: Broadway Books.

Schaefer, C., & Voors, T. (1996). *Vision in action: Working with soul and spirit in small organizations.* Hudson: Lindisfarne Press.

Senge, P. M. (1990). *The fifth discipline: The art and practice of the learning organization.* New York: Doubleday.

Smith, H. (1991). *The world's religions: Our great wisdom traditions.* San Francisco: Harper.

Star, J. (1991). Two suns rising. In A. Ahmad (Ed.) *The Ghazals of Ghalib.* New York: Columbia University Press.

Suzuki, S. (1970). *Zen mind, beginners mind.* New York: John Weatherhill, Inc.

Taylor, C. (1969). Sayings of the Jewish fathers, verse 1.14. In P. Novak (Ed.), (1994). *The world's wisdom: Sacred texts of the world's religions.* San Francisco: Harper. (Original work published 1969).

Torbert, W. R. (1987). *Managing the corporate dream:Restructuring for long-term success.* Homewood, IL: Dow-Jones-Irwin.

Torbert, W. R. (1994). The good life: Good money, good work, good friends, good questions. *Journal of Management Inquiry*, 3 (1), 58–66.

Venkataramiah, M.S. (1994). *Talks with Sri Ramana Maharshi* (6th ed.). In P. Novak (Ed.) *The world's wisdom: Sacred texts of the world's religions.* San Francisco: Harper.

Von Krogh, G., & Roos, J. (1995). *Organizational epistemology.* London: Macmillan.

Wilber, K. (1996). *A brief history of everything.* Boston: Shambhala Publications, Inc.

Wilber, K. (2000). *A theory of everything: An integral vision of business, politics, science and spirituality.* Boston: Shambhala Publications, Inc.

Contributors

Diana Chapman Walsh has since 1993 been the twelfth President of Wellesley College. During her tenure, the college has expanded its programs in global education, experiential and service learning, and religious and spiritual life, and has undertaken a number of initiatives aimed at improving the quality of campus intellectual life. Formerly a professor and department chair at the Harvard School of Public Health, and a professor at Boston University, Dr. Walsh has published widely on issues related to health policy and leadership. She is a trustee of Amherst College, a director of State Street Corporation, chair of the board of the Consortium on Financing Higher Education, and the recipient of four honorary degrees.

Riane Eisler is best known for her international bestsellers *The Chalice and The Blade* and *Sacred Pleasure,* and the award-winning *Tomorrow's Children: A Blueprint for Partnership Education in the 21ˢᵗ Century.* Her most recent book is *The Power of Partnership,* a guide to personal and cultural transformation. She is a pioneer in peace education and human rights, cofounder of the Spiritual Alliance to Stop Intimate Violence (SAIV), keynotes conferences worldwide, and is president of the *Center for Partnership Studies*, dedicated to research and education on systemic change (www.partnershipway.org).

Jennifer Gidley is an educational psychologist and Futures researcher lecturing at the Australian Foresight Institute, Melbourne, Australia. As well as founding and pioneering a Steiner school, she has researched and published on educational transformation, futures of consciousness, and cultural renewal, including coediting two books: *The University in Transformation* and *Youth Futures: Comparative Research and Transformative Vision.*

Daniel Goleman consults internationally and lectures to business, college campus and professional audiences. For many years he reported on brain and behavioral sciences for *The New York Times.* He was cofounder of the Collaborative for Academic, Social, and Emotional Learning at Yale University. Goleman has several published books. *Emotional Intelligence* has sold 5 million copies worldwide; *Destructive Emotions* is an account of a dialogue with the Dalai Lama and a group of philosophers, neuroscientists, and psychologists. His most recent book is *Primal Leadership-Realizing the Power of Emotional Intelligence.* He has received the Career Achievement Award from the American Psychological Association for his communication of science to the public.

Eugene Halton is the author of *Bereft of Reason* and *Meaning and Modernity*, coauthor of *The Meaning of Things*, and is finishing a collection of essays on American culture. He teaches sociology, American studies, and humanities at the University of Notre Dame. Halton has also performed blues harmonica internationally, and his band, *Off the Wall Blues Band*, will be releasing their next CD shortly. His web site is: http://www.nd.edu/~ehalton

Jon Kabat-Zinn is Professor of Medicine Emeritus at the University of Massachusetts Medical School. He is the founding director of its Stress Reduction Clinic and Center for Mindfulness in Medicine, Health Care, and Society. He is the author of *Full Catastrophe Living: Using the Wisdom of Your Body and Mind to Face Stress, Pain and Illness; Wherever You Go, There You Are: Mindfulness Meditation in Everyday Life;* and co-author, with his wife Myla, of *Everyday Blessings: The Inner Work of Mindful Parenting* and *Coming to Our Senses: Healing Ourselves and the World Through Mindfulness.* His work has contributed to a growing movement of mindfulness into mainstream institutions in our society such as medicine, health care and hospitals, schools, corporations, prisons, and professional sports.

Steven Keeva is assistant managing editor of the *American Bar Association Journal,* for which he also writes the column "Keeva on Life and Practice." He is the author of *Transforming Practices: Finding Joy and Satisfaction in the Legal Life,* and he speaks internationally on quality-of-life issues for lawyers and law students.

Mark Kriger is Professor of Strategic Management at the Norwegian School of Management in Oslo, Norway. He has a doctorate from Harvard Business School as well as master's degrees from the University of California at Berkeley and M.I.T., in computer science and philosophy. His publications are in the areas of executive leadership, strategy process, managerial wisdom, and organizational vision, and he serves on the boards of directors of multinational corporations. His passions include writing poetry, meditation, swimming, and traveling to exotic places.

Peter Senge is the director of the Center for Organizational Learning at MIT's Sloan School of Management and founding partner of Innovative Associates in Boston. His books include *The Fifth Discipline, The Fifth Discipline Field Book,* and *Presence: Human Purpose and the Field of the Future.* He has introduced thousands of managers at major corporations such as Ford, Apple, and Royal Dutch/Shell to the disciplines of the learning organization. His work draws on science, spiritual wisdom, psychology and management thought leading to searching personal experience and dramatic professional shifts of mind.

Margaret Wheatley writes, teaches, and speaks about radically new approaches to organizing, where the human spirit is known as the blessing not the problem. She carries this message to organizations of all types and on all continents, as well as writing about it in prose and poetry. She has been a professor of management in two graduate programs, and received her doctorate in Administration, Planning, and Social Policy from Harvard University. She has written several books, including *Turning to One Another, Leadership and the New Science,* and *Finding Our Way: Leadership for an Uncertain Time.*

David Whyte is a poet and a Fortune 500 consultant, using poetry to bring understanding to the process of change. He has helped clients understand individual and organizational creativity in such companies as Boeing and Toyota and to apply that understanding to vitalize and transform the workplace. In addition to his four volumes of poetry, David Whyte is the author of *The Heart Aroused: Poetry and the Preservation of the Soul in Corporate America,* and *Crossing the Unknown Sea: Work as a Pilgrimage of Identity.*

Bruce Wilshire is Senior Professor of Philosophy at Rutgers University. He received the Herbert Schneider Lifetime Achievement Award for 2001 from the Society for the Advancement of American Philosophy. He is the author of many books including, *The Primal Roots of American Philosophy: Pragmatism, Phenomenology, and Native American Thought* and *Fashionable Nihilism: A Critique of Analytic Philosophy.* His most recent work is *Get 'Em All, Kill 'Em: Genocide, Terrorism, Righteous Communities.*

Arthur Zajonc is Professor of Physics at Amherst College, where he has taught since 1978. His research has included the relationship between sciences, the humanities, and contemplation. He is author of the book: *Catching the Light,* coauthor of *The Quantum Challenge,* and coeditor of *Goethe's Way of Science.* In 1997 he served as scientific coordinator for the Mind and Life dialogue with H.H. the Dalai Lama published as *The New Physics and Cosmology: Dialogues with the Dalai Lama* (Oxford, 2004). He again organized the 2002 dialogue with the Dalai Lama, "The Nature of Matter, the Nature of Life." He has also been General Secretary of the Anthroposophical Society in America (1994–2002), President of the Lindisfarne Association, and a senior program director at the Fetzer Institute.

Editors

Susan M. Awbrey is Vice Provost for Undergraduate Education at Oakland University. She received her Ph.D. from Michigan State University. She was a faculty member and administrator at the University of Texas, The University of Illinois, and Michigan State University, and was selected as an American Council on Education Fellow. Her passion is creating education for whole persons.

Diane Dana is a Research Assistant for the SEED Project on Inclusive Curriculum, based at the Center for Research on Women at Wellesley College and supports efforts to make schools, colleges and universities more multicultural, gender fair and globally aware. She joined the team of academics, administrators and community members in the Five College area of western Massachusetts to form the Community for Integrative Learning and Action (CILA).

Vachel Miller is currently Project Manager for the Kenya, Uganda, Rwanda, and Ethiopia Together (KURET) Project in Uganda. His work focuses on education for peace, alternative indicators, and spirituality in education. He has coedited a book of essays entitled *Transforming Campus Life: Reflections on Spirituality and Religious Pluralism* (Peter Lang, 2001).

Phyllis Robinson received her doctorate in International Education from the University of Massachusetts Amherst, Center for International Education, and has worked for many years in support of the Buddhist leadership in Cambodia in their efforts to stabilize their society after decades of war and attempted genocide. She now consults internationally and nationally in exploring and researching the integral role spirit can play in individual healing and in building an ethical society.

Merle M. Ryan was an Assistant Dean of Students at the University of Massachusetts Amherst. She is now retired and teaches *Embracing Diversity*, *Leadership in Higher Education* and *American Sign Language* at the University of Massachusetts Amherst. She was also a coeditor of *Transforming Campus Life: Reflections on Spirituality and Religious Freedom* (Peter Lang, 2001).

David K. Scott received his D.Phil. from Oxford University and has worked as a nuclear scientist and as an educator, most recently as the Chancellor of the University of Massachusetts Amherst. He is now interested in creating a Community for Integrative Learning and Action (CILA) and in exploring the role of spirituality in higher education.

Peter L. Laurence &
Victor H. Kazanjian, Jr.
General Editors

Studies in Education and Spirituality presents the reader with the most recent thinking about the role of religion and spirituality in higher education.
It includes a wide variety of perspectives, including students, faculty, administrators, religious life and student life professionals, and representatives of related educational and religious institutions. These are people who
have thought deeply about the topic and share their insights and experiences through this series. These works address the questions: What is the
impact of religious diversity on higher education? What is the potential of
religious pluralism as a strategy to address the dramatic growth of religious
diversity in American colleges and universities? To what extent do institutions of higher learning desire to prepare their students for life and work in
a religiously pluralistic world? What is the role of spirituality at colleges
and   universities,
particularly in relationship to teaching and learning pedagogy, the
cultivation of values, moral and ethical development, and the fostering of
global learning communities and responsible global citizens?

For additional information about this series or for the submission of manu-
scripts, please contact:

Peter L. Laurence
5 Trading Post Lane
Putnam Valley, NY 10579

To order other books in this series, please contact our Customer Service
Department:

(800) 770-LANG (within the U.S.)
(212) 647-7706 (outside the U.S.)
(212) 647-7707 FAX

Or browse online by series:

www.peterlang.com